Islam, Oil, and Geopolitics

Islam, Oil, and Geopolitics

Central Asia after September 11

Edited by
Elizabeth Van Wie Davis
and Rouben Azizian

ROWMAN & LITTLEFIELD PUBLISHERS, INC.
Lanham • Boulder • New York • Toronto • Plymouth, UK

ROWMAN & LITTLEFIELD PUBLISHERS, INC.

Published in the United States of America
by Rowman & Littlefield Publishers, Inc.
A wholly owned subsidary of The Rowman & Littlefield Publishing Group, Inc.
4501 Forbes Boulevard, Suite 200, Lanham, Maryland 20706
www.rowmanlittlefield.com

Estover Road, Plymouth PL6 7PY, United Kingdom

British Library Cataloguing in Publication Information Available

Library of Congress Cataloging-in-Publication Data

Islam, oil, and geopolitics : Central Asia after September 11 / edited by Elizabeth Van
    Wie Davis and Rouben Azizian
    p. cm.
    Includes bibliographical references and index.
    ISBN-13: 978-0-7425-4128-3 (cloth : alk. paper)
    ISBN-10: 0-7425-4128-2 (cloth : alk. paper)
    ISBN-13: 978-0-7425-4129-0 (pbk. : alk. paper)
    ISBN-10: 0-7425-4129-0 (pbk. : alk. paper)
    1. Geopolitics—Asia, Central. 2. Islam and politics—Asia, Central. 3. Energy
    policy—Asia, Central. I. Davis, Elizabeth Van Wie. II. Azizian, Rouben.

    JC319.I85 2006
    958'.043—dc22

                                                                        2006011874

Printed in the United States of America

∞™ The paper used in this publication meets the minimum requirements of American
National Standard for Information Sciences—Permanence of Paper for Printed Library
Materials, ANSI/NISO Z39.48-1992.

Contents

Part II: Energy Security

Part III: The Geopolitics of Central Asia

Part IV: Central Asia and Asia Pacific

1

Islam, Oil, and Geopolitics in Central Asia after September 11

Rouben Azizian and Elizabeth Van Wie Davis

In a little more than a decade, Central Asia has gone through a dramatic trans-formation as international attention and interest focused on the region. Until the end of the 1980s, Central Asia was treated by the outside world as a Russian periphery and strategically unpromising area. After the breakup of the Soviet Union and since the early 1990s, the region has been experiencing a myriad of problems as part of a painful transition from Soviet authoritarianism to a more open society, from secular orientation to religious revival, from state-run econ-omy to market transformation with valuable energy resources. The interna-tional community was initially slow in offering cooperation to Central Asia in overcoming those challenges. This was a result of many factors. Russia was looking primarily to the West and largely ignoring the ex-Soviet states, while the West was looking at Russia as a natural guide for Central Asia's expected democratization. The Islamic countries did little to empower the Central Asian states politically and economically beyond the general euphoria regarding the expected return of the region to the fold of Islamic civilization. Central Asia is "indebted" to the Taliban for the greater realization by the United States as well as Russia and China of the importance of peace and stability in Central Asia for their own security. Since the tragic events of September 11, Central Asia has been drawn into an intense international struggle against the forces of religious extremism and transnational crime. The great powers were able to put aside their geopolitical differences in order to crush al-Qaeda and the Taliban. Cen-tral Asian states promptly offered their territories and airspace for use by the antiterrorist coalition. At the same time, it is increasingly clear that the great powers have not abandoned their vital geopolitical and geoeconomic interests in the region, which do not always coincide. With the marginalization of the

Taliban and eviction of al-Qaeda from Afghanistan, the tension between the great powers is notably increasing, as is the discomfort of Central Asian states that find themselves in the middle of a renewed Great Game. This competition opens a new stage in Central Asia's evolution, and its interactions with external powers are fueled by a number of factors. As China gains economic weight and political influence, it is becoming increasingly sensitive to attempts to use Central Asia against her national interests. China's growing energy needs prompted energy cooperation with Central Asian states. Vladimir Putin's Russia is desperately trying to hold on to the remnants of its post-Soviet sphere of influence after Georgia and Ukraine opted for closer integration with the West. With the proclamation of the "march for freedom," the second George W. Bush administration has come under significant domestic and international pressure not to let the authoritarian Central Asian states use the common antiterrorist agenda as an excuse for continued abuse of democratic principles and human rights. Central Asia, from an obscure region largely associated with Islamic radicals, has become a strategic magnet and a litmus test of America's ability to be consistent in its promotion of global liberal change, of Russia's *true* foreign policy allegiance, and of China's readiness to translate economic power into a tool of political dominance.

This book examines all of the above issues and the complex dynamic of cooperation and competition within and outside the Central Asian states.[1] It looks at the sources of domestic and external extremism as well as the evolving bilateral relations between the major external actors in Central Asian affairs. The book is divided into four parts.

Part I deals with the internal conflicts and the peace processes in Afghanistan and post-Soviet Central Asia. The five countries of Central Asia unhesitatingly supported the war on terrorism and the elimination of al-Qaeda and the Taliban. From the mid-1990s, they have confronted terrorist actions emanating primarily from Afghanistan and Tajikistan. Their consent to the presence of international security forces was a calculated step toward meeting their own national interests rather than a reluctant concession to great power pressure. The Central Asian states are likely to continue their cooperation with the United States and other members of the antiterrorist coalition as long as they remain the target of extremist forces. They regard the decline in militant activities in the region following the destruction of the Taliban as temporary and tactical. Some call it a pause before a bigger storm.

The situation in Afghanistan remains of paramount importance for stability in the entire Central Asian region. According to Najibullah Lafraie, former foreign minister of Afghanistan, the Bonn Agreement and Emergency Loya Jirga, despite major shortcomings, as well as the Tokyo Conference, the deployment of the International Security Assistance Force (ISAF), and the

Kabul Declaration were important steps toward restoration of peace and stability in Afghanistan, as he writes in chapter 3. However, agreements, conferences, and councils provide only a framework for action. The success of the peace process depends on what is practically achieved on the ground. Warlordism is perhaps the single greatest challenge and obstacle to the peace process in Afghanistan. This is not confined to occasional clashes between warlords. The real problem is that the Transitional Administration has not been able to extend its authority beyond Kabul. The country is divided into fiefdoms of larger and smaller warlords who have their own armies, appoint their own officials, collect their own taxes, and establish their own relations with outsiders, paying little regard to the central government.

The Russian ambassador in Afghanistan and an old Afghanistan hand, Mikhail Konarovsky, reiterates these concerns in chapter 2. The administration in Kabul must simultaneously solve two interconnected problems: maintain stability and security everywhere and address urgent economic and social issues. Lack of efficiency in achieving these goals may allow the Taliban and al-Qaeda remnants to regroup, expand the area of their activities, and close their ranks with such extremist aliens to the Bonn process as Ghulbedin Hekmatiyar. Terrorist formations also exploit growing resentment in different regions of Afghanistan stimulated by the lingering foreign "man with a gun" presence embodied by the Coalition Forces and the U.S. armed forces in particular. The emergence of extremist organizations that openly take responsibility for the acts of terror in Kabul and the Afghan provinces is exemplified by the regrouping Talibs and al-Qaeda. Several groups train kamikaze fighters and are headed by foreign nationals, including the Islamic Movement of Uzbekistan, whose leaders were directly supported from Kabul during the Taliban regime.

The political situation in the Central Asian republics is increasingly volatile, and a relatively localized riot like the March 2002 confrontation in the Ak-Sui region of Kyrgyzstan can potentially spark much broader unrest. The potential for such riots to be hijacked by extremist groups is also high. Parties like the Hizb-ut-Tahrir and the Islamic Movement of Uzbekistan emerged to fill a vacuum that resulted from the failure of Marxism-Leninism, then the Central Asian form of nationalism. According to Alisher Khamidov in chapter 6, the best option for Central Asian governments to combat Islamic radical groups is to vigorously pursue economic reforms and political liberalization. The political reasons for the resurgence of the Hizb-ut-Tahrir and other Islamic groups include the growing authoritarianism and ineffectualness of authoritarian regimes, the radicalization of politics, and official inability to address long-standing economic and social problems. As economic and industrial outputs reach their lowest levels and nearly all Central Asian states face the prospect of civil unrest and large-scale violence, Hizb-ut-Tahrir has effectively cast itself as the promoter of social and economic justice. Hizb-ut-Tahrir's calls for an end to corruption, greed, and abuse of power resonate with many ordinary people in villages and cities where living standards have fallen drastically over the past decade. Some regional reports indicate that in addition to the regional network in Central Asian republics, Hizb-ut-Tahrir receives financial support from sympathizers in Jordan, Egypt, Indonesia, and Pakistan.

Kamoludin Abdullaev, in chapter 5, believes that the main threat to Central Asian security is the general failure of political and economic transformation as well as widespread corruption, not radical Muslim policies. Lack of cooperation between Central Asian governments and rapid militarization of the region further deteriorate the situation. Local regimes and their close non-Muslim neighbors—China and Russia—identify radical Islamist mobilization as a threat to national security interests. A consequence of this is a rapid, burdensome, and dangerous militarization of the region. Governments have chosen repression as the only response to dissent. This concentration of fear, violence, mistrust, and mismanagement is the most alarming problem of the region. Uzbekistan is one of the forerunners of the militarization of Central Asia. Another source of instability is Tajikistan, where the military elite comprises former adversaries, hardened militias from the pro-Communist Popular Front, and the United Tajik Opposition. On the pretext of fighting Islamic terrorists, Kazakhstan and Kyrgyzstan have also strengthened their defense and security. Sadly, in the aftermath of September 11, Central Asian governments have begun to use the rhetoric of the war on terror to justify their pressure on opposition. Instead of weakening the Islamist militancy, this repression has strengthened and radicalized the Islamist groups. Successful bargaining between the government and Muslim militants in Tajikistan showed that Muslim politics are not inevitably radical and antisystemic. To avoid a slide back to militancy, participation must be extended to all political movements committed to act legally, and national economies must be developed.

Gaye Christoffersen, in chapter 4, examines the challenges of Islamic identity. Central Asia has been in a state of flux since September 11, as Muslim and non-Muslim civilizations clash throughout the region and the United States maintains a military presence there. This flux has overflowed into the Xinjiang region of China, with the Chinese military cracking down on Uyghur militants. Western human rights groups are concerned that the Chinese crackdown is spreading too wide a net, detaining innocent Uyghurs in addition to the Uyghur militants. China is accused of bandwagoning in the war on terrorism in a manner similar to New Delhi treating Kashmir as part of the global terrorist threat. The central question is whether China is victimizing the Uyghur minority by using the war on terrorism as an excuse to violate their human rights or whether China itself is a victim of the al-Qaeda network, which trained Uyghurs in Afghanistan for terrorist activities in Xinjiang. Both Uyghurs and Chinese are attempting to take advantage of the current international attention that has transformed Central Asian geopolitics.

As Aleksei Malashenko notes in chapter 7, distinguishing between religious-political radicalism and terrorism in Central Asia is not easy. Efforts to define the notion of "terror" in a precise, scholarly way have not succeeded. Terrorist methods of struggle have characterized the proponents of most diverse ideological and political views—not only of Islamists but also of Communists, for example. So terror is not a "privilege" restricted to Muslim radicals. The ambivalence of the interpretation of terror makes it possible to describe as "Islamic terrorists" nearly all of the opposition forces that appeal to Islam in varying degrees. That is exactly what is being done by the Russian and Central Asian presidents as well as the leaders of China and India. The current global antiterrorist campaign has not led to a definition of terrorism that is shared by Russia and many Western states, which refuse to see the main cause of the Chechen conflict as interference by international Islamic extremism. The correlation between the real and virtual threat of Islamic terrorism is still not clear. After September 11, when military actions by Islamists in Central Asia practically ceased and their political activity was limited to cautious propaganda, the struggle against Islamic terrorism has become one of the main instruments of conducting domestic policy by Central Asian regimes and one of the main focal points of foreign powers, especially the United States.

Part II turns to another important dimension of great powers' interest in Central Asia—the energy lure of the region. Russia, China, and the United States all have a stake in this prospective hydrocarbon reserve to either offset their current Middle East oil imports, as in the case of China and the United States, or control the pipelines needed to move oil and gas out of this landlocked region, as is the case of Russia, China, and the United States. Other regional powers, particularly Japan and India, have some interest in the reserves, but transportation and political difficulties make it unlikely that Central Asia will become a major exporter of hydrocarbons in the next decade.

Countries like Japan and China, wanting to diversify their reliance on Middle Eastern oil, have shown a consistent interest in Central Asian energy exports. According to Manabu Shimizu in chapter 8, Japan has been one of the largest donors of direct overseas aid to Kazakhstan, Uzbekistan, and Kyrgyzstan. Japan also recommended developing a new Eurasian policy with the implicit understanding that Central Asia is strategically important to Japan in terms of overall regional stability and in its potential as a supplier of energy resources. Japan is also interested in gaining access to the development of energy resources in Central Asia, positions now primarily held by the major Western and Russian oil companies.

China is in the market for massive amounts of imported energy, primarily oil and gas, as detailed by Kang Wu in chapter 9. China is developing its western region with its large oil and gas reserves as an important part of its energy strategy. West-to-east pipelines and western energy development will ideally lead to the development of poor western region of China—the region that abuts Central Asia and hosts a large Muslim minority—as well as supply energy needs to eastern coastal areas. Crude output from western China's Xinjiang province was the largest contribution to China's onshore oil production. However, imports remain crucial to fulfilling China's ever increasing demands for energy. China looks to diversify its sources of oil and gas imports with imports from Russia and Central Asia. It is also looking to strengthen the overseas investment by its state oil companies, including in Russia and Central Asia.

September 11 revived interest in the exploitation of Central Asia's energy resources. Some expected the coalition against the Taliban to evolve into cooperation on Central Asia's energy resources. Of the hydrocarbon reserves in Central Asia, oil is of primary interest, according to Robert Smith in chapter 10. Most countries with an interest in Central Asian energy have ample supplies of coal, particularly China and the United States. Although there are good supplies of natural gas in Central Asia, production is hindered by transportation problems. There are significant gas reserves in Kazakhstan, Turkmenistan, and Uzbekistan. Both Turkmenistan and Uzbekistan export gas through the pipeline system built by the Soviets. Gas needs an extensive system of pipelines to be delivered and there is a relative scarcity of ships that can carry gas. Building new long-distance gas pipelines is expensive and almost always involves host country national investment. Pipeline issues, for instance, have hampered Turkmenistan's attempts at gas exports. Currently gas is best used close to its source of production. Oil is more easily transported than gas and more profitable than coal and remains the black gold of the twenty-first century. Landlocked Central Asia has ample energy reserves but faces export obstacles and political obstacles related to religious extremism, social crises, and poorly developed economies.

Part III deals with the broader picture of geopolitics among the great powers in the region. Central Asia was historically a center of confrontation, competition, and conflict among the great powers, then Russia and Britain. Their notorious confrontation was aptly labeled the "Great Game." Both Britain and Russia had extensive global reach and clashed over Central Asia as part of their imperial strategies. The geographical location of Central Asia was crucial. In the current era of post–cold war politics, Central Asia is still strategically pivotal.

The relatively simple pattern of bipolar great power politics, however, has been replaced by a more complex multipolar structure with a single global power, especially in the aftermath of September 11. According to Shi Yinhong in chapter 11, emergent Central Asian geopolitics give the United States a strong advantage with its preponderance of resources and long-distance power projection, Russia has the advantage of geography and historical links, and China has adjacency and shared ethnic groups. Regional politics are also part of the mix, with powers like Iran and Turkey pushing their agendas in Central Asia and the drama of the Indian subcontinent extending into the region. And then there are the Central Asian states themselves with their diverse nationalities, ethnicities, languages, cultures, and histories and a state system that is far from mature. The great powers have different approaches to this new Great Game.

The drastic decline of its national strength, the overwhelming international social and economic problems, and the loss of its external ambitions and positions are central to the Russian position toward Central Asia and the new Great Game, as detailed by Sergey Lounev in chapter 12 and Feng Shaolei in chapter 14. Russia long considered Central Asia its strategic backyard but lacked the political, economic, and military resources to maintain its influence in the decade after the collapse of the Soviet Union. Nonetheless, Russia hopes to maintain its influence in Central Asia. The clear and limited definition of security requirements leads Russia to see Central Asia as a buffer zone, especially from the forces of Islamic revivalism, with the Russian Muslim population of twenty million.

India must also be considered, as Sergey Lounev points out in chapter 12. India is highly interested in obtaining oil and gas from Central Asia as well as in playing a geopolitical role. India is a natural and long-standing partner with Russia, both of them perceiving a threat from China. Islamic revivalism in Central Asia is also a concern for India, which has a population of 140 million Muslims. The Indo-Pakistan rivalry that dominates South Asia has threatened to spill over into Central Asia. Pakistan's Muslim population has close ties with Afghanistan and strong interests in promoting the Islamic revival in the region. While the government of Pakistan has tried since September 11 to stop all links with terrorist activities in Russia's Chechnya, China's Xinjiang Province, and the United States, Pakistan's influence in Central Asia has been limited by its own domestic turmoil and economic difficulties.

Iran and Turkey also act as regional powers in Afghanistan and Central Asia, the Middle East, and the Islamic world. Shireen Hunter in chapter 13 discusses how Iran impacts and is impacted by being a direct geographical neighbor of Central Asia. Although the U.S. war on terrorism provided an opportunity to end the Iranian-U.S. confrontation, the United States chose instead to name Iran as part of the "axis of evil." Iranian influence is limited by several factors. Iranians are ethnically different from Central Asians, being Indo-Aryan rather than Turks or Caucasians like most of the Central Asians. In terms of the Muslim revivalism, Iranians are Shiites rather than the majority of the Central Asian Muslims, who are Sunnis. Financially, Iran does not have enough funds to aid structural modernization in Central Asia. Turkish influence has also been limited in Central Asia. From a Western perspective, the Turkish secular model of development may be attractive to Central Asian states concerned with the emergence of Islamic revival. From a Russian perspective, there were a dozen wars between the Turkish Ottoman Empire and Russia, so Russia is not pleased with the prospect of Turkish influence in its former Central Asian republics. These regional powers, Iran and Turkey, are also influenced by the great power politics descending on Central Asia.

Sergei Troush in chapter 15 outlines Chinese and Russian interests. China's primary interest vis-à-vis Central Asia is to prevent instability, both political and religious, along its long western border and prevent instability from leaking into China. China has a large Muslim population and fears that the Central Asian states, having their independence from the former Soviet Union, will spur the movement for independence among its twenty to thirty-eight million Muslims, many living in the western regions adjoining Central Asia, the most notorious being the Uyghurs. It could also have implications for other regions, such as Tibet. China has cultivated good relations with the Central Asian republics, including stronger diplomatic and economic relations with Kazakhstan, Kyrgyzstan, and Uzbekistan. Additionally, the sale of hydrocarbons has become an important component in the strategic relations between Russia and China. Although China may be attempting to move into the power vacuum left by the departure of the Soviet Union, which also includes the energy sector, Russia and China are also moving closer together with their shared interests in a multipolar world, positions on arms control and disarmament, Taiwan, and Chechnya as well as other areas of geopolitics. Russia and China seek an inclusive cooperative relationship while trying not to harm their relations with the United States.

Part IV deals with Central Asia's relations with the wider Asian region as the Central Asian nations are attempting to diversify their foreign relations, balance the great power politics, and deny any of them strategic preeminence in the region. Little considered in the geopolitics of the new Great Game are the positions of the Central Asia republics themselves, which are often left trying to balance great power influences and regional power concerns with few economic and political resources of their own. Organizations, policies, and agreements are emerging in an attempt to address the multitude of issues surrounding the religious revival, the lure of oil, fears of terrorism, and desires for political and social vibrancy.

In chapter 16, Pan Guang discusses the multifaceted role of the new multilateral phenomenon transcending the Central Asia region—the Shanghai Cooperation Organization (SCO). Its background and evolution have been unique. The events of September 11 posed a host of new challenges to the SCO revealing the organization's inexperience and lack of cohesion particularly in the area of security cooperation and counterterrorism campaigns in Central Asia. The increased U.S. military presence in Central Asia after September 11 made the United States the major player in the antiterror war in the region. The SCO has, however, been stepping up in its role of a regional security cooperation grouping, particularly on the antiterrorist front. Due to the sluggish pace of economic cooperation, the SCO has not been able to compete with the rapid growth of American influence and investment in Central Asia. If this is not changed soon, warns Pan Guang, the SCO will be "hollow" and its existence and development seriously undermined.

Kazakhstan has been particularly active in promoting multilateralism and diversification of foreign policy. Murat Laumulin outlines Kazakhstan's role in confidence-building measures in Asia in chapter 17. Kazakhstan has a strong industrial base compared with the other Central Asian republics and is removed from the front line with Muslim revivalists; thus it feels stronger geopolitically and militarily. Nonetheless, Kazakhstan, like other Central Asia states, is interested in cooperating with other countries in the region regarding security. One form of institutionalization might be the CICA (Conference on Interaction and Confidence Building Measures in Asia), which was initiated by Kazakhstan in 1992 and held its first summit in 2002. The CICA is envisioned as a pan-Asian security forum bringing together countries from diverse subregions into a common security space.

Among Asian countries, Mongolia is one of the most promising candidates for being a natural partner for Central Asia due to similarities in geography, history, and geopolitical challenges posed by powerful neighbors as well as to transformation from authoritarian communist background to democratic rule. In chapter 18, Orhon Myadar analyzes those similarities as well as specific peculiarities. While the Mongolian conquest left an imprint on Central Asian society, Mongolia has also been impacted by the political influence of the Soviet Union and then the Soviet Union's demise and the rise of nationalism in ways both like and unlike the Central Asian republics. Like many Central Asian republics, Mongolia is experiencing a growing religious revival, although it is Buddhist rather than Islamic. There is also a strong nationalism and a less than successful economy. Currently the countries in Central Asia and Mongolia are facing an uncertain future.

Central Asia is increasingly involved in wider Asian politics. Be it through the involvement of China, expansion of SCO to the South Asian continent, or expansion of CICA to include members of the Southeast Asian subregion. At the same time, both Central Asia and the Asia Pacific remain distinct and incoherent. Because Asia encompasses extraordinary diversity, bringing it under a single rubric is difficult. In chapter 19 Thomas Simons Jr., who served as U.S. ambassador to Pakistan, explains that the U.S. involvement throughout Asia does not provide a common denominator for the region or for U.S. policy. It provides for great flexibility, however, and over the years the United States has successfully defended and promoted its interests in Asia in ways that are advantageous to its local partners too but make it difficult to set a coherent policy for the whole Asian region. Therefore, U.S. policy in Central Asia must address the specific attributes of the Central Asian republics.

Thomas Simons's suggestion that America should be more specific in dealing with individual Central Asian states is particularly relevant after a serious deterioration of U.S.-Uzbek relations since the Andijan events of May 2005, when President Islam Karimov ordered the use of force against what seemed to be a peaceful protest and refused to allow an international investigation of the incident. This presents a serious dilemma for the United States, and it is not just about the loss of the U.S. military facility in Uzbekistan or mounting difficulties of retaining another one in Kyrgyzstan. It is about justifying the U.S. military presence in Central Asia overall, and, more importantly, about reprioritizing the Central Asian states in America's foreign policy. For many years Uzbekistan played the role of America's closest strategic partner in Central Asia; recently it dramatically changed course and is likely to become America's worst critic. Who will fill the vacant position? Will it or can it ever be filled given the increasing pressure from Russia and China and the widespread concern in Central Asia about the spread of "color revolutions"? Finally, is it the idealism of democracy or the materialism of energy security that will prevail in the Central Asian geopolitics in the coming years?

The book may not have answers to these new questions, but it offers many insights that can help predict the most likely development of the fascinating Central Asian saga.

NOTE

1. The views expressed in this book are the academic opinions of the various authors and do not represent any official positions.

I

CONFLICT AND PEACE

2

Central Asia and the War against Terrorism: A View from Russia

Mikhail A. Konarovsky

In the 1990s, terrorism, extremism, and organized crime arose in Central Asia as a result of many factors, principally the critical social and economic situation, the tough domestic struggle within the local elite (including a struggle to reallot property and repartition the spheres of political influence), and a drastic weakening of state power in general and of its individual official structures among other elements. Meanwhile, certain political activities of different groups and movements, especially those guided by religious dogma, aimed at undermining the ruling regimes brought them in direct contact with the criminal element. In particular, that was reflected in the close association of those movements with known international terrorists operating in the region and with drug and weapons smuggling coming from Afghanistan to Tajikistan and Kyrgyzstan and then to Russia and Europe.

The spread of terrorism into Central Asia and the North Caucasus region of Russia imperiled the security and stability in those regions in the second half of the 1990s as a result of events in Afghanistan and after the radical regime of Talib fundamentalists took control and established close ties with the top of the al-Qaeda international terrorist syndicate guided by Osama bin Laden. As a result, the situation in and around Afghanistan added a multifaceted regional and international dimension to the internal conflict in that country. Since 1996 the Afghan territory was transformed into a principal center of international terrorism and religious extremism. As a strategic goal, those extremists attempted to change political regimes in Central Asia by force, create a caliphate in this region, and then transfer that process to other parts of the world, including Russia. Those forces began consolidating under a joint political, ideological, and organizational command and started creating joint military formations. Al-Qaeda and the World Jihad Front (WJF) played the key coordinating and mobilizing role in this, both headed by Osama bin Laden. A majority of other extremist organizations in Afghanistan, including the Islamic Movement of Uzbekistan (IMU) (its leader, T. Yuldashev, was Osama bin Laden's deputy in WJF), sided with them.[1] By some estimates, up to sixty thousand mercenaries from twenty countries were trained on Afghan soil.

Virtual disintegration of Afghan statehood, along with the social and economic degradation of a society exhausted by civil war, added to that country's consolidation as the main base of international terrorism and Islamic extremism. The mercenaries drilled in training camps in the Talibs' Afghanistan later operated in Iraq, Kashmir, and the Xinjiang-Uyghur Autonomous Region of China. Chechnya and the nations of Central Asia—Uzbekistan, Kyrgyzstan, and Tajikistan—were gradually coming into focus as areas of particular interest.[2] At the same time, Afghanistan was turning into a center of world narcotics trade. Narcotics began to play a role as a major currency, which provided regime survival and financed training on its territory to international terrorists.

The threats of Islamic terrorism and extremism from Afghanistan together with the prolonged conflict in that country were considered by Moscow as a real threat to Russian interests in the region and to the security of the southern borders of the Commonwealth of Independent States (CIS). In this regard, Russian foreign policy priority becomes to do everything necessary to secure a durable and just political settlement of the Afghan issue and to prevent the export of terrorism and extremism from that country.[3]

Central and South Asia were the main breeding grounds of international terrorism by the mid-1990s. Because of their geographic location, the CIS member states found themselves on the cutting edge of battle with this evil, which had detailed plans to radically change the political map of whole regions. Having come face-to-face with advancing international terrorism and extremism, those Central and South Asia countries identified international terrorism and extremism as a global menace that requires joint international efforts to fight it.

The worsening situation in Afghanistan, especially the Talibs' drive to strengthen their control over the whole country, required additional cooperative efforts by Russia, the Central Asian republics, and Kabul's other neighbors. In June 1999, the Treaty on Cooperation in Terrorism Prevention between CIS member states was signed. It became the legal basis of cooperation between concerned agencies of CIS nations in warning, preventing, and investigating acts of terror. Regular consultations of the Collective Security Treaty Organization (CSTO) member states were held in October 1999 in Moscow (the treaty was concluded on May 15, 1992). The parties stated that the aggravated events in Afghanistan had further proved the significance of the treaty to its members, since that very document played an important role in the settlement of the internal conflict in Tajikistan by barring external interference. The extraordinary meeting of CIS internal ministers held in Moscow in March 2002 resulted in the creation of an antiterrorist center. In less than six months, the presidents of the Central Asian republics at their meeting in Bishkek signed the treaty on joint efforts in preventing terrorism, political and religious extremism, and transnational organized crime.[4]

Accomplishing national reconciliation in Tajikistan in the second half of the 1990s helped reduce political extremism and terrorism and undercut their use as instruments and levers in an internal political struggle. As a result of measures undertaken by the governments of other Central Asian states, similar positive tendencies were observed there too, especially in Uzbekistan and Kyrgyzstan. But the antigovernment uprising in southern Kyrgyzstan in March 2005, which resulted in the ousting of President Askar Akayev (the March Revolution), was a clear sign that urgent economic and social reforms in the country—one of the poorest in the region—were required. Russia, along with other neighboring nations, is interested in the stabilization of Kyrgyzstan and thus has to be ready to provide more assistance to the new authorities in Bishkek. Some understandings in this respect were reached during consultations of acting Kyrgyz foreign minister Roza Otunbayeva in Moscow in April 2005. The tragic events in Uzbekistan's Andijan City in May the same year revealed serious flaws in the domestic situation of that key Central Asian nation too. The Uzbek events caused grave anxiety both in the region and in a broader geopolitical context, affecting Russia as well. A matter of special concern was the perceived involvement in the Andijan uprising of a number of international and regional terrorist organizations such as al-Qaeda, Islamic Movement of Uzbekistan, Islamic Jihad, and probably Chechen extremists, who continue their aggressive operations in the region, including Afghanistan. Bombings and kidnappings in Kabul and Kandahar that happened simultaneously with events in Andijan could have been coordinated.

Political extremism and terrorism is regarded by the leadership of the respective countries as one of the most significant potential threats to national security. Russia adheres to the same opinion. This predetermines the necessity to perfect their cooperation in every possible way, both on bilateral and multilateral regional bases, including the framework of the Collective Security Treaty Organization and of the Shanghai Cooperation Organization (SCO) created in 2001. Russia's participation in the international antiterrorist coalition reduced the threat coming from the Afghan territory to its own security and that of its Central Asian neighbors. The signing of the memorandum on respective cooperation between the Ministries of Internal Affairs of

Russia and Kyrgyzstan to prevent terror and illegal drug trafficking became an important element of Moscow teamwork with the Central Asian republics to counter terrorism and drug trafficking. This was also influenced by the agreement to establish a base in Kyrgyzstan for the Russian air force brigade as a part of the collective rapid reaction forces (CRRF). The agreement reached during the visit of President Vladimir V. Putin to Bishkek in December 2002 is meant to increase CRRF capability in neutralizing extremist and terrorist threats to the nations of Central Asia.

AFGHANISTAN AFTER SEPTEMBER 11

The removal of the Talib regime from power in late 2001, the conduct of anti-terrorist operations in Afghanistan, and the new Kabul administration's first steps toward economic revival of the country have all significantly decreased the immediate danger of the international terrorism proliferation from its territory and of renewal of the Taliban and al-Qaeda's activities. Principal terrorist training camps were destroyed. Such odious leaders as Osama bin Laden and Mullah Omar now have less opportunity to operate openly from the territory of Afghanistan. According to the Bonn Agreement of December 5, 2001, the transitional government was created and the main directions of the country's economic and political revival were determined. In twenty years of civil war, especially escalating in 1992, Afghanistan was turned into ruins, both literally and physically. Aside from economic dislocation, the country lost all the elements of the modern state and social institutions. To restore the country enormous international assistance has been in need.

In June 2002, the extraordinary Loya Jirga (National Assembly) approved the creation of the Transitional Administration, which adopted new decisions to further stabilize the country and restore its economy. Some of the highest identified priorities are to build new armed forces, consolidate the influence of the central government and limit the influence of local and regional leaders and warlords, adopt basic laws regulating trade and economic relations inside the country and with the outside world, conduct fiscal, judicial, and civil service reform, and adopt a long-term strategy to rationally utilize over $4 billion allotted to Afghanistan by the donor nations at the Tokyo Conference in January 2002. A principal task was to work out a new constitution for the country, so that the 2004 general elections could take place on the basis of that constitution. After long, conflicting debates at the Constitutional Loya Jirga in late 2003 and early 2004, a new constitution was finally adopted, with the election of a new president earlier the same year.

The Afghan administration has achieved a lot since the signing of the Bonn Agreement, and that gives rise to optimism.[5] At the same time, official Kabul and international donors are often criticized for ineffectiveness, sluggishness in accomplishing economic and social projects, and insufficient efforts to maintain security throughout the country.[6]

The administration in Kabul must solve two intertwined problems: maintaining stability and security everywhere and addressing urgent economic and social issues. Lack of efficiency in achieving these goals may give an opportunity for the Taliban and al-Qaeda remnants to regroup, expand their activities, and close ranks with extremists like Ghulbedin Hekmatiyar.[7] Terrorist formations are also using a growing resentment in different regions of Afghanistan set off by the lingering foreign "man with a gun" presence in the person of the coalition forces, and U.S. armed forces in particular.[8] By a Pakistani assessment, since the beginning of the counterterrorist operation, 1,800 members of al-Qaeda and more than 3,500 Talibs crossed the Pakistani border from Afghanistan, and only about 600 of them were captured.[9] When the bloc of religious parties—the United Action Council—strengthened its presence in Balochistan and the North-West Frontier provinces of Pakistan, a serious alert was raised not only in Kabul but also by Pakistan's neighbors. Official Afghan representatives repeatedly pointed to escalating pro-Taliban and pro–al-Qaeda activities originating from those provinces.[10]

The rise of new extremist organizations openly taking responsibility for acts of terror in Kabul and the Afghan provinces is an example of regrouping of the Talibs and al-Qaeda. One of these new extremist organizations is the so-called Secret Army of Muslim Mujahideen, which was identified attempting to commit acts of terror near the ground location of the ISAF peacekeepers and near the U.S. and Russian embassies.[11] Several of these groups train kamikaze fighters and are headed by foreign nationals, including those belonging to the Islamic Movement of Uzbekistan, whose leaders were directly supported from Kabul during the Taliban regime. The same level of alert was caused by the information that al-Qaeda in Afghanistan was involved in research on biological weapons and is still trying to obtain nuclear weapons.[12]

High-ranking Afghan military officials, however, believe that the remnants of the Talibs and al-Qaeda do not directly threaten the Transitional Administration.[13] The coalition forces make statements in the same spirit.[14] Nevertheless, extremist activities loosen the already fragile stability and security in the eastern regions of the country. The U.S. military operation against Iraq has also aggravated the situation, having been effectively used for their ends by the Taliban and al-Qaeda groups in Afghanistan and in the so-called Tribes Strip along the Afghan-Pakistani border.

The unanimous approval by the U.N. Security Council (UNSC) in January 2003 of Resolution 1455, as well as Resolution 1566 in October 2004 to intensify control over the remnants of the Taliban and the al-Qaeda network, affirmed the international community's concern over continuing subversive activities of al-Qaeda and the Taliban. Despite the undertaken efforts, including those in Afghanistan, the threat to the international community from al-Qaeda and the Taliban remains high; thus the UNSC members voted to create a more effective mechanism that would prevent the activities of these organizations throughout the world.[15] Moscow highly praised their adoption as a significant step to consolidate the sanctions regime, which is a key factor in a successful eradication of the Talibs and the terrorist operations affiliated with them and an important move to assist international efforts to stabilize the situation in Afghanistan.[16] A timely step undertaken by the United Nations in a broader context of combating international terror was also made at the special open U.N. Security Council session on January 20, 2003, which confirmed the determination of the international community to improve effectiveness of the counterterrorism efforts under the U.N. leadership.

The accomplishment of this mission will be furthered by consolidating the antiterrorist coalition on the basis of the U.N. charter and international law and refraining from unilateral steps capable of threatening the coalition's unity. Strengthening the international legal basis of counterterrorism may also provide a fundamental change in combating terrorism. Against this background, Russia has been concerned about delays in U.N. discussions on an Indian draft Comprehensive Convention on Preventing International Terrorism and a Russian initiative in respect to a convention on preventing the acts of nuclear terror. The U.N. members' inability to overcome political and ideological differences has affected interests of the world community and, as it was underlined by the Russian foreign minister, cast a shadow on U.N. ability to act effectively and responsibly in difficult situations.[17] (The latter document was adopted in April 2005.) Clearly it is necessary to pay serious attention to preventing poverty, settling national conflicts and tensions, and overcoming negative consequences of globalization, because they remain the main nutrient medium of political extremism and terrorism.[18]

In this context, the overall continuation of antiterrorist operations in Afghanistan is significant. The international community's material assistance to social and economic revival of that country as well as Afghanistan's involvement in international and regional institutions with the aim of collective development and implementation of counterterrorist and antinarcotics strategy is also of great importance. The Kabul Declaration on Good Neighborly Relations of December 22, 2002, was a significant document focused on coordination of Kabul and its neighbors' efforts, including those in Central Asia, in addressing new challenges and confirming their interest in joining measures to counter terrorism, extremism, and narcotics trafficking.[19] An understanding reached in December 2002 by the member states of the Central Asian Cooperation Organization to make their interaction in preventing transborder crime, illegal migration, and drug trafficking more active and to invite Afghanistan to participate as an observer in this organization seems to be a positive expression of the regional nations' interest to cooperate with that country. [20]

REGIONAL COLLECTIVE RESPONSE TO TERRORISM: THE SHANGHAI COOPERATION ORGANIZATION

Changes in the international political climate in the mid-1980s marked considerable improvement in relations between China and the former USSR and the elimination of border tensions between them. The disintegration of the Soviet Union and the emergence of independent states designed a new political landscape in the former Soviet-Chinese border as well. By the mid-1990s, with the emergence of three new states (Kazakhstan, Kyrgyzstan, and Tajikistan), it became necessary to transform the bilateral Soviet-Chinese negotiation mechanism into a multilateral one. In 1996 the leaders of Russia, China, Kyrgyzstan, Kazakhstan, and Tajikistan, having met in Shanghai, signed the agreement on military confidence, strengthening the border region and creating the "Shanghai Five." The total territory of the participating countries covers three-fifths of the Eurasian continent and encompasses approximately one-quarter of the world's total population. This predetermined the significance of the regional summits of their leaders who meet to solve pressing issues of the region in a new international environment. When the forum started its work, it became clear that the established mechanism of cooperation is very effective not only in the sphere of regional security but also in other fields of mutual interest. Adoption of joint documents on border issues and reduction of armed forces in the region of common borders allowed the Shanghai Five to make topics of expanding regional security cooperation as well as trade and economy exchange—with possible participation of other interested countries (initially the adjacent ones)—a main point of discussion by its third meeting in July 1998 in Almaty.

The next stage was marked on June 15, 2001, by the creation of the Shanghai Cooperation Organization (SCO) at the meeting of the leaders of Russia, China, Kazakhstan, Kyrgyzstan, Tajikistan, and Uzbekistan. The main task of this regional organization was identified as one to strengthen cooperation between the participating states on the issues of security, defense, law enforcement, foreign policy, economy, and culture.

Addressing such new challenges as international terrorism, illegal drug trafficking, weapons smuggling, illegal immigration, and other criminal transborder acts became one of the main sections of joint work of the Five and later of the Six. The most important outcome of the Bishkek summit (June 2002) was elaboration of unified approaches to prevention of international terrorism and extremism. Considered against the lack of stability and the potentially explosive situation in Central Asia and adjacent regions, previous agreements were further developed into the Shanghai Convention on Terrorism, Separatism, and Extremism Prevention. Its objective is promoting interactions among law enforcement agencies of the member states to counter those challenges, first of all in Central Asia.[21] The Bishkek Group, which consists of the heads of such SCO agencies, has been functioning since December 1999. Also, a process was under way to make a draft interstate program of cooperative measures for 2003–2005 to combat terrorism, separatism, extremism, and other dangerous crimes. It also intends to prevent illegal drug production, illegal weapons trade, and illegal migration.

Today a visible common interest of the SCO states is to interact closely and effectively with other states as well as respective international and regional structures. By now, the ASEAN Regional Forum (ARF), India, Iran, Pakistan, Sri Lanka, Mongolia, the United States, and Japan have all demonstrated interest in the SCO activity. However, the requests to broaden the SCO's ranks will not be reviewed until the respective charter documents of the organization come into force. Experts propose to use the G8 experience as well as different levels of participation: permanent members, partners in separate projects that are implemented by the permanent members, and observers. Those countries, enthusiastic to join the SCO, may be required at first to go through participation in its separate thematic sittings and projects.[22] Mongolia, Pakistan, Iran, and India have observer status in SCO in 2006.

Meanwhile, the Moscow meeting of the SCO's foreign affairs ministers in December 2002 adopted a provisional scheme for mutual relations between the Shanghai Cooperation Organization and other International Organizations and States.[23] It will be used until the respective SCO legislation comes into force. Supposedly, representatives of states and international organizations that are not members of the SCO may be invited to participate in the SCO Council of Ministers sittings or the international consultations of the organization. The tragic events of October 23–26, 2002, in Moscow reinforced the general feeling to consolidate the organization faster. All Russian partners in the SCO firmly supported measures undertaken by the Russian authorities to free the hostages.[24] The SCO foreign ministers meeting underlined the global nature of antiterrorist struggles, stressing that terrorism is still the most serious threat to international peace and security. SCO members have supported the international community's efforts aimed at cutting the channels of terrorist financing and fully agreed with the provisions of the declaration on financial measures of terrorism prevention adopted by ARF in July 2002. In April 2005 a memorandum of understanding between SCO and ASEAN (Association of Southeast Asian Nations) was signed in Jakarta.

Russia believes that the most urgent task of the international community in the near future is to strengthen the international legal basis of counterterrorism and adopt as quickly as possible a comprehensive convention to prevent acts of nuclear terror. At the same time, the leading role of the United Nations in the antiterrorist struggle must be reinforced. Another important result of the Moscow meeting was a general understanding that the strengthening of stability in Central Asia remains the paramount security task of the SCO member states. The member nations are seriously concerned over separatist tendencies in different Asian countries and by a growing symbiosis between terrorism and separatism. They underline that it is inadmissible to excuse terrorism and separatism by religious, national, or political motives.

The SCO nations, proceeding from the fact that efficient counteraction to new challenges and threats to international and regional security and stability needs their closer cooperation, are interested in drawing up a comprehensive program that would include joint and coordinated efforts in fighting terrorism, separatism, and extremism. The events in Uzbekistan in spring of 2005 made this objective even more pressing. The Astana summit of SCO in July 2005 adopted a special declaration aimed at coordination against the "three evils."

THE SCO AND AFGHANISTAN

The SCO member states paid careful attention to the dramatic developments in Afghanistan in the recent past, especially because that country became a main breeding ground for regional and international terrorism and illegal drug trafficking after the Talibs came to power in 1996. The SCO nations' interest in the Afghanistan situation was not accidental: their security was directly affected by the country which the Talibs transformed into the center of training and export of international terrorism and of narcotics. As President Vladimir Putin noted at the SCO summit held in Tashkent in June 2004, dramatic developments in Afghanistan were impelling motives of that structure, and the SCO members are vitally interested in restoring peace and economic rehabilitation on that soil.

In late 2002 in Moscow the SCO's ministers of foreign affairs extensively discussed developments in post-Taliban Afghanistan. They confirmed the common interest in a peaceful path for that country, expressed support for the Kabul administration in its efforts to normalize and stabilize the situation in Afghanistan and to recover its economy on the basis of the Bonn Agreement. They also supported the Extraordinary Loya Jirga's decisions and the corresponding resolutions of the U.N. Security Council. International action to eliminate terrorism in Afghanistan was also favorably appraised. At the same time, the Six expressed grave concern in connection with illegal drug production in that country. They stated that drug trade remains the most important source of financing international and regional terrorism. Underlining the remaining drug threat to the SCO members, the ministers have positively characterized proposals to create antinarcotic "security belts" along the Afghan borders. The high-level Tashkent Declaration, having confirmed the U.N.'s central role in implementation of international programs in Afghanistan, affirmed the SCO intention to promote international cooperation in the fight against terrorism and drug trafficking with a view to achieving security, peace, and order in Afghanistan.

A temporary mechanism of enlisting other countries to participate in organization activities, worked out by the SCO countries, creates favorable conditions for Afghanistan as well. In the beginning, Kabul might be interested in antiterrorist and counternarcotics tracks of the SCO. Later, the practice of time checks and concrete cooperation can be applied to other areas, including the economic one. To meet these objectives as well as to consolidate cooperation in implementation of Russia's initiative concerning regional antidrug security belts, the SCO-Afghanistan Contact Group was set up in 2004, with Kabul being invited as an observer at the SCO's regular sessions.

ILLEGAL DRUGS AND FINANCING OF TERRORISM

The Transitional Administration of Afghanistan is aware that the mass production of opium poppies inflicts tremendous damage not only to the national economy but to the international prestige of the government as well.[25] Official Kabul also realizes that illegal drug trafficking undermines internal stability, provides considerable financial feeding to unlawful and terrorist military groups in Afghanistan, visibly displeases its neighboring countries together with Russia and other European nations, where up to 90 percent of heroin originates in Afghanistan. That is why, on coming to power the government of Afghanistan undertook a number of measures to address this threat. By January 17, 2002, a decree was adopted that forbids opium poppy cultivation, opium and heroin production, as well as transportation of illicit raw materials and drugs.[26] In May 2003, the National Strategy of Drug Control was announced too.

However, the lack of effective governmental levers of influence in provinces, weakness of state authorities, and lack of financing has impeded Kabul's ability to implement the intended course. And what is more, in 2002 the opium poppy sowing area became ten times larger than in 2001.[27] In recent years the consumption of narcotics in Afghanistan itself has grown sharply.

The acuteness of the drug problem for Afghanistan is deepened by the fact that the income from selling opium poppies grown on one hectare of land is dozens of times higher than the income from grain from an equal area. Measures undertaken by international donors and Kabul to reorient farmers to growing different crops and to pay compensation if they eliminate sown poppy ($375 per hectare) did not manage to visibly decrease land under poppy cultivation in 2002 because the proposed compensation was significantly smaller than the poppy price (up to $600 per hectare). Open resistance has been observed among the farmers, especially in the southern provinces of Afghanistan.[28] If such a tendency continues, it is not improbable that the production and export of narcotics will increase considerably. Nevertheless, for the present, neither Kabul nor the international community is capable of dealing with the drug problem in that country. Considerable international assistance, from the United Nations as well as from European and regional countries, is required.

The growth of Afghan narcotics production (which is 70 percent of the world's production) caused substantial increase of the drug traffic through Central Asia, particularly through Tajikistan, into Russia. In 2002, Russian border guards confiscated about five tons of illegal drugs on the Afghan-Tajik border.[29] Illegal drugs have been shipped through Kyrgyzstan and Kazakhstan to Russia and Europe and recently to Japan as well. This situation raises a growing concern in Moscow. To this effect, the issues of bilateral cooperation with Afghanistan in prevention of terrorism and drug contraband were discussed during the visit of the Afghan foreign minister, Abdullah Abdullah, to Moscow in November 2002, as well as in political consultations with his deputy A. Aziz in May 2005.[30]

One should combat the drug threat emanating from Afghanistan with the backup from new Afghan authorities and with the highest possible participation of the international community. Among the first and most important tasks in that direction would be increased efforts to strengthen the structure of Tajik border forces after the full authority on border control with Afghanistan has been transferred to them from the Russian border guards group in Tajikistan. In August 2002 at the ASEAN regional forum the Russian side proposed that an additional second "counternarcotic security belt" on the Russian-Kazakh border be created. On this path, the cooperation between Russia and the United

States already started. Russia also added to this task accomplishment by contributing $500,000 to the United Nations Drug Control Program (UNDCP). Primarily, these funds are designated to complete respective projects in Central Asia.

RUSSIAN ANTITERRORISM COOPERATION IN ASIA

As a result of counterterrorist operations by coalition forces in Afghanistan, regional terrorist hotbeds moved into the area of the Afghan-Pakistan border, including the "Tribes Strip," and to Kashmir, thus predetermining the necessity to expand certain cooperation between Russia and such non–Central Asian Afghan neighbors as Iran, India, and Pakistan. The activity of bilateral antiterrorist working groups is an effective mechanism of such cooperation. Consultations between Russia and Iran, which took place in January 2003 in Moscow, underlined interactivity of the terrorist groups operating in the regions of Afghanistan, Pakistan, Chechnya, and Trans-Caucasus, declared readiness to expand counterterrorist cooperation and to deepen coordination to prevent narcotic threat from Afghanistan.

Russia and India are generally united in their approach to the main international issues. That also includes terrorism prevention, which was never a subject of abstract theory for either Russia or India. Long before the tragic events of September 11 in the United States, these nations tried to attract attention to that problem, pointing at the international nature of the terrorist organizations. The main principles of the parties' interaction were reflected in the Moscow Declaration on International Terrorism of November 6, 2001: the key role of the United States in preventing the terrorist threat, the necessity of decisive measures against terrorists and countries that support, shelter, finance, and thus promote them. At the same time both Moscow and Delhi recognize the unproductiveness of a simplified approach to the problem of terrorism, of attempts to identify it with certain ethnic groups or religious beliefs. Both countries have energetically assisted in addressing dangerous instability in Afghanistan and are involved in a dialog on the Afghan issues in which the working group on terrorism prevention created in 2000 plays an important role. Their vision of postconflict restoration of Afghanistan is identical. Serious concern of both parties is additionally raised by growth of illegal drug production in that country. The working group meeting in July 2002 described the progress in Afghanistan in a positive way, confirmed the determination to assist Kabul in restoring the country and strengthening the political settlement process, which will also add to the final eradication of terrorism in the region. The special significance of Russian-Indian cooperation, which is of crucial importance to the strategic partnership between Moscow and Delhi, was emphasized.[31]

Cooperation between Moscow and Islamabad was expanded recently, including the framework of bilateral consultative group on strategic stability. Its first meeting took place in January 2003. The group discussed preventing the proliferation of weapons of mass destruction and their delivery means, particularly into this region, first of all, in the light of growing threats on behalf of international terrorism.[32]

Regular Russian-U.S. consultations on the issues of international terrorism within the framework of the working group (since 2000) are quite productive. Formerly its activity was aimed to elaborate joint response to the Talibs' Afghanistan threats. Today, however, the working group is considered—by both Moscow and Washington—to be one of the most effective mechanisms of bilateral cooperation in addressing new challenges of the present and a convenient instrument of "time checks" on Afghanistan and the situation around it.[33]

The same context preordains the necessity to create similar consultative bodies directly between Moscow and Kabul. The first step in this direction was, undoubtedly, a protocol on consultations between the foreign ministries of both countries, signed during the official visit of the minister of foreign affairs of Afghanistan, Abdullah Abdullah, to Moscow in November 2002.

Instability in Central Asia and Afghanistan can affect the overall security in this vast region, affecting Russia's interests as well as those of China, India, the United States, and the European Union, which keeps an eye on regional developments too. That fact predetermines the need for their close antiterrorist cooperation in the region, including Pakistan.

NOTES

1. For more information on the subject, see Z. Nabiev and M. Arunova, "Talibanskiy Afghanistan ili opornaya baza mezhdunarodnogo terrorizma," v *Islamism i extremism na blizhnem vostoke* (Afghanistan under Taliban and as Support Base of International Terrorism, in *Islamism and Extremism in the Middle East)* (Moscow: Nauka, 2001), 158–63. In Russian.

2. V. Sazhin, "Vooruzhennye konflikty: Porozhdenie narkobiznesa i terrorisma," v Z. *Islamizm i extremism na blizhnem vostoke* (Armed Conflicts as Product of Narcobusiness and Terrorism, in *Islamism and Extremism in the Middle East)*, 231–37.

3. "Konzepziya vneshnei politiki Rossiskoi Federazii," *Diplomaticheskiy vestnik* (The Concept of the Foreign Policy of the Russian Federation, *Diplomatic Herald)*, January 2001. In Russian.

4. Yu. Rakhmaninov, "O presechenii mezhdunarodnogo terrorisma kak opasnogo vyzova miru i mezhdunarodnoi bezopasnosti," v *Islamizm i extremism na blizhnem*

vostoke (On Eradication of Terrorism as a Dangerous Threat to Peace and International Security, in *Islamism and Extremism in the Middle East*) (Moscow: Nauka, 2001), 222–23. In Russian.

5. Khamid Kharzai, speech on the occasion of the first anniversary of the Transitional Administration, Ministry of Foreign Affairs, Afghanistan.

6. M. Kapila and K. Weamester, "The Afghanistan Job Is Bigger Than Expected," *International Herald Tribune,* January 14, 2003.

7. *Farda*, December 15, 2002; General Mirza Aslam Beg, "Afghan Turmoil: Security Imperatives for Region," *The News,* January 18, 2003.

8. *Daily Times,* January 7, 2003; *Sahaak*, December 14, 2002.

9. Statement, January 8, 2003.

10. *Kabul Times,* January 1 and January 22, 2003; *Christian Science Monitor,* December 26, 2002.

11. *Dawn,* January 13, 2003; *Sahaak*, January 13, 2003; *Frontier Post*, January 22, 2003.

12. *Frontier Post,* January 11, 2003; Interfax News Agency, January 17, 2003.

13. Minister of Defense of Afghanistan M. Fakhim, interview, *Armane Melli*, November 16, 2002.

14. *The News*, January 12, 2003.

15. Resolution 1455 (2003), Security Council 4686th meeting (AM), press release, SC/7636.

16. Ministry of Foreign Affairs of the Russian Federation on the UNSC Decision to Adopt a Resolution Against the Talibs and al-Qaeda, press release, www.mid.ru (January 20, 2003).

17. Russian foreign minister Igor S. Ivanov, speech to the opening session of the UNSC dedicated to the prevention of terrorism, press release, www.mid.ru (January 20, 2003).

18. Russian foreign minister Igor S. Ivanov, speech to the opening session of the UNSC.

19. Kabul Declaration of Good Neighborly Relations, December 22, 2002.

20. *The News,* December 28, 2002.

21. The convention was ratified by both chambers of the Federal Assembly of Russia in December 2002.

22. Dmitry Trofimov, "Shanghaiskiy process—ot 'Pyatyorki' do 'Organizatsii sotrudnichestva'" (The Shanghai Process: From the Five to Cooperation Organization), *Centralnaya Asia i Kavkaz,* February 2002, 102. In Russian.

23. "The Provisional Scheme for Mutual Relations between the Shanghai Cooperation Organization and Other International Organizations and States," www.mid.ru (November 23, 2002).

24. Russian foreign minister Igor S. Ivanov, speech to a press conference at the end of the SCO Foreign Affairs ministerial meeting, www.mid.ru (November 23, 2002).

25. *The Nation*, January 1, 2003.

26. Dr. Zalmai Rassoul, statement to the Second International Drug Control Meeting, *The Nation*, October 17, 2002.

27. The main cultivation areas are located in the southwestern provinces of Hilmand, Uruzgan, and Kandahar and in the eastern provinces of Nangarhar and Kunar. In the northern part of the country there are poppy fields in Badakhshan, Badghiz, Baghlan, Faryab, Kunduz, Samangan, and Takhar. The largest areas are in Badakhshan.

28. *The News,* December 30, 2002.

29. *The Statesman,* January 9, 2003.

30. *Kommersant Daily*, November 30, 2002.

31. Joint statement of the fifth meeting of the Joint Russian-Indian working group on Afghanistan, New Delhi, July 17–18, 2002.

32. "On the Meeting of the Russian-Pakistani Consultative Group on Strategic Stability," Ministry of Foreign Affairs of the Russian Federation Informational Bulletin, www.mid.ru (January 16, 2003); *The News,* January 18, 2003.

33. In May 2002 it was transformed into the Working Group on Counterterrorism, www.mid.ru (January 17, 2003).

3

The Afghanistan Peace Process: Progress and Problems

Najibullah Lafraie

Afghanistan has been in the grip of turmoil and instability for more than a quarter of a century, ever since the pro-Moscow communists overthrew the existing regime and seized power in April 1978. The country has passed through different stages: from spontaneous resistance against the communist regime to organized liberation war against the Soviet army, and from the imposed factional fighting among mujahideen in the first half of the 1990s to the brutal Taliban rule in the second half of that decade. Circumstances have dictated militancy, but extremism has been limited to certain groups, even when the infamous Taliban brought most of the country under its control. With the removal of the Taliban, a light for peace and stability appeared at the end of the long tunnel of the Afghan people's suffering for the first time after the short-lived hopes for peace that had followed the downfall of the communist regime in April 1992.

The peace process that began with the Bonn Conference in November 2001 has come a long way. It is marred with countless difficulties, however, and is far from assured to bear the desired fruits. This chapter will first look at the peace process itself and what has been achieved so far. Then it will discuss the problems that have beset the peace process and how they came about. Finally, it will consider future prospects for the peace process and make recommendations for further action to secure peace and stability in the country.

ACHIEVEMENTS

The Bonn Agreement, Emergency Loya Jirga, Constitutional Loya Jirga, Tokyo Conference, and Berlin Conference have been important steps toward restoration of peace and stability in Afghanistan. However, agreements and conferences only provide a framework for action. The success of the peace process depends on what is practically achieved on the ground. In a speech to the nation on the first anniversary of his assumption of power, President Hamid Karzai listed ten areas of success for the peace process and his administration:

1. Making Afghanistan a common home for all Afghans
2. Restoring Afghanistan's prestige
3. Establishing security and reconstructing a national army and police force
4. Rehabilitating the civil administration
5. Rehabilitating the economic infrastructure
6. Launching the reconstruction process
7. Establishing some independent commissions
8. Reviving educational and higher educational institutions and cultural activities
9. Assisting people stricken by natural disasters such as earthquakes
10. Conducting an active foreign policy[1]

There was some substance in this overly optimistic assessment of the situation. At the time of the speech, more than 1.7 million refugees had returned to the country. Many countries resumed diplomatic relations with Afghanistan and reopened their embassies in Kabul. President Karzai became a well-known international figure. Relative security was established in Kabul and other major cities, and some steps were taken for establishment of national army and police. Civil administration, which was almost totally destroyed by the Taliban, was rehabilitated, at least in Kabul. Steps were taken toward financial and economic reforms, including introduction of a new currency and enactment of a new foreign investment law. Some reconstruction work had begun, especially to rebuild national highways. Radio and TV stations in Kabul and other cities resumed broadcasting. Several newspapers and magazines, both government and privately owned, were published in Kabul with relative freedom of speech. Schools and universities reopened all over the country, and millions of children and youth of both sexes enjoyed the opportunity to seek knowledge and build a brighter future.

The list of achievements has grown longer in the past two and one-half years since Karzai's speech. Now he will certainly put passage on the new constitution and the presidential election on top of his list. Moreover, a million more refugees have returned, and the number of students going to schools and universities has increased substantially. Civil administration has extended to most provincial capitals. Police and army training and recruitment have continued. More than 55,000 armed militias have surrendered their weapons under the Disarmament, Demobilization, and Reintegration (DDR) program—supported by the United Nations and Japan. Reconstruction work has continued and some projects have been completed, for example, the Kabul–Kandahar highway. Economic reforms have been continued by passage of new laws and bringing border customhouses under central government control. Business seems to be booming in Kabul with expatriate Afghans and foreign companies joining local businessmen in ventures such as telecommunications and hotels.

SHORTCOMINGS, DIFFICULTIES, AND FAILURES

In his anniversary speech, President Karzai also noted some shortcomings and failures of the peace process and his administration. They included:

1. Warlords
2. Slow progress in disarming illegal armed forces
3. Highway robberies and other crimes
4. Administrative corruption including bribery and embezzlement
5. Failure to form some necessary independent commissions
6. Lack of a trained police force
7. "Extortionists" holding other people's houses and estates
8. Inability to return all internally displaced people to their homes

Grave as this list may seem, the actual situation was even worse. A January 2003 report by the International Development Committee of the British Parliament painted a bleak picture of Afghanistan. It categorically stated, "Afghanistan has no institutions that work, no legitimate economy, no security and a serious lack of capacity within the government."[2] Moreover, according to a December 2002 report by Human Rights Watch, "because of the conscious choices made by key actors, notably Afghan military leaders and the United States, the processes set in motion by the Bonn Agreement are now faltering in key areas such as human rights, public security, the rule of law, and economic reconstruction."[3]

The Karzai government and its foreign supporters do not seem to have overcome many of the problems he identified. And the specter of another monster—narcotic drugs—now looms large on the horizon. Even the apparent successes may be less than they seem. Two examples will suffice. Disarming more than 55,000 militias under the DDR program is a great accomplishment. Yet the number of medium and light weapons collected reaches only 33,500, which forms a fraction of several hundred thousand illegal arms in the country.[4] As an observant journalist notes, "Most militia fighters [have] simply concealed their best weapons and turned in old, ineffective ones."[5] Rebuilding the Kabul–Kandahar highway is another example. It is the single largest reconstruction project so far, and completion of its first phase was inaugurated by Karzai and Khalilzad with a lot of fanfare in mid-December 2003. After only three months, however, the road "became full of potholes and bumpy." A Kandahar resident complained, "We don't know what kind of reconstruction project this was, it only lasted a few months."[6]

The main problems and shortcomings of the peace process will now be discussed. Most of these problems are interrelated.

Warlordism

Warlordism is perhaps the single most important challenge and obstacle to the peace process in Afghanistan. It is the main reason why the Karzai government has not been able to extend its authority much beyond Kabul. The problem dates back to the war against the communist regime and the Soviet army. As the authority of the central government collapsed, local commanders amassed more power by virtue of receiving arms as well as financial resources. Until the downfall of the Najib regime, they paid allegiance to one of the political parties of the resistance movement based in Pakistan and Iran, and in the case of the pro-government militias, to the central government in Kabul. In the aftermath of the imposed factional fighting that followed the establishment of the Islamic State of Afghanistan, local commanders slowly asserted their autonomy, relying on revenues from custom duties, road tolls, exploitation of local natural resources, and production and smuggling of narcotics.

Atrocities committed by warlords motivated the Afghan people to welcome the Taliban movement and support it initially. The Taliban's subsequent repression and abuses of human rights rivaled those of the warlords. Nonetheless, they were able to unify most parts of the country militarily and remove the warlords from the territories under their control. The commanders who joined the Taliban were not allowed to operate in their traditional power base. Instead, they were sent to other parts of the country.

The current problem of warlordism in Afghanistan is largely the result of U.S. policies. As Human Rights Watch notes, "Although the Taliban had effectively unified the military command of most of the country and thereby undermined the country's endemic military feudalism, the United States and others helped to re-establish this system as part of their strategy for removing the Taliban from power."[7]

Karzai's attitude toward warlords has been ambivalent. He has spoken harshly against warlordism and has vowed to end it. During his presidential campaign, he sidestepped some prominent members of the Northern Alliance and dismissed others, winning praise for fighting warlordism. The practical effects of those measures are questionable, however. All those commanders and warlords have largely retained their influence even after losing their official positions in their regions. This is evident from an incident in May 2005, when a Dostum rival was prevented from launching his political campaign for parliamentary elections in a district under Dostum's influence.[8] A June 2005 news report by the U.N. Integrated Regional Information Network (IRIN) quotes the police chief of Badakhshan province as saying, "We need commandos, we need police, we need helicopters. Commanders [warlords] are strong [and 'have no shortage of heavy or light weaponry at their disposal to enforce their will']. They must be brought under control."[9] This is the region described as one of the safest in the country; despite "all the militia forces in the northeast [being] supposedly decommissioned by the UN-backed Disarmament Demobilisation and Reintegration programme" and despite "the support of a 200 strong NATO-led group of international peacekeepers stationed in Faizabad [the provincial capital]."[10]

Insecurity and Violation of Human Rights

Warlordism has damaged security and resulted in human rights abuses in most parts of the country. According to Human Rights Watch annual report for 2005, "Political repression, human rights abuses, and criminal activity by warlords . . . are consistently listed as the chief concerns of most Afghans." Such crimes include rape, murder, illegal detention, forced displacement, and trafficking in women and children. "In some remote areas, there are no real governmental structures or activity, only abuse and criminal enterprises by factions." The report also blames the local military and police forces, even in the capital, for involvement in "arbitrary arrests, kidnapping, extortion, torture, and extrajudicial killings of criminal suspects."[11]

The capital city, Kabul, enjoys a greater measure of peace and security thanks to the presence of International Security Assistance Force (ISAF) troops. Even there, however, the security situation is less than satisfactory. Abuses committed by the police and other security forces are only part of the problem. In May 2005, for example, several major robberies took place in Kabul, a bomb attack on a downtown Internet café killed an expatriate U.N. staff and two Afghans, and an Italian aid worker was abducted.

The United States and its allies have also been blamed for violations of human rights in Afghanistan. The Human Rights Watch, Amnesty International,

and even the U.N. independent expert on the situation of human rights in
Afghanistan have continuously criticized U.S. treatment of prisoners in the
country. In his last report, the latter noted that he had received information on
"forced entry into homes, arrest and detention of nationals and foreigners
without legal authority or judicial review . . . forced nudity, hooding and sen-
sory deprivation, sleep and food deprivation . . . sexual abuse, beating, torture, and use of force resulting in death."[12] Unfortunately, instead of the report finding receptive hearing, the independent expert was dismissed and the
post was eliminated.[13]

Limited Deployment of ISAF

Two weeks after endorsing the Bonn Agreement on December 6, 2001, the
Security Council passed another resolution authorizing establishment of the
ISAF on December 20, 2001. It was not a U.N. peacekeeping force. It con-
sisted of troops from volunteer countries who were responsible for their
own expenses. In practice it became a mainly European force with one non-
European member — New Zealand — and one Muslim country — Turkey. On
December 22, a ceremony for transfer of power was held in Kabul and the
Interim Administration under chairmanship of Hamid Karzai took office.

The ISAF mission was initially limited to providing security to Kabul.
From the beginning, however, there were calls for its deployment to other
parts of the country. At that time the European countries contributing to ISAF
seemed open to the idea,[14] but it did not happen due to U.S. opposition.[15]
Later when the United States changed its position to favor expansion, those
countries had become reluctant to commit more troops and resources to
Afghanistan. "The Americans and Europeans have blamed each other for the
failure to expand peacekeepers."[16] In this debate, an important observation
has been lost: "Unless the international community is prepared to give the
kind of security support [provided to Kabul] to Afghanistan as a whole, it is
going to start to fracture."[17]

To compensate for the absence of ISAF troops, the U.S. military command
in Afghanistan prepared a program to deploy provincial reconstruction teams
(PRTs) to some population centers around the country starting in January
2003. A PRT consists of about 100 to 200 soldiers, engineers, medical staff,
and civil affairs officers. The aim is to "help President Hamid Karzai expand
the still dormant authority of his government and begin construction projects
outside Kabul."[18] However, the program was sharply criticized by humanitarian organizations at the outset for several reasons. It was argued that such
enclaves needed to rely on the goodwill of the local warlords. Thus the program would strengthen warlords' power and further legitimize it.[19] It would

take the focus away from security prematurely, duplicate coordination of reconstruction efforts, and "blur the line between humanitarian workers and a combatant military force, [thus creating] security risk for civilian aid workers."[20] Those fears proved true when Doctors without Borders, the French NGO that operated in Afghanistan for more than twenty years under harsh conditions of Soviet occupation and Taliban rule, decided to terminate its activities in Afghanistan after coming under frequent attacks by antigovernment forces.[21]

Despite the PRT's shortcomings, it became a model for ISAF expansion in late 2003. Until then, New Zealand and Germany were the only countries other than the allied forces to have established PRTs in Afghanistan. NATO assumed command and coordination of ISAF in August 2003, and in December the German-led PRT in Kunduz was transferred to ISAF authority as a pilot project. By June 2005, ISAF was operating five PRTs in the north and two in the west. There were also fourteen American PRTs in the south and the east and one New Zealand PRT in Bamian, central Afghanistan. The number of military and civilian staff serving in these PRTs is relatively small and their role seems mostly symbolic and psychological. A comparison of the number of international peacekeepers committed to Afghanistan with that in other postconflict situations is instructive. In East Timor, for each 111 Timorese there was 1 peacekeeper. In Bosnia the ratio was 67 to 1, and in Kosovo it was 45 to 1. In Afghanistan the ratio is about 2,500 to 1.[22]

Problems in Raising a National Army and Police Force

Afghanistan badly needs international peacekeepers because it lacks a professional army and police force of any size. Work to train a 70,000-strong army began in May 2002. The program was beset with numerous problems from the outset, however, and progress has been slow. The number of recruits undergoing training is small, and the desertion rate is high. In June 2005 the *Daily Telegraph* reported, "Thousands of soldiers are deserting Afghanistan's new British- and American-trained national army, their morale undermined by poor conditions and the threat from the Taliban." According to the report, 31,000 Afghans have undergone training, but the number of those serving the army reaches only 20,000.[23] The Karzai government and its foreign supporters hoped the army would reach its full capacity by 2007. At the current rate, however, it may take at least a decade to reach a minimum of 70,000.

While American, British, and French troops train the army, Germans have been training the police force. "The police training program . . . is also in trouble."[24] Salaries are low; the program is limited to Kabul and a few other cities, and the police lack the basic equipment necessary for carrying out their operations.[25] To make its presence felt at least in provincial capitals, the government has tried to enlist tens of thousands of Afghans as police— 50,000 according to Karzai[26]—but fewer than 5,000 have been trained by Germany,[27] thus making police unprofessionalism a major cause of concern.

Regrouping of the Taliban, Hikmatyar's Hizb Islami, and al-Qaeda Remnants

Lawless warlords and common criminals are not the only security problems in Afghanistan. Activities of those opposed to the U.S. presence and committed to the overthrow of its handpicked government have been increasing. The enormous use of force by the allied troops was not able to wipe out the Taliban. Most of the rank and file threw away their turbans, trimmed their beards, and melted among the local population. Some of their leaders were captured, but most—including the top leader, Mullah Omar—went into hiding. A large number of al-Qaeda leaders and their fighters also escaped unharmed. The Taliban and al-Qaeda found a new ally when Gulbuddin Hikmatyar, formerly a mujahideen leader, was forced out of exile in Iran in May 2002 and returned to the tribal areas between Afghanistan and Pakistan. There are signs that Hikmatyar has joined forces with remnants of the Taliban and al-Qaeda.

The Taliban and its allies failed to disrupt the first presidential election in October 2004 and lowered their activity level in the subsequent winter, raising hopes that they might be a "spent force." With the advent of the spring, however, they resumed their activities, and at the time of this writing—June 2005—carry out several operations every week. As a *New York Times* reporter puts it, "During the last six months, American and Afghan officials have predicted the collapse of the Taliban. . . . But the intensity of the fighting here in Zabul Province, and in parts of adjoining Kandahar and Uruzgan Provinces—roughly 100 square miles of mountain valleys in all—reveals the Taliban to be still a vibrant fighting force supplied with money, men and weapons."[28]

The insurgency is active not only in the "jagged hills" but also in the cities and elsewhere. For example, a pro-Karzai religious leader who had denounced the Taliban just a week earlier was assassinated in Kandahar toward the end of May 2005. A bomb explosion at his funeral in a mosque killed twenty people, including the Kabul police chief, and wounded more than fifty. "Hours after the bombing, unsigned 'night letters' were distributed in parts of Kandahar threatening to kill people who cooperate with the government or the U.S.-led military coalition."[29]

FOREIGN INTERFERENCE

Before the first presidential election in October 2004, President Karzai and his spokesman, Ambassador Khalilzad, and even Pakistani journalists accused the Pakistani government of hypocrisy in its relations with Afghanistan and active support of the Taliban. Ahmad Rashid, an eminent Pakistani journalist, for example, wrote, "Pakistani leaders promise both aid and trade to bolster Karzai's government. At the same time, Islamabad has effectively undermined Kabul's authority by allowing senior Taliban leaders and other antigovernment renegades, including Gulbuddin Hikmatyar and Jalaluddin Haqqani, to find de facto sanctuary in Pakistan's tribal belt."[30] He also reported retired Pakistani army officers saying that the Pakistani army units operating along the Afghanistan-Pakistan border had split into two parts. Some senior officers and their staff worked with American forces to find and capture al-Qaeda members while others "work out deals with the Taliban."[31]

In the aftermath of the presidential election, however, relations between Afghanistan and Pakistan seemed to experience a complete overhaul. President Pervey Musharraf's trip to Afghanistan in November 2004, as the first foreign leader to visit the country after Karzai's official assumption of presidency, was described as "a major comeback and a diplomatic coup."[32] The United States seemed to play an important role in the rapprochement. It was also noted that "the symbolism of the visit could not be lost on anyone. Karzai's victory means that the Pashtuns are, once again, at the center of Afghan politics and that Pakistan is prepared to back them as it had done with the Taliban."[33] However, after an increase in antigovernment activities in spring 2005, Afghan authorities started blaming foreign hands for the unrest and acts of terrorism. They refrained from naming Pakistan, but their tone demonstrated clearly what they meant.[34]

Pakistan is not the only country interfering in Afghanistan. Again according to Ahmad Rashid, "Sources say that Russia is arming one warlord, Iran another and India and Pakistan are secretly backing different claimants to power. Wealthy Saudis have resumed funding Islamic extremists and some Central Asian republics are backing their ethnic allies."[35] Finally the United States, which has about 18,000 troops in Afghanistan, is backing President Karzai, to the extent of providing his personal bodyguards as well as supporting various warlords around the country.

Insufficient International Assistance for Reconstruction

To rebuild Afghanistan at the prewar level, tens of billions of dollars are needed. The Asian Development Bank estimates Afghanistan's need at $27.5

billion.[36] The amount of aid pledged falls far short of the country's needs and compares unfavorably with international assistance to other countries in similar circumstances. According to one report, the "US gave Iraq $18.6 billion for reconstruction in 2004 and Afghanistan only $1.2 billion," while the two countries are comparable in population and Iraq is much richer in resources and income.[37] It has also been noted that "Cambodia, Sierra Leone and the Congo received more per capita spending in their first two years of reconstruction than Afghanistan, to say nothing of expensive efforts in Kosovo, Bosnia and East Timor." This is why Karzai's former finance minister labeled the U.S. efforts in Afghanistan "state building on the cheap."[38]

Narcotic Drugs

Narcotic drug production, processing, and trafficking have become a major problem in Afghanistan. According to the 2004 report of the International Narcotic Control Board, opium production reached an unprecedented level of 4,200 tons in 2004, jumping from 3,600 tons in 2003. The area under poppy cultivation rose from 80,000 hectares in 2003 to over 130,000 hectares in 2004.[39] An estimated 2.3 million people, representing about 10 percent of the population, are involved in opium-related activities; the annual income from opium reaches $2.8 billion, or 60 percent of country's legitimate GDP.[40] Ridding Afghanistan of this illicit economy, dealing with drug-related law and order problems, dealing with the warlords who benefit from narcotic drugs, cleansing the government of high-level officials with drug mafia connections, and depriving the Taliban and other antigovernment forces of their drug-related income have posed major challenges to the Karzai administration and its foreign supporters.

Narcotics production has a long history in Afghanistan. It was boosted by several decades of chaos and instability and was officially sanctioned by the Taliban during its rule, except for the last year when it successfully banned cultivation. Its unprecedented level in the post-Taliban era, however, is directly related to the U.S. policies in its "war on terror." Many of the warlords who cooperated with the allied forces in the removal of the Taliban had a history of drug involvement. The support and resources they received from the United States enabled them to expand their drug-related operations. Initially the United States and its allies turned a blind eye on such activities, and the U.S. forces in Afghanistan refused to get involved in anti-drug campaigns until March 2005.[41] The modest antinarcotic campaigns carried out by the U.S. and British civilian authorities worsened the drug problem instead of solving it, due to their ad hoc nature and lack of a well-planned and coordinated strategy. The attempt to compensate farmers for switching to alternative crops encouraged those who had not cultivated poppies before to do so with the hope of receiving free cash. Consequently, poppy cultivation spread from fourteen provinces during Taliban rule to more than thirty provinces. Relying on the governors, most of whom benefit from narcotics, to curb poppy cultivation also backfired. Aerial sprays damaged other crops and affected only the poor farmers, creating a backlash among the Afghan people and government officials alike and leading the assistant secretary of state, Robert Charles, a staunch proponent of the policy, to resign. Manual eradication carried out in some provinces in spring 2005 was marred by security problems, stiff resistance from farmers, and compromises by the authorities.[42] The Afghan government and the foreign agencies supporting it are unlikely to solve the narcotic drugs problem in the foreseeable future.

FUTURE PROSPECTS

Despite great strides, the future of the peace process in Afghanistan does not seem bright. In a speech accepting an award in early 2003, Lakhdar Brahimi, the U.N. secretary-general's special representative to Afghanistan at the time, noted that "just over one year into the Bonn process, it is too early to draw conclusions about the peace process." Then he went on to say, "If Afghan authorities search for themselves attainable objectives, if the international community can help them help themselves, if we can admit that we don't know what's better for them than they do, then we can be optimistic about the stabilization of the peace process."[43] This statement puts the responsibility squarely where it belongs: on the shoulders of the Afghans themselves. It does not, however, absolve the international community of its duty. As noted earlier, the coalition forces complicated the situation in Afghanistan for apparently being more interested in the "war on terror" than in peace in Afghanistan. Moreover, the international community's actions have not matched its verbal commitment to peace and security in the war-ravaged country.

It may not be too late to save the peace process in Afghanistan. Drastic measures are needed soon, however. The events of the last decade bring home the truth of what the philosopher-poet Iqbal wrote more than seventy years ago:

> The continent of Asia is a body of water and clay;
> The Afghan nation, a heart in that body;
> Its prosperity leads to prosperity all over Asia;
> Its disorder brings disorder all over Asia.

The international community ignores the issue of genuine peace in Afghanistan at its own peril. Before it is too late, the following measures— among many others—need to be seriously considered:

- Formation of a new peacekeeping force under direct U.N. command is urgently needed. There will be several advantages. Many Muslim countries may be able and ready to participate in such a force. When ISAF was being formed, some countries (e.g., Bangladesh) showed interest in participation but only if their troops served under U.N. command. It is advantageous to have the majority of the peacekeeping forces from Muslim countries—especially those who have not been directly involved in Afghanistan affairs such as Bangladesh, Malaysia, Indonesia, and the North African states. Afghans will be more accommodating to such troops than to those associated with past colonialism and anti-Muslim activities.
- More emphasis should be placed on training and equipping the national army and police force. Sufficient financial resources must be provided to train the army and police in a relatively short time and support their proper maintenance and function. A program should be designed to facilitate the return and recruitment of hundreds of experienced military and police officers who live abroad as refugees and have no criminal record.
- The United States and its allies should try to withdraw their troops from Afghanistan as soon as possible. Their effectiveness in fighting the antigovernment forces is counterbalanced by the excuse that their presence provides incentives to recruit more fighters for those groups. Their longer stay will intensify the resentment of the general population and legitimize the cause of antigovernment insurgency. In the meantime, strong pressure must be exerted on Afghanistan's near and far neighbors to stop their interference. The United Nations, the United States, and the European Union are in a position to play an important role in this if they are ready to use both the carrot and the stick.
- Begin a genuine intra-Afghan dialogue. In a genuine Loya Jirga, all prominent Afghans—the number of whom may come to several thousands—should be given the opportunity to participate. It may not be advisable to exclude the warlords. They are a reality and cannot be just wished away. They should not be allowed, however, to dominate the discussion and set the agenda. Nor should there be time limits on discussions or the duration of the Jirga. Grievances accumulated over decades need to be voiced.
- The international community needs to be more generous with humanitarian and reconstruction assistance than it has been so far. Assistance to

Afghanistan should not be viewed as charity but as an investment that will benefit the whole international community. Dividends of such an investment will include eliminating terrorist threats and narcotic drugs and promoting economic prosperity throughout the region. Afghanistan's strong agricultural potential, rich natural resources, and geoeconomic location will help its resilient and hardworking people put the country back on the road to development—as long as an initial impetus for economic growth is provided and the peace process succeeds.

NOTES

1. "President Karzai Reviews Achievements of the Past Year," www.afghanembassy .net/n_news.html (January 2003).

2. Michael Drudge, "Afghanistan Could Fall Back into Anarchy, Warns British Parliament," *Voice of America,* January 24, 2003, www.afghan-web.com/aop/today .html (January 25, 2003).

3. Human Rights Watch, "Afghanistan's Bonn Agreement One Year Later: A Catalog of Missed Opportunities," *Human Rights News,* December 5, 2002, www.hrw .org/backgrounder/asia/afghanistan/bonn1yr-bck.htm (January 2003).

4. "Nearly 60,000 Ex-combatants Disarmed in Afghanistan—UN," UN News Center, June 10, 2005, www.un.org/apps/news/story.asp?NewsID=14541&Cr=afghan &Cr1 (June 11, 2005).

5. Pankaj Mishra, "The Real Afghanistan," *New York Review of Books,* March 10, 2005, www.nybooks.com/articles/17787 (May 2005).

6. Zainab Mohaqiq, "Afghan People Say Donor Money Hasn't Been Spent Effectively to Reconstruct Their Country," *Pajhwok Afghan News,* March 10, 2005, www.aopnews.com/today.html (March 11, 2005).

7. Human Rights Watch, "Afghanistan's Bonn Agreement One Year Later."

8. "General Malek Comments on Unrest in Northern District," *AIP,* May 19, 2005, www.e-ariana.com/ariana/eariana.nsf/0/988358843EDA984C8725700600475 E94?OpenDocument (May 20, 2005).

9. IRIN, "Afghanistan: Focus on Warlordism in Northeast," Reuters AlertNet, June 1, 2005, www.alertnet.org/thenews/newsdesk/IRIN/1e8de30de17e6459cded3b 553a69a946.htm (June 2, 2005).

10. IRIN, "Afghanistan: Focus on Warlordism in Northeast."

11. Human Rights Watch, "World Report 2005: Afghanistan," *Human Rights Overview,* hrw.org/english/docs/2005/01/13/afghan9827.htm (May 2005).

12. "Report of the Independent Expert on the Situation of Human Rights in Afghanistan, M. Cherif Bassiouni," Commission on Human Rights, Economic and Social Council, Document E/CN.4/2005/122 (March 11, 2005): 16, daccess-ods.un .org/access.nsf/Get?Open&DS=E/CN.4/2005/122&Lang=E (May 2005).

13. The excuse for sacking Professor Bassiouni and eliminating the position of U.N. independent expert on human rights in Afghanistan was very curious. According

to the U.S. State Department spokesman, "more than three years after the Taliban, the human rights situation in Afghanistan had evolved to the point where it could be monitored under the ordinary procedures of the high commissioner for human rights without the need of an independent expert." See Warren Hoge, "Lawyer Who Told of U.S. Abuses in Afghan Bases Loses U.N. Post," *New York Times,* April 30, 2005, www .nytimes.com/gst/abstract.html?res=F30A15FF35550C738FDDAD0894DD404482& incamp=archive:search (May 1, 2005).

14. Ahmad Rashid, "US Placing Greater Emphasis on Economic Stabilization in Afghanistan," *Eurasianet,* September 6, 2002, www.eurasianet.org/departments/business/articles/eav060902.shtml (February 2003).

15. Human Rights Watch, "Afghanistan's Bonn Agreement One Year Later."

16. CARE International, "A New Year's Resolution to Keep: Secure a Lasting Peace in Afghanistan," CARE International in Afghanistan: Policy Brief, January 2003, www .careinternational.org.uk/news/what_do_care_think/afghanistan.htm (February 2003).

17. Drudge, "Afghanistan Could Fall Back into Anarchy."

18. Ahmad Rashid, "American Commander Alters Military Strategy in Afghanistan," *Eurasianet,* January 13, 2003, www.euroasianet.org/departments/ insight/articles/eav011303.shtml (February 2003).

19. Human Rights Watch, "Afghanistan's Bonn Agreement One Year Later." See also Ahmad Rashid, "US Officials Prepare New Campaign for Afghan Security," *Eurasianet,* December 3, 2002, www.euroasianet.org/departments/insight/articles/ eav120302a.shtml (February 2003).

20. CARE International, "A New Year's Resolution to Keep."

21. See "MSF leaves Afghanistan after 24 Years," *Medecins Sans Frontieres,* August 24, 2004, http://217.29.194.251/msfinternational/invoke.cfm?component=article &objectid=19FA7761-67AF-4540-A6F3C81E6164F1CF&method=full_html (May 2005).

22. East Timor has a population of a little more than 1 million, and the number of UNTAET peacekeepers was 9,000. Population of Bosnia is about 4 million, and the number of IFOR troops was 60,000. Population of Kosovo is about 2.7 million, and the number of KFOR troops reached 45,000. Population of Afghanistan is estimated at more than 25 million, and the number of ISAF troops is fewer than 10,000.

23. Tom Coghlan, "Afghans Flee Army over Taliban and Low Morale," *news.telegraph,* June 10, 2005, www.news.telegraph.co.uk/news/main.jhtml?xml=/news/2005/ 06/09/wtal09.xml&sSheet=/news/2005/06/09/ixworld.html (June 7, 2005).

24. CARE International, "A New Year's Resolution to Keep."

25. CARE International, "A New Year's Resolution to Keep."

26. "Karzai Says Terrorism Defeated in Afghanistan," *IRNA,* May 10, 2005, www.irna.ir/en/news/view/line-16/0505101072171607.htm (May 15, 2005).

27. Germany trains about 1,500 police per year. See "Afghanistan: Handover of New Building to Accommodate Female Police Recruits in Kabul," Afghanistan Online, May 20, 2005, www.aopnews.com/today.html (May 21, 2005).

28. Carlotta Gall, "Despite Years of U.S. Pressure, Taliban Fights in Jagged Hills," *New York Times,* June 4, 2005, www.nytimes.com/2005/06/04/international/asia/ 04taliban.html (June 5, 2005).

29. "Bombing a Warning to Afghan Moderates," *AFP,* June 3, 2005, www .afghannews.net/index.php?action=show&type=news&id=2735 (June 4, 2005).

30. Ahmad Rashid, "Afghan-Pakistani Tension Prompts Kabul to Develop New Trade Routes," *Eurasia Internet,* January 25, 2003, eurasia.org.ru/cgi-bin/datacgi/ database.cgi?file=News&report=SingleArticle&ArticleID=0000806 (June 2005).

31. Ahmad Rashid, "Jockeying for Influence, Neighbors Undermine Afghan Pact," *Eurasianet,* January 15, 2003, www.eurasianet.org/departments/insight/articles/ eav011503.shtml (February 2003).

32. Amir Taheri, "Kabul Visit a Diplomatic Coup for Musharraf," *Arab News,* November 8, 2004, www.benadorassociates.com/article/9071 (June 2005).

33. Taheri, "Kabul Visit a Diplomatic Coup for Musharraf."

34. For example, in a live forum on BBC Persian program for Afghanistan on June 10, 2005, Jawaid Ludin, spokesman for the president, was asked which countries he blamed for the problems in Afghanistan. In response, he made remarks to the effect that, "It is quite clear to our compatriots which foreign countries have been interfering in Afghanistan's domestic affairs in the past several decades." Most Afghans would understand this to mean Pakistan.

35. Rashid, "Jockeying for Influence."

36. Ari Berman, "Abandoning Afghanistan," *Nation,* February 24, 2005, www.thenation.com/blogs/outrage?pid=2218 (May 2005).

37. Berman, "Abandoning Afghanistan."

38. Berman, "Abandoning Afghanistan."

39. "Report of the International Narcotic Control Board for 2004," International Narcotic Control Board, 2005, www.incb.org/incb/annual_report_2004.html (May 2005).

40. "Afghanistan's Opium and Heroin Production Background," *Report for the Subcommittee on Criminal Justice, Drug Policy, and Human Resources; Committee on Government Reform; U.S. House of Representatives,* May 2005, http://reform.house .gov/UploadedFiles/Afghanistan%20Backgrounder%20-%20updated%205-18-05.pdf (May 2005).

41. And even then, on a very limited scale. See Thom Shanker, "Pentagon Sees Aggressive Antidrug Effort in Afghanistan," *New York Times,* March 25, 2005, www .nytimes.com/gst/abstract.html?res=F40917F73C5B0C768EDDAA0894DD404482 (March 26, 2005).

42. For earlier approaches, see Michael Bhatia, Kevin Lanigan, and Philip Wilkinson, "Minimal Investment, Minimal Results: The Failure of Security Policy in Afghanistan," AREU Briefing Paper, June 2004, www.areu.org.af/download_pub .asp?id=150 (May 2005). For aerial spray and Charles's resignation, see Ramtanu Maitra, "Washington's Afghan Poppy Policy Withers," *Asia Times* Online, February 18, 2005, www.atimes.com/atimes/Central_Asia/GB18Ag01.html (May 2005). For the latest attempts, see "War on Opium Falters in Southern Afghanistan Taliban Stronghold," *AFP,* April 17, 2005, www.afgha.com/?af=article&sid=48634 (May 2005).

43. Thomas Wigg, "U.N. Ambassador Urges Afghanistan's Development," *Georgetown Hoya,* January 28, 2003, www.afghan-web.com/aop/today.html (January 29, 2003).

4

Islam and Ethnic Minorities in Central Asia: The Uyghurs

Gaye Christoffersen

A vital issue for Central Asia and its neighbors is the role of political Islam in creating both stability and instability within states and within nationalities. Islam can be a rallying point or a divisive force in a community. Nowhere is this clearer than among the Uyghurs, an Islamic people of Central Asia and China.

A painful fact of Uyghur existence is the fragmentation of what it means to be Uyghur, in Xinjiang, China, and throughout the diaspora, a topic that Uyghurs themselves rarely address. Uyghurs form a loose "nation," with fractious local "oasis identities." The war on terrorism may further fragment the Uyghur community. Additionally, different groups of Uyghurs are drawn to different foreign visions, resulting in further divisions among them. As a result of internal fissures and external influences, there are approximately twenty different separatist groups in Xinjiang. Uyghurs are easily incorporated into the agendas of outside powers and transnational movements. Who the Uyghurs are defined as depends on who is defining them.

The Uyghur people, lacking a state of their own, are in a perpetual search for a patron or protector. Each agenda the Uyghurs encounter provides some patronage, promises protection, and gives hope that it will sustain the Uyghur struggle for cultural survival. However, these globalizing agendas, by their very nature, practice hegemonic domination on the particular group of Uyghurs they encounter and further complicate Uyghur identity. Outside forces, attempting to construct a monolithic identity that fits their particular definition, tend to assume there is a "universal Uyghur" with an unchanging essence and fixed properties, whether living in China, the Central Asian diasporas, Afghanistan, Turkey, Germany, or the United States.

This chapter asserts that there are multiple definitions of "Uyghur" and the pan-Islamist identity occupies the smallest space. Other possibilities for Uyghur identity include the sinified Uyghur, who has been made invisible by Western discourse and foreign projects. A more diverse understanding of "Uyghur" is required. Chinese and Central Asian definitions of the Uyghur converged during the 1990s, but Americans, Chinese, and Islamists have clashed, as each defined the Uyghur to fit their own political agenda. Each definition believes that it captures the "true Uyghur identity." The war on terrorism has brought these alternative definitions of the Uyghur into focus.

WAR ON TERRORISM

Central Asia has been extraordinarily agitated since September 11, 2001, partly because a clash of Muslim and non-Muslim civilization spilled over into the region from Afghanistan, and partly because of the U.S. military presence in the region. This agitation has overflowed into Xinjiang, with the Chinese People's Liberation Army (PLA) cracking down on what are either Uyghur terrorists or freedom fighters but will simply be called militants in this chapter. Western human rights groups have been concerned that this crackdown is spreading a wide net, trapping innocent Uyghurs in addition to the Uyghur militants. Beijing is accused of bandwagoning in the war on terrorism in a manner similar to Jakarta's effort to categorize Aceh separatists as al-Qaeda–trained terrorists, and New Delhi arguing Kashmir is part of the global terrorist threat.

China expected the international community to accept its post–September 11 crackdown in Xinjiang as part of the global war on terrorism. The Chinese State Council in January 2002 issued a report, *East Turkestan Terrorist Forces Cannot Get Away with Impunity,* which detailed the extent of terrorist activities since 1990. The report listed more than 200 incidents that resulted in 162 deaths and 440 injuries and included bombings, assassinations, armed assaults on government organizations, poisonings and arson, establishing training bases, and plotting riots such as the Yining incident in 1997.

In the past, Beijing had always publicly downplayed the level of violence in Xinjiang and tried to manage it discreetly through state-to-state negotiations with Turkey and Pakistan, the two countries where Uyghur militants trained. Beijing sought to quietly lobby Pakistan's secret service Inter-Services Intelligence (ISI) to exercise some control on Xinjiang's Islamic activists, which it was fully aware had received training and funding from ISI. Given this quiet approach, it is not surprising that Beijing's January 2002 report was met with disbelief by Western human rights organizations that accused Beijing of cracking down on peaceful demonstrators unconnected to terrorist organizations. The post–September 11 world moved beyond individual government management of domestic terrorists and required Beijing to manage terrorism in ways that could be scrutinized by the outside world.

Beijing initially overestimated the extent of al-Qaeda influence, with claims that there were 300 Uyghurs in Afghanistan in late 2001 and all Uyghur separatists in Xinjiang were linked to al-Qaeda. Later this claim was reduced to 100 Uyghurs in Afghanistan, with 1,000 Uyghurs in Xinjiang trained by al-Qaeda and the Taliban. That claim is supported by the United National Revolutionary Front of East Turkestan (UNRF), which also claimed that more than 100 Uyghurs in Afghanistan at that time were helping the Taliban. The UNRF's support for figures that support the more modest Chinese claim is given credence because the UNRF stridently opposes sinification of Xinjiang and has assassinated imams with pro-China views.

The United States initially refused to recognize any al-Qaeda involvement in Xinjiang, despite numerous pre–September 11 reports of Taliban activity in Xinjiang. For example, the December 25, 2000, *Turkestan Newsletter* carried a UPI article, "Pakistan, China Collide over Islam," that was based on information obtained from U.S. administration officials. The article claimed Chinese security forces had arrested 200 Taliban and other Islamic militants near China's border with Pakistan. They were charged with arming and training Muslim separatists in Xinjiang. It was only in the post–September 11 era that Uyghur involvement with the Taliban was questioned.

Uyghur militants hope for a Kosovo-style humanitarian intervention by a U.S.-led military force into Xinjiang. Uyghur interest in U.S. support stems from a loss of previous patrons. During the twentieth century, the Soviet Union offered refuge to Uyghurs who fled Chinese rule. This accounts for the 500,000 members of the Uyghur diaspora in Central Asia. Today, Russia and the Central Asian states are less sympathetic and more concerned that the Uyghur exiles in their midst are becoming increasingly Islamicized and radicalized by outside forces. Their high rate of unemployment and extreme alienation make young Uyghur men receptive to recruitment by Islamic groups.

The new geopolitical situation in Central Asia, the war on terrorism, the mixing of human rights and terrorism issues, and the definition of Uyghur have generated debate in U.S.-Chinese relations. Pro-Uyghur forces urge the U.S. government not to sacrifice Uyghur human rights in its cooperation with Beijing in the war on terrorism. Uyghur activists are hoping that, now that the U.S. military has established a presence in Central Asia, Uyghurs will receive U.S. patronage similar to that given to Tibetans in the past—military training and arms transfers that assisted Tibetan terrorism against the Chinese in

Tibet. Uyghurs have depicted their situation as closely parallel to the Tibetan situation, thus worthy of comparable assistance, because they have lost their old patrons—the Soviet Union and Central Asian states, the Taliban, and al-Qaeda.

The question revolves around whether China is victimizing the Uyghur minority, using the war on terrorism as an excuse to violate their human rights, or whether China itself is a victim of the al-Qaeda network, which trained Uyghurs in Afghanistan for terrorist activities in Xinjiang. As both Uyghurs and Chinese attempt to take advantage of the current global war on terrorism that has transformed Central Asian geopolitics, Uyghur identity has become malleable in the U.S.-Chinese-Uyghur debate.

GLOBALIZING VISIONS FROM AFAR

There is an expectation that Uyghurs, with their fragmented identities, could easily be incorporated into a foreign definition of Uyghur. Four different foreign definitions or visions have attempted to colonize Uyghurs and create an identity for them. There are consequently four different identities available to Uyghurs that partially correspond to a foreign definition. Each foreign definition has a site for training Uyghurs, an emphasis on one type of human rights, and a dark side of the project to transform the Uyghur.

Chinese Vision of Uyghur Identity

The Chinese definition of Uyghur identity spans most of the twentieth century. There are parallels in Soviet and Chinese projects of russification or sinification of Central Asians, which encouraged them in goals of modernity: economic development, industrialization, and secularization. Both socialist countries hoped to create socialist men and women out of Turkish minorities. China's recent Western development program is the latest effort. Russification was relatively successful in Central Asia compared to sinification in Xinjiang.

The Chinese government borrowed Soviet ethnic policy to classify ethnic groups. Justin Rudelson argues that the Chinese Nationalist government labeled a disparate group of Muslim oasis dwellers as "Uyghur" in the mid-1930s, a term that had not been used for 500 years as an ethnic label. It was then that "Uyghur" became associated with Islam, and the newly created Uyghurs claimed the ancient Uyghur Buddhist kingdom as their ancestry.[1]

In 1994, the Xinjiang Academy of Social Sciences published a book, *Pan-Turkism and Pan-Islamism in Xinjiang*, which warned of the dangers these two movements posed to the unity of nationalities in Xinjiang and to the unity of China. The movements were disparaged as religious fanaticism driven by reactionary mullahs. Every uprising, violent confrontation, incident, bombing, and assassination was linked to organizations suspected of maintaining links abroad. The book was widely distributed as *neibu* (internal) to Chinese officials and candidly recounts every violent incident in the twentieth century.

This Chinese linking of pan-Turkism and pan-Islamism became fixed in Chinese thinking so that no distinction would be drawn between Uyghurs who were pan-Turkic in orientation and those who were pan-Islamic, no distinction between those trained in Turkey and those trained in Afghanistan, no distinction between those advocating Deobandism, a puritanical form of Sunni Islam that includes groups like the Taliban, and those advocating modernity. All were labeled as feudal and antimodern. Since both movements glorify "freedom fighters," the violence each would instigate would be indistinguishable.

This Chinese definition of Uyghurs facilitates the military approach to terrorism, which Beijing continues to rely on in conjunction with the economic development approach. A post-9/11 article in *Jiefang ribao* advocated expanding the PLA's traditional role of war preparation to include nonwar activities to counterterrorism, separatism, extremism, and organized crime. The PLA would assist local authorities, which it has done previously but has not trained for these activities. It would be similar to the U.S. Army's Delta shock force and Russia's Alpha group. The PLA would continue to rely on the militia units, the *bingtuan*.[2]

The Chinese definition of the Uyghurs as an underdeveloped minority means that Uyghur human rights are largely economic rights and are given priority over all other rights. Uyghurs are primarily expected to attend Han Chinese universities, but there is also the Islamic Institute of China, a national religious college that trains Islamic scholars who support the Chinese Communist Party. Sinification in Xinjiang and russification in the Central Asian Uyghur diaspora has made more progress than is usually acknowledged by Uyghur radicals. After the collapse of the Soviet Union, many Central Asians retained identities from the Soviet legacy while some looked toward Afghanistan. A lament of Turkic activists is the ease with which Uyghurs assimilate in China and the Central Asian diaspora after migrating there. Within the Central Asian diaspora, 50 percent of diaspora Uyghurs identify themselves as "Russian" or even state they have "no nationality." These assimilated Uyghurs are criticized for not having a "Turkic" national identity, and are sometimes assassinated by radical Islamists.[3]

The dark side of this process means the Uyghur loss of cultural identity and second-class citizenship in a sinified or russified society. Uyghur government employees are discouraged from entering mosques and threatened with losing their jobs if they do. Uyghur military officers and soldiers feel mistrusted. Beijing holds fast to the idea of economic development and modernization, secularization, and sinification. A problem with this Chinese approach is that it benefits few Uyghurs. An estimated 90 percent of the unemployed in Xinjiang are Uyghur. The economy of southern Xinjiang, where Uyghurs are concentrated, needs to be better integrated with the relatively prosperous economy of northern Xinjiang, where Han concentrate in Urumqi. Despite the limited appeal of sinification, Beijing resents outside powers imposing their alternative visions on this sinified modernization.

Pan-Turkic Vision

The pan-Turkic definition of Uyghurs has endured since the collapse of the Ottoman Empire. It revived during the 1990s after collapse of the Soviet Union as a dream of a Turkic empire stretching from northern Cyprus to northwestern China, populated by Turkic people and led by Ankara. With this kind of pan-Turkic territory under its leadership, Turkey would be able to assume a seat on the U.N. Security Council. A pan-Turkic region would psychologically be a way for Turkey to surmount its "traditional fear of isolation."[4] This pan-Turkic approach to the Uyghurs views their human rights as the right to self-determination for Turks in a Turkestan homeland that stretched across Central Asia into Xinjiang.

There is a radical wing of the pan-Turkic vision. The Xinjiang Liberation Organization/Uyghur Liberation Organization (ULO), based in Uzbekistan and Kyrgyzstan, is scattered throughout the Uyghur diaspora in Central Asia. The ULO claims responsibility for assassinations of "Uyghur collaborators" in China and Central Asia. Another radical organization is the Home of East Turkestan Youth radical youth group with 2,000 members, training in Afghanistan and operating in Xinjiang.

Most of the Central Asia Uyghur diaspora was traditionally more pan-Turkic than pan-Islamic.[5] However, the violent tactics employed by the two movements now make them difficult to distinguish. The United Revolutionary Front of Eastern Turkestan, based in Kazakhstan and originally moderate, claims it was radicalized in 1997 as a result of the Chinese crackdown called Operation Strike Hard following the Yining incident.

There is also a moderate wing of the pan-Turkic vision. Nonviolent East Turkestan groups, such as the East Turkestan Information Center, are based in Turkey and Germany. This moderate wing of pan-Turkism has promoted fusion with the Western liberal vision, which is matched by U.S. advocacy of the Turkish model for Central Asia. A fusion of pan-Turkism with liberalism has inherent limitations as liberals reject the violence of militants.

Human Rights Watch argues that increasing restiveness of Uyghurs in Xinjiang is motivated by this pan-Turkic movement rather than the pan-Islamic movement. Although well intentioned, the Human Rights Watch report marginalized the identity of Uyghur Islamic militants, recreating and presenting them in a form more acceptable to Western visions.[6] Amnesty International also issued a report critical of China's antiterrorism legislation and denied Uyghur participation in pan-Islamic movements, also marginalizing the Islamic militants' identity.[7] Amnesty International acknowledges that it relied on the Uyghur diaspora for its information.[8] Because Amnesty International is known to work closely with Erkin Alptekin, leader of the pan-Turkic East Turkestan Information Center (ETIC), it would seem that this one category of Uyghur identity, a fused pan-Turkic liberalism, attempts to speak for all Uyghurs.[9]

Sinified Uyghurs, who have no voice in the Western world, have no opportunity to point out that the Chinese antiterrorism legislation would protect them, since they are often the targets of terrorist violence. Human Rights Watch and Amnesty International seem to draw most of their information about Uyghurs from the ETIC, and in turn shape the Western world's understanding of Uyghur identity.

In this pan-Turkic definition of Uyghurs, Turkey accepts the current world order but wants a stronger leadership position in it, which it would only get with all of Central Asia as its sphere of influence. Ankara would represent Turkic people's interests against European and East Asian dominance. The darker side of this definition involves violence carried out on assimilated and sinified Uyghurs, including assassinations, further fragmenting Uyghurs. To some extent, this violence is instigated for the purpose of mobilizing the quiescent Uyghur majority. Turkey does train Uyghur militants. A retired Turkish colonel and former NATO officer ran a military training camp for Uyghurs in Turkey. Uyghurs have tried to assert that this military training camp is no longer providing military training but rather instruction in cultural survival.

By some accounts, the Turkish definition has failed because the Central Asian states preferred to consolidate their national identities, Turkey lacked the resources to fund its vision in the region, and the Russian definition did not completely lose its influence. The events of September 11 cemented the trend of the 1990s, in which most Turks abandoned the pan-Turkic vision as unrealistic due to Central Asian "nationalisms."[10] This created more political space for Islamists.

Pan-Islamic Vision

Al-Qaeda and Pakistan fund the pan-Islamic definition of Uyghurs. It is based on a dream that Central Asia could break away from non-Muslim Russian, Indian, and Chinese domination and form a Central Asian caliphate, an Islamic state that would afford Muslims protection. The hope is to establish an autonomous Islamic identity in an alliance spanning the Middle East and Central Asia into Xinjiang and Southeast Asia. Uyghur participation in the Islamic vision was strengthened when the Karakorum highway opened in 1986, combined with Beijing's liberalized policies on religious practices. The route of the haj always included a stopover in Pakistani religious schools, or madrassas, on the way to Saudi Arabia. In this manner, thousands of Uyghur men developed connections with Pakistani religious schools and organizations. The exact number of Uyghurs, and other Chinese Muslims, who have gone on the haj is uncertain. When Osama bin Laden created al-Qaeda in 1988, American intelligence sources knew it had set up a network of Islamic terrorist cells in twenty-six countries, including an al-Qaeda cell in Xinjiang. Beijing had not thought through how this would impact the insurgency in Xinjiang, and Washington thought al-Qaeda would not impinge on U.S. interests.[11]

China realized the consequences by the 1990s. Almost all the explosives and arms that Uyghurs used in Xinjiang have come from Afghanistan. Since 1992, Beijing asked Islamabad to end its support of Uyghur militants. In the words of one author, China "paid a terrible price during the blowback period after the war's end."[12] In 1999, Beijing executed a Pakistani citizen, accusing him of entering Xinjiang in 1995 and assisting in Islamic terrorist activities, including the bloody riots in Yining in February 1997. The Uyghurstan Liberation Front and the United National Revolutionary Front of East Turkestan (UNRF) overcame their differences in 1997 and joined in a jihad in Xinjiang. The UNRF fears sinification of Xinjiang most of all, and announced that it had assassinated an imam of the mosque in Kashgar in 1996 because of his pro-China views. It also claimed that there were more than 100 Uyghurs in Afghanistan at that time helping the Taliban.

Pakistani militants—Jamaat-e-Ismali, Tablighi-Jamaat, and Laskar-e-Toiba—were sneaking into Xinjiang along the Peshawar–Karakorum highway, a symbol of Chinese-Pakistani friendship, for the purpose of assisting Uyghur militants. Covert Inter-Services Intelligence (ISI) operations along the Silk Road gave Islamabad a strategic influence it would not have had otherwise.[13] However, the status of Uyghurs in Afghanistan and Pakistan training camps was precarious even before September 11. A Uyghur source reported in April 2000 that nine Uyghur trainees were gunned down at a Pakistan training camp near Mirpur by the Pakistan army.[14] The Uyghurs held the Chinese government responsible for the attack since a Chinese delegation had visited Kabul seeking thirteen Uyghur trained by the Taliban.

Incidents such as this indicate that Pakistan was an unreliable patron for Uyghurs. The East Turkestan Information Center reported on December 2, 2000, that "two Uyghur Community Centers which had provided shelters for new Uyghur immigrants in Pakistan for decades were closed, Kashgar Center on December 1 and Hotan Center on December 2, by Pakistan Army. Hundreds of Uyghurs who had been living in those centers were evicted by Pakistan soldiers. They became helpless."[15] Joint Pakistani-Chinese military exercises in Xinjiang in August 2004 demonstrated that the Pakistani government was no longer a protector. However, a former Pakistani ISI officer indicated that some (less than 100) Uyghur Islamic militants in the diaspora are still in Pakistan, located in South Waziristan under the protection of tribal leaders.

Under this pan-Islamic attempt to define the Uyghurs, religious rights are most important, especially the right to practice Islam under Sharia in an Islamic state. The Free Turkestan Movement is the primary Islamic fundamentalist organization and it claims responsibility for organizing the Baren uprising in April 1990, which initiated the cycle of violence during the 1990s of violent Uyghur uprisings and violent Chinese crackdowns. Although there had been violent clashes before, Baren is considered different because of the quantities of weapons and explosives, the foreign money and backers. The purpose of Baren was to provoke Chinese repression and polarize Xinjiang, mobilizing Uyghurs from passivity. Led by Zahideen Yusuf, smuggled weapons had been stockpiled, and organizers had been spreading the message of jihad beforehand. The Baren riots began with the organization's mobilizing efforts in a mosque, followed by a mass protest. At Baren, fifty Uyghurs and several Chinese police were killed, initiating a process of increasing radicalization of Uyghurs, which was the intention of the Free Turkestan Movement. Zahideen was killed, but songs are still dedicated to him. Afterward, a thousand Uyghurs were rounded up in Xinjiang and imprisoned by Chinese forces. Militants report that in prison, identities were strengthened and Islamic education continued. Baren became a symbol of the liberation struggle. Bombings began in 1992 in Urumqi and reached Beijing in 1997, when two buses were bombed.

The most important Islamic organization for influencing and recruiting Uyghurs within the Central Asian Uyghur diaspora is probably the Islamic Movement of Uzbekistan (IMU). It originated in 1991 but was transformed in 1996 by the Taliban as an armed auxiliary. The IMU obtained financial support and training in al-Qaeda camps and operated in the Ferghana Valley. Most financing comes from control of the heroin and opium trade in Central

Asia. The IMU has direct links in Xinjiang with the Islamic Movement of Eastern Turkestan, providing military and financial assistance.

IMU changed its name to the Islamic Party of Turkestan (Hezb-e Islami Turkestan) in June 2001 in Deh Dadi, near Mazar-e Sharif, northwest of Kabul in Afghanistan. The original goal of the IMU was to overthrow the Uzbek government and install an Islamic state in Uzbekistan. When IMU changed its name to the Islamic Party of Turkestan, its goal expanded to creating an Islamic state for all of Central Asia and Xinjiang, which led to increased recruits of Uzbek, Uyghur, Chechen, Arab, and Pakistani members. The IMU subsequently broadened its activities beyond Uzbekistan and the Ferghana Valley to attacks on surrounding countries. The total size of IMU is estimated to be about 5,000 serving in the armed wing. The Uyghur component is unknown but not large.

The ethnic similarities between Uzbeks and Uyghurs might explain why Uyghurs were drawn to IMU. It found sanctuary in Afghanistan after the Tajikistan civil war in 1992, and may have found sanctuary in Tajikistan after the Afghan war. IMU strength in Afghanistan was estimated at 2,000, which included Xinjiang Uyghurs, diaspora Uyghurs, Chechens, and other Central Asians. In 2001, IMU had units stationed at Koh-e-Siah Boz and Deh Dadi (west of Mazar) and participated in the Taliban campaign.[16]

This pan-Islamic vision sees an expansion of an Islamic world order with Islamic law, Islamic economies, Islamic education, and an Islamic state stretching from North Africa, the Middle East, and Central Asia into maritime Southeast Asia, including Xinjiang. Al-Qaeda funded IMU camps in Afghanistan and Islamic schools throughout Central Asian republics and Xinjiang, both under- and above ground. *Jane's* reported that Uyghurs were found at several camps in Afghanistan: al-Badr, Salman Farsi Gkhund, and Korps-9.[17] In Urumqi, Chinese Public Security reported that in 2001 it had closed down 357 underground organizations, unauthorized madrassas and mosques, but it is uncertain how many had links to radical organizations. Post–September 11, a small number of Uyghurs captured in Afghanistan and held in Guantanamo confirmed the Islamic Movement of East Turkistan's links to the IMU and al-Qaeda.

The darker side of this vision has meant that the 1990s in Xinjiang were extremely violent as Uyghurs trained in Afghanistan returned to wage jihad in China. The year 1997 witnessed several bombings, riots, and assassinations in Xinjiang. The cycle of violence that continued from 1998 to 2002 became a vortex that sucked in many others. Reliable reports indicate Islamists have been known to lop off the heads of Han PLA soldiers and place them on stakes along the road in Xinjiang, a practice that seems to go beyond activities of pan-Turkists.

Western Liberal Vision

The Western liberal vision of the Uyghurs is essentially an American vision that views Central Asian republics as economies and polities in transition to some form of market economy and liberal democracy. This vision promises to give Central Asians autonomy from Russian, Chinese, and Islamic influence. There is support for the rights of the individual, political, and religious rights, with emphasis on the right to peacefully demonstrate.

There are several organizations that support this Western liberal vision. Many of the pan-Turkic groups in the Uyghur diaspora, which advocate nonviolent means and are based in Germany, the United States, and Turkey, present themselves as candidates for recruitment into the liberal vision, hoping for a fusion of pan-Turkism and liberalism. This includes the East Turkestan Information Center (ETIC), the East Turkestan National Congress, the Uyghur American Association, and others.

Their projected world order focuses on a democratic peace in Central Asia and a human rights regime that extends across Eurasia. This would essentially be an expansion of European civilization into the region. They train Uyghurs in projects for encouraging community activists and civil society in Central Asia combined with a liberal education in American and German universities, as well as pluralist democracy learned through participation in forming and running a transnational network of interest groups in the United States and Germany advocating the rights of Uyghurs. The Uyghur American Association (UAA) renounces the use of violence to achieve political ends. The UAA claims that Beijing's military approach to militants in Xinjiang is state terrorism and is planting the seeds for future violence among young Uyghurs. As a lobbying group in the United States, UAA has created the identity of "Uyghur" to be almost identical to "Tibetan" and encouraged American NGOs and government agencies to think of Uyghurs with the same amount of sympathy they accord Tibetans.

The darker side of this vision includes promoting the right to national self-determination in Wilsonian terms and expanding NATO into Central Asia to defend these emerging democracies from Russian or Chinese hegemony. The Uyghur diaspora supporting this Western liberal vision understands its realization in realpolitik terms, viewing the balance of power shifting in Central Asia from Russia and China to American military and economic power. They believe that the United States unsuccessfully sought access to this Central Asian region for the past decade and only after September 11 could realize its strategic plans for Central Asia and Xinjiang's resources. This has presented an opportunity to the Uyghur diaspora to align itself with this American strategy. They believe that the United States condones the Uyghur armed struggle in Xinjiang and hope Uyghurs will be enlisted by the U.S. military as partners in a war in Central Asia against Han Chinese that culminates in a humanitarian intervention by a U.S.-led force into Xinjiang.[18] The United States has not encouraged these hopes, which are not an integral part of the liberal vision.

Uyghurstan Autonomy Vision

This is not the product of a foreign globalizing vision, and so it does not have foreign financial assistance or arms suppliers, nor sites for training Uyghurs. Yet it is the vision that attracts the quiescent Uyghur and everyday resisters, much more than any of the foreign visions. Of the organizations promoting this vision, Erkin Alptekin's East Turkestan Information Center is generally considered pan-Turkic but claims to work for a peaceful solution to constructing a Uyghurstan within the Chinese state, a negotiated settlement between Beijing and Uyghurs that would create a federated system with a more autonomous Xinjiang. Human rights are seen as the right of indigenous people to develop autonomously.

CONCLUSION

There is a clear divide between those Uyghurs who use violence and consider it legitimate and those Uyghurs who are the targets of violence or are meant to be mobilized by the violence. Further differences, identified by Joanne Smith, are generational differences, urban-rural differences, and gender differences. The separatist movement is an urban, not a rural, phenomenon. There is a north–south difference over whether there should be a Uyghurstan (supported by northern Xinjiang and rejecting Turkish identity) or an East Turkestan (supported by southern Xinjiang and reflecting influence from Turkey, the Middle East, and Afghanistan). The Uyghur diaspora is divided over whether there should be an East Turkestan or a Uyghurstan. Women are more pacific than men. Generational differences exist: the elderly are grateful for improved living standards; the middle-aged remain wary, remembering the ravages of the Cultural Revolution; the younger generation experienced the Han-Uyghur social distancing of the 1990s in Xinjiang.[19] From these numerous differences it is clear who the recruits for the pan-Islamic vision are: young males, urban unemployed, restless and angry, a phenomenon that can be observed and felt in any Xinjiang urban area.

The one foreign approach that has not yet had a discernible impact on Uyghur identity is the Western liberal vision, except for a few iconic figures such as Rabiya Kadeer. The Uyghur activists who hope to make the United States their patron in a manner similar to previous patrons will in all probability engage in illiberal activities that will undermine a pan-Turkic/liberal fusion. It is a stretch to imagine the liberal vision attracting the quiescent majority, which will probably continue to resist outside influence and promote the vision of Uyghurstan autonomy.

There are several consequences of Uyghur identity fragmentation. No Uyghur or East Turkestan group speaks for all Uyghurs, despite any claims otherwise. Intra-Uyghur violence reflects the fragility of Uyghurs as an ethnic identity and reflects diverse outside influences that attempt to pit one Uyghur fragment against another. The pan-Turkic movement seeks and receives support from the West, one fragment of it communicating in the language of human rights and presenting itself as "the Uyghur." Other fragments are violent militants. The pan-Islamic movement in its Deobandist form remains vehemently anti-Western and anti-American. Despite these differences, before September 11, the pan-Islamists and pan-Turkists appeared to be merging. They both glorified militants and violent struggle. In operational terms, their behavior was hard to distinguish. Post–September 11, the relationship between the pan-Turkists and pan-Islamists is contentious. Turkish military forces were originally designated by the United States to head up a peace-keeping operation (PKO) in Afghanistan, while many Islamist Uyghurs remained under attack or were incarcerated.

The pan-Turkic/pan-Islamic convergence shattered after September 11 as the pan-Turkic movement scrambled to distance itself from Deobandism, the Taliban, al-Qaeda, and the pan-Islamic militants in Xinjiang. There seemed to be a tactical realignment in some of the statements by pan-Turkic representatives after September 11 to encourage Uyghurs to shed their anti-American Taliban image for a more pro-American image and to try to explain away the Islamic Movement of Eastern Turkistan's links to the IMU. And it was recognized that Uyghurs need better public relations strategies for constituting Uyghur identity.

The pan-Turkic movement, having the strongest links to the Western world, would use all its contacts to establish its distinctiveness from the Islamic movement. A Human Rights Watch report, issued in October 2001, stressed this very point, that the Uyghur activists are pan-Turkic, not pan-Islamic. The report depicted Uyghur identity as similar to Tibetan, struggling for cultural survival and nonviolent. Amnesty International also issued a report critical of China's antiterrorism legislation and denied Uyghur participation in pan-Islamic movements.

The post–September 11 world has witnessed new understandings and new alliances. The Western liberal vision, as it is implemented in Central Asia, needs to distinguish the numerous identities of Uyghurs. The West demonstrated its understanding of the fragmented nature of Uyghur identity in August 2002 when the United States, Kyrgyzstan, and China jointly placed one organization, the East Turkestan Islamic Movement (ETIM), on the U.N. list of terrorist organizations, but not other Uyghur organizations. Kazakh TV claimed that joint operations by Chinese, U.S., and Kyrgyz special forces tracked down two Uyghur terrorists accused of planning to bomb Bishkek's Manas airport (where the U.S. military is based) and the U.S. embassy outside of Bishkek.

In future dialogues, Beijing and Washington could both attempt to advance their respective visions for Uyghurs, further fragmenting the Uyghur community. Alternatively, both powers might recognize that the weak and fragmented identity of Uyghurs leaves them vulnerable to foreign, globalizing visions that promise to provide patronage and/or protection, as al-Qaeda did. The best defense against al-Qaeda–type forces making inroads into Uyghur society is to strengthen Uyghur identity. This would create Uyghurs who are not so easily recruited by movements promising them an identity. Thus the Uyghur autonomy vision, not supported by Beijing or Washington, might be the best for stability in Xinjiang and should be considered. This would require the United States to broaden its support for Uyghur identity beyond the pan-Turkist vision, which has lost favor among Turks.

The protector/patron for this Uyghur autonomy vision should be the Chinese state, but it should receive help from the United States, Central Asia, the U.N. Human Rights Commission, numerous NGOs from global civil society, Europe, and Russia, now that the pan-Islamic patron/protector has failed the Uyghurs. If China, other countries, and global civil society fail to become patron/protectors, Uyghurs can be expected to continue their search for the independent state they feel they need to protect themselves and continue to seek foreign patrons.

NOTES

1. Justin Jon Rudelson, *Oasis Identities: Uyghur Nationalism along China's Silk Road* (New York: Columbia University Press, 1997), 4–7.

2. Chen Yutian, "Incorporating the Anti-Terrorism Struggle into the Military Scope of Responsibility: The Struggle against Terrorism Has Become a Just War with Invisible Battle Lines," *Jiefangjun bao* April 23, 2002, 6, Foreign Broadcast Information Service (hereafter FBIS), April 23, 2002.

3. "Chinese Communist Dictators Are Madly Waiting for Their Death," January 14, 2002, in FBIS, January 16, 2002.

4. Igor Torbakov, "Turkish Foreign Policy in the Post-Soviet Space," *Eurasia Insight*, December 23, 2002, at eurasianet.org.

5. Dewardric L. McNeal, *China's Relations with Central Asian States and Problems with Terrorism*, Washington, DC: Congressional Research Service Report for Congress, December 17, 2001.

6. Human Rights Watch, *China: Human Rights Concerns in Xinjiang*, Human Rights Watch Backgrounder, October 2001.

7. Amnesty International, *People's Republic of China: China's Anti-Terrorism Legislation and Repression in the Xinjiang Uighur Autonomous Region*, March 2002, 14. AI Index: ASA 17/010/2002.

8. Amnesty International, *People's Republic of China*, 20.

9. "China's Growing Problem with Xinjiang," *Jane's*, June 13, 2000, www.janes.com.

10. Igor Torbakov, "Ankara's Post-Soviet Efforts in the Caucasus and Central Asia: The Failure of the 'Turkic World' Model," *Eurasia Insight*, December 26, 2002, eurasianet.org.

11. Rahul Bedi, "Why? An Attempt to Explain the Unexplainable," *Jane's*, September 14, 2001, www.janes.com.

12. John Cooley, *Unholy Wars: Afghanistan, America, and International Terrorism* (London: Pluto, 1999).

13. Yossef Bodansky, "Islamabad's Road Warriors," www.kashmir-information.com.

14. Uighur-l, "Pakistan Killed 19 Uyghurs," April 5, 2000, www.mail-archive.com/uighur-l@taklamakan.org/msg00304.html. In a letter written by the Uyghur American Association to the Pakistani ambassador and placed on the Uyghur American Association website, the Association complained of Pakistan's treatment of Uyghur immigrants and mentioned this massacre. The letter has since been removed from the UAA website but is cached at www.uyghuramerican.org/recentevents/lettertopak.html.

15. "Pakistan Killed 19 Uyghurs."

16. "Foreign Pro-Taliban Fighters inside Afghanistan (Pre-hostilities)," *Jane's*, October 8, 2001, www.janes.com.

17. S. Troush, "China's Pressure on the Uyghurs," *Jane's Islamic Affairs Analyst*, February 1, 2003.

18. Perhat Muhemmidi, "Let Us Make Use of Present World Situation and Overturn the Chinese Oppression," *Spark* (Munich), January 30, 2002, in FBIS, March 6, 2002.

19. Joanne Smith, "Four Generations of Uyghurs: The Shift towards Ethno-political Ideologies among Xinjiang Youth," *Inner Asia* 2 (2000): 195–224.

5

Integrating Political Islam in Central Asia: The Tajik Experience

Kamoludin Abdullaev

Is Islamism strengthening or weakening in post-Soviet Central Asia? Does it present a force for terrorism or an energy for democracy? Various international centers of power (Western governments, the United Nations, Organization for Security and Cooperation in Europe, etc.) are primarily concerned with the practical implications of the issue: should they support local, secular post-communist elites that have taken steps to strengthen their defenses combating Islamists? Is the best solution to encourage governments that strive to marginalize political Islam or "domesticate" Islam within the limits of their respective countries and subjugate it to national projects? Another may advocate an "ideal" solution and include Islamists in legal politics. Does the Tajik model of inclusion represent a positive example of demilitarization of Muslim politics? Could the legalization of Islamists in this country and other countries of the region finally result in moderation of their politics in general? Can it reveal a "paradox of democracy" phenomenon—illiberal political groups using democratic procedures to impose their domination and undermine democracy from inside? And finally, can the current Tajik regime be called democratic, and is it capable of moderating arguably radical Islamists?

All Central Asian states are following secular, democratic (at least de jure) nation-state building projects with no clearly articulated formula of dealing with Islam as an ideology and a political institution. Outwardly, all pay respect to Islam and claim Islamic civilization as a part of their national legacy, yet exclude it from open political participation and competition. All have forbidden political parties and movements based on religion and all underline the equality of all confessions and their separation from the state. Driven by atheism from the Soviet era, all strive to strengthen the hand of the secular president by bringing Islam under bureaucratic control. Weakening the Muslim opposition has been one of the Central Asian presidents' unchanging policy objectives; its final aim was to destroy active and potential opponents. This secularization and domestication attempt, however, did not find a democratic formula capable of securing mass approval as the antithesis to a virtual Islamic one. As recent political developments in the region show (particularly in Kyrgyzstan and Uzbekistan in 2005), political systems of all Central Asian states have proved politically unstable both in short- and long-term perspective. The facade of Western-patterned legal arrangements hide a blend of secular, religious, and traditional features that cannot connect civil and political society or promote the interests of individuals and pluralist solidarity groups.

BACKGROUND

When Russian rule ended in 1991, no one, not even Islamists, expressed an intention to restore "Islamic order" typical to pre-Soviet times. Yet Central Asia is a Muslim majority region, and there is nothing odd in local people's opting for a secular state in the aftermath of the collapse of communist atheist domination. Islam has played a vital but not decisive role in societal and political life in Central Asia. There were never theocracies in Central Asia, even during the Bukharan emirate or Kokand khanate. Of prominent importance in religious affairs were experts *(ulamo)*. Since only religious education was operational, so it can be said that *ulamo* possessed virtual monopoly to intellectual production. They served, taught, censored, and advised, but never ruled. *Ulamo* took on themselves the responsibility to advise secular emirs and insist on complete implementation of Sharia, without directly interfering in the political process, let alone taking over the state. Political power always belonged to secular chieftains, bearing the title of Emir al-Muslimin. Ideally the emir was not an uncontrolled tyrant but one of the equal coreligionists ruling in accordance with sacred doctrine. In fact, however, emirs as high administrators were independent from direct influence of *ulamo* or the Muslim community. Emirs relied more on traditional political institutions than on Islamically (ideologically) charged structures. In truth, the orthodox *ulamo*'s advice was cautious not to challenge emirs' unrestricted monopoly to power. Moreover, orthodoxies often compete for the benevolence of power holders, be it the emir or the later Russian tsar.

In general, there has always been a division between state and religion in the region. In Sunni Central Asia there have never been institutionalized religious hierarchies, while existing religious authority's charisma rarely embraced devotees beyond inward-looking communal (sectarian, ethno-regional, tribal) networks. At the local level this religious network was intertwined with the communal one to the extent that made them hard to distinguish. This combination of communal spirit and religious zeal was responsible, in particular, for the spontaneous defensive jihad of Bukharan and Ferghanan communities known as Basmachism in the 1920s against forceful establishment of Soviet rule.

In contrast to conformist orthodoxies, sectarian and Sufi leaders led rebellions against violations—real or imagined—of Islamic principles by enemies of Islam, be it Central Asian (secular) monarchs with their corruptive governments, Islamic reformers, or foreign invaders. The scale of this antagonism never reached the level of an antigovernmental, oppositional, alternative ideology or political project. This unstructured interference of religiously motivated opportunists in politics was a manifestation of antimodern traditionalism and fundamentalism ("cleansing" Islamic society or protecting it from modernity) rather than a drive for political power. This spontaneous communal intervention into politics aimed at an extraordinary "rescuing of Islam" has always had negative societal consequences. It quickly radicalized and slid into uncontrolled violence. This was exemplified by the execution at a peaceful rally of Islamic reformers (known as the Jadids) by reactionary mullahs and the Shia-Sunni bloodshed in Bukhara in 1917.[1]

In Central Asia, political Islam as a force aimed at introducing alternative political order appeared in the late Soviet period. It was a product of modernity rather than a manifestation of Central Asia's old-fashioned communal fundamentalism. Yet a tradition of providing services to Islamically charged leaders and nationalist-minded modern secular political entrepreneurs by a fundamentalist, mutinous periphery—as happened in Tajikistan in first half of the 1990s—is clearly rooted in Central Asian history and the culture of prestate (or stateless) communal society.

REGIONAL DIVERSITY

Islam has a different stand in various Central Asian states as local elites respond to the rise of political Islam in different ways. Uzbekistan adopted a law "on liberty of conscience and religious organizations" on May 1, 1998, while Tajikistan a year later amended article 28 of its constitution. The measures were opposite in content. The former has confirmed previous restrictions and added the right of the state to limit liberty of conscience "if it is needed for securing national safety, civil order, life, health, ethics, rights and liberties of other citizens." This law has legalized severe oppression of the Islamic activism in Uzbekistan. In this country, 5,500 individuals remain jailed on charges of religious extremism.[2] In May 2005, hundreds of people were executed in Andijan on the same charges. The main challenger of official Tashkent, Islamic Movement of Uzbekistan (IMU), has been persecuted and excluded from legal political engagement. Nevertheless, it advocates the forceful overthrow of the regime. IMU has been Central Asia's most dangerous terrorist organization, al-Qaeda and Osama bin Laden's closest regional ally.

In 1999 Tajikistan amended its constitution, authorizing the formation "among others, parties of a democratic, religious, or atheistic character." This legal formulation suggests that parties can be either democratic or religious, but not both. This formal imperfection underlines an abnormality of this rash procedure. Only several months prior this event, a high-ranking Tajik official claimed before the U.N. General Assembly that Tajik society, "especially educated people . . . are clearly against the Islamists that have been among major instigators and perpetrators of criminal and political acts that led to a bloody civil war."[3] Nevertheless, under the pressure of international guarantors of the Tajik peace process, changes in its constitution were made, and the Islamic Renaissance Party of Tajikistan (IRPT) was legalized. Today Tajikistan is the only state in the region where the Islamic movement, after ten years of open confrontation, opted to participate in the political process legally, within quasi-democratic structures.

In Kyrgyzstan, especially in the south (Osh, Batken, and Jalalabad), the neo-fundamentalist movement known as Hizb-ut-Tahrir (HT), an outwardly peaceful party that supports military jihad against the United States, is getting increasing support. Kyrgyz authorities launched a dialogue with Hizb-ut-Tahrir. In contrast, Kazakhstani Islam does not show visible political activity, yet it may emerge, again as in the case with Kyrgyzstan, in the south (especially in the cities of Shymkent, Turkistan, known as traditional centers of the region's Islam). So far, in a virtually secular Kazakhstan a missionary Islam prevails over political Islam. In outwardly secure Turkmenistan, with its totalitarian regime based on a stable tribal hierarchy, Islam is intertwined tightly in the social fabric and shows no intention to form political parties yet. It is steadily privatized by tribal network and the government. State agencies of Turkmenistan succeed in controlling the selection, promotion, and dismissal of all mullahs.

Central Asia proposes three basic state responses to the Islamic challenge: combat/control (Uzbekistan), control (Turkmenistan), and control/cooperation (Tajikistan). A general profile of political Islam in Central Asia is provided in table 5.1.

All Central Asian Islamist movements have related goals but different strategies. IRPT claims to build a just Islamic society not simply by imposing Sharia but by promoting "Islamic ideals" through political action in existing legal (non-Islamic) space. Mysterious Hizb-ut-Tahrir is an example of a

Table 5.1.   Profile of Today's Political Islam in Central Asia

	Islamic Renaissance Party of Tajikistan	Islamic Movement of Uzbekistan	Hizb-ut-Tahrir (Central Asian Section)
Formed in	1990	1996	1996
Centered in	Central, Southern, and, from 2000, northern Tajikistan	Uzbek part of Ferghana Valley	Ferghana Valley (mostly Uzbek, but also Tajik and Kyrgyz parts)
Nature	Sunni Islamist movement	Sunni Islamist militant movement	Supranational Islamic movement
Aim	Islamic state	Islamic state	Islamic state
To be achieved by way of . . .	militant jihad against Tajik regime (1991–1997); gradual introduction of basic Islamic principles through participation in legal politics (since 1999)	militant jihad against Uzbek regime	nonviolent jihad in three stages: clandestine indoctrination, open public campaign, and taking over power
Targeted against Christians / Jews?	no	no	yes
Legal status	legal from 1991 to 1993 and since the end of 1999	illegal, under severe repression, leaders sentenced to death in absentia	illegal, clandestine, under severe repression
Attachment to ethnic nationalism	close	moderate	none
Today it . . .	is integrated into national politics	is joined with regional geopolitics (al-Qaeda and the Taliban) and most likely defeated	has a tendency to rise in secrecy in spite of severe repression

radical transnational movement imported from the West to Central Asia. This London-based radical organization has a vague and utopian goal of establishing the caliphate without a declared intention of taking power in a particular territory. HT avoids violence and insists on a strict implementation of Sharia yet without conciliation with secular legislation. On that ground HT denies its participation in March 2005 "revolution" in Kyrgyzstan and May 2005 popular unrest in Uzbekistan. Finally, IMU is a fundamentalist militant movement striving to forcefully implement Sharia while overlooking legal procedures and failing (in contrast to their Tajik IRP counterparts) to set up political alliance with secular Uzbek nationalists.

None of the Central Asian Islamic militants target non-Muslims—Russians and/or Christians and Jews. The anti-Christian and anti-Jewish rhetoric of HT is not targeted against a particular group of non-Muslim population in Central Asia. Seemingly this imported slogan has to do with the Arab-Israeli conflict or with the so-called Islamic anti-Semitism of Euro-Muslim groups.[4]

The multiplicity of Islamic responses in post-Soviet Central Asia shows that the dominant religion has not yet been a central strategic factor in the region. It is mostly preoccupied with local concerns. Political configurations here have to do with state-based ethnic nationalism(s) but not religions or ideologies. Even in extreme situations Central Asian Islamists never thought of creating a unifying political movement to pose an Islamic threat to other civilizations. Moreover, terrorists' call for international jihad elicits no interest among local Muslim political activists who adopted nationalist positions. In the early period of the Tajik civil war there were signs of international terrorist involvement, but it disappeared as soon as the jihad in Tajikistan turned into civil strife. The international terrorists whose primary target is the West (especially the United States) may interfere with local politics, if jihad is already there (as in Chechnya). But they avoid setting up jihads in such complicated sociopolitical and cultural settings like the one in Central Asia.

INTEGRATING ISLAMIC POLITICAL ACTIVISM INTO THE TAJIK GOVERNMENT

Tajikistan has undergone the most painful state building of all the former Soviet republics of Central Asia. Since 1991, the country has experienced a rapid rise in political activism, followed by civil war, an internationally led peace process, the integration of opposition forces into government, disarmament of former combatants, and redistribution of power among warring political factions. In general, Tajikistan is widely considered an important success story of internationally supported peace building. Today this country is ready to pay a robust price to avoid further violence after the 1992–1997 conflict that resulted in an estimated 50,000 dead and disappeared.[5] The implications for integrating political Islam into a pluralist system, however, have been mixed.

The most valuable and instructive part of the Tajik experience relates to the search for the most effective formula for dealing with religion-based political activism. Proclaimed Islamist ideals notwithstanding, the Islamic Renaissance Party of Tajikistan from its inception has been closely attached to ethnic nationalism and the Tajik state-building mission. Since the first days of independence, it created a coalition that included official clergy (which used to cooperate with Soviet authorities), newborn nationalist-minded democrats, and a non-Sunni (Shi'a Ismaili) minority against the Communist Party candidate in the presidential election of 1991. After independence in 1991, through the civil war in 1992–1996, the peace process in 1994–1997, and the integration into government in 1999–2000, Tajik Islamists and the nationalist-democratic movement were part of a unified political front based on common Tajik nationalism, which appeared to be unexpectedly strong. During the U.N.-sponsored peace process in 1999, under the pressure of international guarantors of Tajik peace, changes in the constitution were made, and the IRPT, which constituted a core of the United Tajik Opposition (UTO), was legalized.

The fortune of Tajik Islamists sharply differs from one of their Uzbek party comrades. The Islamic Movement of Uzbekistan (IMU) started as a relatively peaceful fundamentalist Islamic movement, but by 1992, it had taken steps to forcibly introduce an Islamic state in Ferghana Valley. Persecuted by the Uzbek regime, most IMU activists left Uzbekistan for Tajikistan, where they fought alongside the Tajik Islamists against the secular Tajik government in 1992–1996. This Islamist alliance of Tajiks and Uzbeks proved to be short-lived. It was ruined in 1996–1998 in favor of ethnic nationalism. First, the rise of the Pashtun-dominated Taliban in Afghanistan heralded the end of the Tajik civil war. It was northern Afghanistan's Jamiat-i Islami led by Burhanuddin Rabbani, then president of Afghanistan, an ethnic Tajik, who was the first to prefer nation-state interests to romantic cross-border nationalism and supranational Islamic solidarity. To secure Russian support in the fighting against the Taliban, the Jamiat-i Islami supported their Tajikistani counterparts who were in conflict with Moscow-backed official Dushanbe. After a period of confusion, under the pressure of Burhanuddin Rabbani and Russian and Iranian governments, the Tajik opposition came to the U.N.-sponsored negotiating table to make peace with its ideological rival, the secular pro-Russian government. The Taliban's capture of Kabul in September 1996 provided further incentive for the peace process and moderation of Tajik

Islamists' agenda. This is how the overall international situation in the region favored the Tajik peace and gradual decline of the Taliban. As a result, the religious coalition of Afghan, Uzbek, and Tajik Islamists split, revealing the inability of Islamic factors to become strategic. In 1998, a year after the peace accord was signed, under the pressure of Tajik government the leader of Tajik Islamists Sayyid Abdullo Nuri managed the withdrawal of Uzbek Islamists from Tajikistan. The families of IMU members were driven in several vans to the Uzbek border, while the fighters crossed the Afghan border soon afterward to leave Tajikistan forever. That is how IMU, being deprived of political participation in Uzbekistan and finding no place in reconciled Tajikistan and having been frustrated by betrayal of Tajik Islamists, was pushed to Afghanistan. (Tajik Islamists were first to be upset by their Afghan counterparts' lack of Islamic solidarity.) In Afghanistan, IMU had nothing to do but to join illegal trafficking and the regional geopolitical terrorist network—the Taliban and the bin Laden group. In spring 2001, the IMU changed its name to the Islamic Movement of Turkistan (the imagined "Land of Turks") in an attempt to follow the Tajik example of Islamic nationalism, but the bid came too late; the IMU was placed on the list of American terrorist targets in the war on terrorism after September 11, 2001. Most likely, IMU was defeated in fall 2001 during the Enduring Freedom operation in northern Afghanistan, yet Tashkent claims IMU still poses a threat to regional security.

ISLAM AND POLITICAL PLURALISM

Promoting political pluralism in Tajikistan has been more difficult than legalizing IRPT. To begin with, the conflict between the secular-oriented postcommunist elites and the Islamic opposition involved open civil warfare that took thousands of lives in 1992–1998. The problem of relations between the secular state and Islamism in Tajikistan was not discussed at all. Instead, the issue was resolved in the context of the power-sharing dispute during the U.N.-sponsored implementation of the General Peace Accord in 1997–2000. The Islamic Renaissance Party was legalized, while secularism remained central to Tajikistan's constitution. This meant that the dilemma of secularism versus Islamism remains unresolved in Tajik politics. The Tajikistani formula of dealing with political Islam can hardly serve as an ideal example for other Central Asian countries, not only because the inclusion was forced from outside as a part of the conflict resolution agenda but also because the peace process was not open and transparent to the wider Tajikistani public. Despite the relative success of the Tajik peace process, there has been no open debate on Islamism in Tajik politics. Both sides refrain from dispute, fearing that it may instigate another conflict. Consequently the legal Islamic opposition seems nontransparent and often unnamed and appears radical and hostile in the eyes of outside observers and most Tajikistanis.

Openness and nonconfrontation failed to become a regular feature of Tajik policy for several reasons. First, the weak Tajik regime possesses limited resources and an insufficient level of political institutionalization to adopt the U.N.-supported multiparty system. Additionally, the Tajik elites that appeared more than ten years ago—the Kulabi- (a region in southern Tajikistan) dominated secular government and IRPT-dominated UTO—have secured and maintained their position through civil war. They are inclined to choose violent responses for future challenges. As well, the IRPT and other Central Asian parties emerged from the Soviet past, with no tradition of democratic development and political dialogue. Furthermore, the party of Tajik Islamists is built on the model of Muslim Brotherhood, based on loyalty to the leader, and does not yet act as a modern political party. Finally, limited public knowledge of the tenets of Islam due to the regional isolation from the Muslim world and restrictions on religious education also hampers a public Islam-related dialogue.

The international community's effort to push Tajik society toward democracy notwithstanding, Tajikistan failed to become a pluralistic quasi-democratic state with an open arena of political competition, an unfettered media, an independent judiciary, and a market economy. For many Tajiks, the IRPT is a regionalist group of Gharmis (a region in central part of Tajikistan and a stronghold of Islamic opposition) that formerly were underrepresented in government and recently came to power through violence. Trying not to spoil a fragile peace, today the IRPT functions as a potential opponent of the ruling elite, rather than as an Islamic (ideological) party and/or political institute. Legal but excluded from principal decision making, it nevertheless enjoys access to state resources and involvement in illicit activities. The government is well aware that in case of open competition with the state authority, Islamists have the ability to facilitate social mobilization, a mechanism that lies outside of the transparent political field, an informal religious arrangement (schools, registered and unregistered mosques, etc.), as well as Ishan-Murid (master-disciple) groupings, the Sufi network, capable of providing destructive mass involvement, rapid breakdown of civil-military relations, and hazardous destabilization of the system as occurred in the first half of the 1990s. For that reason the Tajik state strives to control the activities of religious institutions and networks. In case of social unrest, the government may rely mostly on external, notably Russian, support. The few Tajik institutions that could theoretically play a mediating role—opposition political parties, independent media, an effective judiciary, active civil society—lack capacity.

So far, the government and opposition are in relative harmony. In the end of the 1990s the opposition, driven by a desire not to break a fragile peace, stopped its activity, opting for nonconfrontation with government and promoting nationalism. As of summer 2005, the main reason for the relative stability in Tajikistan is an agreement among the Tajik elites, based on mutually accepted balance of power and wealth. Both support a need to avoid violent conflict and the necessity of protecting national state building, but neither has created the necessary institutional framework for a more pluralistic democracy.

IS ISLAM A POLITICAL THREAT?

Local regimes and their close non-Muslim neighbors—China and Russia—identify radical Islamist mobilization as a threat to national security interests. Both tend to see Islamists as marginalized terrorist radicals rejected by the populace. They try to hamper Islam-related dialogue in Central Asia to protect their own Muslim "underbelly" (Caucasus, Tatarstan, Boshkortstan for Russia, and Xinjiang for China). Central Asian governments have chosen repression as the principal response to dissent, beginning with the Islamic one. A consequence of this is a rapid, burdensome, and dangerous militarization of the region. The main threat to Central Asian security, however, is not radicalization of Muslim policies but the general failure of political and economic transformation as well as the rise in authoritarianism and widespread corruption. Lack of cooperation between Central Asian governments further deteriorates the situation. This concentration of injustice, fear, violence, mistrust, and mismanagement is the most alarming problem of the region.

Uzbekistan has a sad reputation as a forerunner of the militarization of Central Asia. The Tashkent regime strives to become a regional superpower, the strongest among the weak. Uzbekistan's president was the Americans' closest regional ally in the war on terrorism and Central Asia's most tyrannical dictator. Uzbekistan has the region's strongest and largest army, trained to resist Islamic terrorists in any part of the region. Yet no one forecast the possible consequences of "antiterrorist" operations by Uzbek commandos in the Tajik mountains, for instance. Uzbekistan is unilaterally fixing national boundaries, harming the national interests of all its neighbors. On the pretext of defense from Islamists, Tashkent mines the prefrontier territory of Tajikistan, and this killed about sixty Tajik citizens. For the United States and its war on terrorism, the way Uzbekistan behaves in the international arena is more important than internal discrepancies, including mass human rights violations that take place in this country.

Tajikistan is another source of instability because the military elite is comprised of former adversaries—hardened militias from pro-communist Popular Front and United Tajik Opposition. There are still imprecise numbers of nonstate gunmen loyal to regional political entrepreneurs and field commanders who control the remote regions. They "protect" the Tajik-Afghan border and are heavily involved in illegal trafficking.

Not capable of resolving problems arising from Islamist mobilization and driven by Soviet era authoritarian impulses, Central Asian governments receive millions of dollars from the United States to suppress Islamic dissent. In the aftermath of September 11, Central Asian governments have begun to apply the rhetoric of the "war on terror" to justify their pressure on the opposition. In reaction to governmental moves against real and imagined Islamic militants, youth in particular risk hardening their position and turning to the extreme forms of dissent associated with HT and IMU. This occurs most frequently among hundreds of thousands of Tajik, Uzbek, and Kyrgyz youth who are illegal migrants, returning from Russia where they may have been the victims of anti-Muslim racism.

ON TAJIK POLITICS

Islam is not a strategic factor but a matter of local concern. The preoccupation of Tajik Islamists by nationally charged (secular) issues at the expense of mere religious ones is not surprising, however. The historical legacy of the region is responsible for such metamorphosis. All post-Soviet states and Tajikistan have artificially drawn borders embracing disaccorded ethnic communities. All states of the region suffer from a shortage of public consensus, largely due to the discord between the state and various groups of population. In Tajikistan (as well as in most of the Central Asian states) there is no one commonly accepted legitimate political center. The main element of power generation is nonideological competing peripheral subnational structures, while in the core of national conciseness is ethnic nationalism, constantly undermined by ethno-regional localism and clanism. Those afraid of radicalization of Islamic politics or a reemergence of communism in Central Asia and Tajikistan particularly and those expecting political consolidation on ideological (communist, for example) principle may relax. The time of clashing ideologies has passed while the competition of different programmatic political platforms has not yet come in Central Asia. The divides go not along "Islam versus non-Islam" or a left-right political spectrum, but in accordance with ethno-regional and tribal principle in most of post-Soviet Central Asia. That means that a communist from district A would prefer to support an Islamist from district A instead of supporting his party comrade from district B. Following the same logic, a Tajik academician from a mountainous region, yet having spent his entire life in capital city, would hardly support his colleague whose parents came from the nearby valley. In result, communists, academicians, Islamists from region A will form a distinctive and stable solidarity group, while their colleagues and party comrades from region B would form another one. The Tajik contest in 1992–1997 as well as the recent Kyrgyz "revolution" in March 2005 and the Andijan uprising in May 2005 were initiated by regional, family, and clan networks, not political parties or religious movements. These traditional solidarity groups are most likely to remain central in regional politics in years to come.

Among all subnational Central Asian identities, Tajiks' attachment to their regional milieu is the strictest one. Tajik localism (or *mahalgera-i*) is a symptom of an apolitical prestate culture of Tajiks.[6] Its ideal is simple: to provide community stability, with members who know each other personally. The main reasons of *mahalgera-i's* durability—or, more precisely, the inability of Tajik communities to create a nationwide network—are historical, that is, a lack of experience of living in one state and entrenched distrust toward central power, caused by Soviet-era regional clientelism and asymmetrical regional development. Traditional solidarities are emotional and quasi-kin and resist impersonal institutionalization. Naturally the incumbent central power would prefer to bargain with local leaders at the expense of pushing forward political process through direct dialogue with emerging civil society and political parties.

The main problem of Tajik society lies in the weakness of central power and lack of societal agreement on key political issues. What power should be recognized as legitimate? Previously an inviolability of power had been secured by strong ideology (communism) or religion (Islam). But how to convince people today that this is their power and that it must be supported? To what extent is the regional (Kulabi-dominated) profile of a central power acceptable today? In the light of recent political development in Uzbekistan and Kyrgyzstan, it is hard to envisage that Tajiks would accept nonalternative dynastic succession, widespread corruption, and lack of freedom. Also, there is no agreement in the society on how the power should be applied. According to the Freedom House rating, Tajikistan stays on one level with Kyrgyzstan, Kazakhstan, and Russia. Is it good or bad, bearing in mind the recent color revolution in Kyrgyzstan (this color revolution was one of several that began with massive street protests in postcommunist societies following disputed elections and led to the resignation or overthrow of leaders considered by their opponents to be authoritarian) and spontaneous mass protests in Uzbekistan? Would the Tajikistanis accept benign authoritarianism as conducted in

2000–2003? Or it is better to reconcile with the Uzbekistan president's model of harsh repression of all political opponents in the name of keeping a minimum of security? But the most important is the following issue: when would the process of political consolidation be completed to allow transition from postwar reconstruction to stable development? The consensus-seeking and conflict-avoiding environment entered into contradiction with the new situation that calls for sustainable development, inevitably associated with open political competition, conflict management, and pluralism. Since these questions remain unanswered, since central power is weak and no genuine national unity exists in Tajikistan, people would look for protection and luxury in their communities, putting the interests of "cousins" above national and personal ones.

The Tajik Islamists' involvement in nation building while putting aside the construction of a chimerical Islamic state, is not therefore surprising. The Islamists, as members of Tajik society and followers of traditions, associated with Soviet-era popular Islam, which has always been preoccupied with community concerns, did finally join local politics, having distanced themselves from an initial political agenda of religious character. Promoting an Islamic state for them seems counterproductive to the central idea of coopting diverse elements of Tajik society into the nation.

ON THE APPLICABILITY OF THE TAJIK MODEL

Briefly put, the Tajik model is the inclusion of Islamist parties in a legal environment of a secular nation-state secured by the international community in the context of a wider conflict-resolution program. The transition from exclusivist, fundamentalist, and militant to more flexible and open is central in the agenda of Tajik Islamists. All previous Islamist forces that succeeded in winning political power (in Afghanistan, Sudan) failed because they were unable to practically implement their ideas and solve internal discrepancies in a peaceful manner. The moderates from IRPT, which represent the interests of a religious, educated middle class, have to clearly condemn international jihadi terrorism and get rid of the radicals within the party in order to deserve support from the side of the Tajik, predominantly secular, society. The violence of the 1990s, despite assurances that it was instigated by provocateurs from a "third camp" (Russia, Uzbekistan) still are being associated in the Tajik society with aggressive semieducated mullahs pushing to impose their domination in politics. In other words, a main challenge for IRPT is to complete a difficult transition from a radical illegal religious movement to a legal political party predisposed to democratic procedures and compromises. Time will show if this transmutation is real, given the fact that this would inevitably mean denial of the party's programmatic principles.

Despite its numerous shortcomings, the Tajik model of inclusion seems a more promising form of dealing with Muslim policies in Central Asia compared to the "combat/control" model proposed by Tashkent. The severe repression of opposition, instead of weakening the Islamist militancy, has strengthened and radicalized the Islamist groups in Uzbekistan. In comparison, the Tajik case has been an encouraging example of successful bargaining of the government and Muslim militants. It illustrates that Muslim politics is not inevitably radical and antisystemic. So far, the legal recognition of Islamic policies has not led to the clericalization and a clash with secularism in Tajikistan. Dialogue and inclusion are unlikely to help Islamists come to power in Tajikistan or in any other Central Asian states. Surely the outcome of inclusion depends mostly on the efficiency of secular regimes and secular political parties' ability to cooperate with Islamists in creating a genuine democratic environment. To keep Islamists from sliding back to militancy, there is a need, in addition to the supporting national economic development, to provide advocacy to all political movements committed to acting legally. For international centers of power, it means changing attitudes toward repressive Uzbekistan politics and paying attention to the Tajik model of inclusion.

CONCLUSION

What can we say that Islam is not? First, it is not a strategic and geographical factor. Islam has been unable to defeat nationalism and communalism in Tajikistan and elsewhere in Central Asia. It also failed to mobilize force(s) capable of targeting United States and the West. There is no unified Islamic threat emanating from this region. Prior to the 1980s Islam did not exist as a political canon in the region. In Central Asia it appeared in the late Soviet period under the direct influence of the Afghan war and the Iranian revolution. Since the collapse of the USSR, however, political Islam has not succeeded, even in Tajikistan and Uzbekistan, in creating a sensible mass movement. In 1992–1999 Tajiks and Uzbeks failed to create a unified Islamic front against secular postcommunist governments. Under the pressure of various factors of both internal and external character, Tajik Islamists abandoned Islamic state dreams and joined nation-state–making, while their Uzbek party comrades who were excluded by the extremely repressive Tashkent regime from national politics were pushed toward noncommunal, socially uprooted, and vague U.S.-targeted "international terrorism" and unholy illegal trafficking. Accordingly, Afghan mujahideen from the Northern Alliance blocked their Islamic support to Tajik Islamists, forcing them to make peace with the infidel Tajik government when it appeared rational to their contest for leadership within Afghanistan as a nation-state. The logic of internal political action pushed Tajik and Afghan Islamists toward compromises and normalcy. Keeping Islamism territorialized and officially authorized makes it prone to nationalism. In the opposite, the suppression of political process and exclusion and territorial dislocation of IMU cells made them violent and terrorist. Not surprisingly, neo-fundamentalist Hizb-ut-Tahrir and al-Qaeda avoid political action in a particular territory. Al-Qaeda and bin Laden groups know that Muslims openly negotiating new identities within the existing secular environment would be unwilling to focus on remote Western targets.

Serious risks exist in Central Asia. But as usual those risks come not from Islam but from Muslims. The bankruptcy of a secular, democratic, national state, which came to replace Soviet order, may instigate a noninstitutionalized and dangerous mass involvement in protest politics. Failure of social and economic reforms, injustice, and growing corruption at all echelons of power may fertilize the soil for those interested in discrediting democracy and its basic principles. If this failure occurs, Tajik society may search for a way out of crisis in an "Islamic order."

NOTES

1. In contrast, the Jadids in the early twentieth century failed to gain the support of the masses and put reformation and modernization efforts in people's Islam and mobilize masses. Instead they focused on education reform. It resulted in a split between the reformist secular-oriented minority and a fundamentalist-led traditionalist majority. This split promoted the Bolshevik takeover of Central Asia in 1920s.

2. U.S. Mission to the OSCE, Statement of Freedom of Thought, Conscience, Religion or Belief, www.usosce.rpo.at/archive/2004/10/Freedom_Thought_HDIM_2004.pdf.

3. Remarks by H.E. Academician Talbak Nazarov, Columbia International Affairs online, Working Papers, New York, September 1998, www.ciaonet.org/conf/asoc_spch98/nat01.html.

4. See Olivier Roy, *Globalized Islam* (New York: Columbia University Press, 2005).

5. See Kamoludin Abdullaev and Catherine Barnes, eds., *Politics of Compromise: The Tajikistan Peace Process* (London: Conciliation Recourses, 2001).

6. *Mahalgera-i*—an expression has appeared in Tajik vocabulary in Soviet times. French scholar Olivier Roy uses it to denote Tajik localism. Olivier Roy, "Groupes de Solidarite au Moyen-Orient et en Asie centrale," *Les Cahiers du CERI* 16 (1996): 8.

6

Countering Religious Extremism in Central Asia: Hizb-ut-Tahrir and the Islamic Movement of Uzbekistan

Alisher Khamidov

The continuing international campaign against terrorism in Central Asia brings new security challenges to the region. While operations by armed Islamic militants have ceased, other groups have emerged to exploit growing social sensitivities connected with state repression, official corruption, and deteriorating living standards. Despite being officially banned by Central Asian governments, Hizb-ut-Tahrir al-Islamiyya (HT), a party of Islamic liberation, is operating in most countries in the region. Striving toward its ultimate goal of restoring the Ottoman-era Islamic caliphate, the party is harnessing public popularity through its commitment to nonviolence and its appeal for social and economic justice in society. Meanwhile, increasing suppression of the party by secular authorities and serious differences between competing factions within the party indicate that the party could breed new recruits for violent groups in the region such as the Islamic Movement of Uzbekistan (IMU) or al-Qaeda.

Central Asia, with its vast energy resources and strategic geopolitical location, has become an arena for greater cooperation among the United States, Russia, and China. It is also a region of turbulent ethnic and religious tension, illicit drug trafficking, environmental degradation, and pervasive poverty. There is a real basis for concern that public support for extremist views advocated by such parties as HT will grow amid the ongoing political and civil turmoil. The political situation in Central Asian republics is increasingly volatile, and a localized riot could potentially spark broader unrest. Given the history of violent confrontations between secular rulers and religious insurgents, as in Tajikistan's civil war (1992–1997) and the more recent incursions into Kyrgyzstan and Uzbekistan by militants of the Islamic Movement of Uzbekistan, the potential for religious parties to hijack such unrest is high.

Hizb-ut-Tahrir represents a complex policy challenge in Central Asia and the world primarily because of its commitment to nonviolent social change and its growing grassroots support base. Nevertheless, the party's commitment to nonviolence as a form of political protest places it in a different category from religious groups that have engaged in terror tactics. As of now, the prospect of involving the party in the political process has not been explored by regional governments and their international partners due to their unwillingness to recognize the party's doctrine and its growing popular base. However, a manner in which the party will be induced to move from the arena of religiously inspired extremist protests to engagement in mainstream political life may provide key lessons for crafting a well-informed policy toward similar movements elsewhere in the world.

PROBLEM IDENTIFICATION

Hizb-ut-Tahrir is a transnational religious movement founded by Taqiudding an-Nabhani al-Falastani, an ethnic Palestinian, in 1953. The first HT recruits came from the Palestinian section of the Egypt-based al-Ikhwan al-Muslimin (Muslim Brotherhood). Presently headed by Abd al-Kadim Zallum, also an ethnic Palestinian, HT expanded its membership to countries with Muslim populations all around the world. Hizb-ut-Tahrir pursues international Islamic solidarity in countries with a large *umma*. In what appears to be a utopian view of political Islam, HT members strongly adhere to the belief that only the formation of an Islamic state regulated by Sharia—Islamic law—can address the ills and problems of society. HT sees the process of modernization and secularization in many Muslim-populated countries as a Western plot against the Muslim *umma*.

Despite rejecting modernization, the party has been enjoying its fruits. In recent years, the HT has set up offices in several European countries, including Germany and the United Kingdom. With its headquarters based in London, HT raises funds and trains recruits to spread the movement across the world, including Central Asia. In doing so, HT relies on new technological advancements and facilities, including the Internet, e-mail, web casts, audio and video appliances.[1]

While HT's mission and objectives may appear as fringe elements in most Muslim-populated countries, the growing appeal of its extreme views is a cause of concern for local, national, regional, and international actors, including the U.S. government. HT's rhetoric incites anti-Semitic and anti-American sentiments. Following the events of September 11, 2001, HT has focused on casting itself as the voice of all Muslims while presenting the cooperation of Central Asian governments with the U.S.-led anti-terrorist campaign as treason and war against Islam and Muslims.

Without the Russian colonization of Central Asia and the subsequent collapse of the Soviet Union, HT never would have acquired a mobilized ideological identity and collective Muslim consciousness among its members in Central Asia. Following the collapse of the Soviet empire, millions of Central Asians turned to their "Islamic roots" in search of a new identity. The sudden euphoria of independence that engulfed the region in the early 1990s opened up Central Asia to the outside world, ushering in various outside brands of Islam that had their own agenda. Busy with bolstering their own legitimacy and grappling with new economic challenges, the regional authorities have largely neglected religious affairs and abandoned the Soviet methods of control. The first HT cells, consisting of five or six people, were established in Central Asia by foreign missionaries. These branched off so rapidly that by the late 1990s their membership was estimated to be in the thousands across the republics of Central Asia

Increasing numbers of ordinary people in Central Asian republics have come to equate democracy and market reform with official corruption and lawlessness. One potential implication is the violent overthrow of existing authoritarian regimes and the hijacking of this social outburst by extremist religious groups such as Hizb-ut-Tahrir or the IMU. Most illustrative of this prospect is the eruption of the Tajik civil war in 1992, when the resurgent Islamic parties mobilized public support in an effort to replace a weak post-Soviet regime with an Islamic state.

Another potential danger is that HT's vast transnational network, underground organizational structure, financial and technical capacities make it attractive to sponsors of terrorism. Although HT's links with more violent groups are yet to be determined, the official repression and demonization of its activists could push disillusioned members to join the ranks of militant and terrorist groups such as the IMU or al-Qaeda. The challenge that policy makers must now address is how to keep HT's activities nonviolent while, at the same time, ensuring that its activists do not join terrorist groups. A greater challenge is to create mechanisms under which HT could cease its violent and aggressive rhetoric and become involved in the official political process.

The pattern in which the Hizb-ut-Tahrir will be induced to enter the mainstream political process can offer invaluable insights on crafting more viable policy strategies toward similar movements elsewhere in the world. Hizb-ut-Tahrir members often cite a desire to participate in political and social life as important reasons for joining.[2] At present, it appears worthwhile for the United States to explore the option of encouraging regional actors to maintain communication and strive for peaceful dialogue with HT activists who appear willing to do so. A steady communication with HT may facilitate the monitoring of the movement's activities and future plans firsthand. It could also provide insights into how to keep the resources and structures of the movement away from terrorist groups and to prevent its activists from joining terrorist organizations.

HIZB-UT-TAHRIR AND THE ISLAMIC MOVEMENT OF UZBEKISTAN

Within broader Islamic movements, HT falls under the category of the so-called *al-da'wa al Islamiya* (the Islamic Call) camp as opposed to *al-thawra al-Muslimin* (the Muslim Revolution) camp. While al-da'wa al-Islamiya doctrine seeks to change society gradually and indirectly by concentrating first on the structures and value systems of a society, the al-thawra al-Muslimin groups opt to change society directly through political, possibly violent means. However, the ultimate goal of both camps is the same—to establish an Islamic form of governance. Vivid examples of the al-thawra camp are the Islamic Movement of Uzbekistan and the Tajikistan-based United Tajik Opposition (UTO) dominated by the Islamic Renaissance Party (IRP).

The IMU was founded in 1999 by Tahir Yuldoshev and Juma Namangani, ethnic Uzbeks from the Namangan Province of Uzbekistan. The movement's main goal was to oust the regime of President Islam Karimov in Uzbekistan. The IMU is believed to have received active support from Islamist networks in the Middle East and South Asia, including the Taliban. It had also reportedly maintained links with Osama bin Laden and trained in al-Qaeda's military camps in Afghanistan. The Garm Valley, a mountainous region of Tajikistan, became the stronghold of the IMU in late 1990s.

Namangani and Yuldoshev fought alongside the United Tajik Opposition in the Tajik civil war (1992–1997). In August 1999, with a band of 800 militants, the IMU infiltrated southern Kyrgyzstan, where it captured villages and hostages and threatened to attack Uzbekistan. In August 2000, IMU rebels led by Namangani made incursions into southern Uzbekistan, mountainous areas just outside of Tashkent, and several areas in southern Kyrgyzstan. During the U.S.-led military action in Afghanistan, the IMU fought alongside the Taliban. Recent international media reports indicate that the organization was destroyed and its membership scattered after its leader Juma Namangani was reportedly killed during U.S. aerial bombing. Local reports also suggest that the remnants of the IMU were able to escape through porous borders to the north. Regional security services estimate the current IMU membership at some 300 disorganized, unarmed fighters.

According to regional security services, the IMU's hidden agenda was to secure channels for trafficking drugs from Afghanistan to Central Asian countries. However, local experts in the Ferghana Valley suggested that negotiations with the Uzbek authorities were a likely aim of IMU leaders. These experts indicated that the IMU was hoping to gain power via the "Tajik peace talks scenario"; the settlement that ended the 1992–1997 Tajik civil war provided for the sharing of power between President Imomali Rakhmonov's government and the United Tajik Opposition, which is dominated by Islamic opposition leaders. Both Kyrgyz and Uzbek authorities moved to eradicate unsanctioned Islamic activity before the crackdown came under wider international scrutiny. Apparently they were concerned that if the insurgency dragged on, the international community may have begun to promote the notion of a negotiated settlement. Karimov's government, in particular, was steadfastly opposed to engaging the insurgents in peace talks. The United States branded the IMU a terrorist organization in late 2000, thus tacitly supporting regional military action against the Islamic fighters.

While the IMU and the HT seem to share the ultimate goal of constructing the Islamic state, there are significant differences in their tactics and strategies. In recent years, the Hizb-ut-Tahrir has sought to distance itself from the IMU and other violent Islamic groups, both in rhetoric and in practice. When addressing local Muslims, Hizb-ut-Tahrir regularly juxtaposes its pledge to nonviolence to violent campaigns of the IMU. HT members continuously lambaste militants by calling the path of the IMU misleading.

The IMU claimed public interest by its violent incursions and statements. In contrast, HT activists distribute leaflets and books that often contain scathing criticisms of regional governments. They also rely on underground meetings rather than public speeches. These techniques make Hizb-ut-Tahrir operatives hard to find and to silence. They also let Hizb-ut-Tahrir members send messages more quickly than the government can suppress or discredit them.[3]

Significant differences also exist in their recruitment strategies. In contrast to the IMU's methods of enticing new members by offers of cash and intimidation, the HT emphasizes the recruitment of new members on a voluntary basis by means of persuasion and conviction. While IMU's ranks were filled by only Muslim males, HT accepts Muslim men and women as its members regardless of whether they are Arabs or non-Arabs, since it is a party for all Muslims.[4]

Despite regional governments' exaggeration of HT's link with the IMU, local media reports indicate that members of these two groups interact.[5] During a widespread crackdown on HT in 1999 and 2000, some individual members of the HT found refuge in the Taliban-controlled regions of Afghanistan, where they reportedly joined the IMU ranks. The IMU has reportedly used HT literature to eliminate religious illiteracy of its members.[6]

HT'S ORGANIZATIONAL STRUCTURE AND STRATEGIES

In a pattern resembling the Muslim Brotherhood in the Middle East, HT appeared in Central Asia as a reaction to the secularization and nationalism imposed by authoritarian governments in the postcolonial years that followed the collapse of the Soviet Union. From the start of its penetration into Central Asian republics, HT has striven to fill the ideological and political void created by corrupt governments that offered few public services.

HT doctrine seeks to achieve its goals in three distinct stages. The first stage is mainly a proselytizing or recruitment stage in which the party reaches out to Muslims around the world in an effort to persuade them to accept the idea, mission, and goals of the party. Convinced individuals are invited to join the party and assume its methods and strategies. They are then expected to join the outreach effort.

The second stage is interaction with the *umma* (taking the message to broader Muslim communities). In this stage, HT attempts to persuade the *umma* to embrace and carry Islam so that the Islamic way of life becomes an everyday practice for each Muslim and encompasses all affairs of life.

The third stage includes establishing an Islamic government, implementing the norms and practices of Sharia generally and comprehensively, and carrying it as a message to the world.[7] Some observers suggest that this stage is likely to be violent, as it is reminiscent of the Iranian revolution in 1979. As the Iranian Islamists attacked their opponents after Ayatollah Khomeini sanctioned violence in later stages of the revolution, so will Hizb-ut-Tahrir after it gains a sufficient popular base. According to some observers, in the third stage HT activists are likely to attempt to seize control of major government structures such as law enforcement, army, and broadcasting services. Some local media reports indicate that HT activists are successfully implanting their activists in these key structures.

In Central Asia, HT appears to be in its initial stage—the recruitment stage. While the precise figures depicting level of support for HT are unavailable, local observers in the Uzbek part of the Ferghana Valley suggest that the current active support is less than 10 percent of Uzbekistan's 26 million population.[8] In Kyrgyzstan, officials estimate HT membership at 3,000.[9] But many observers suggest that the membership of HT is much higher and is constantly growing in all republics. In Central Asian republics, the bulk of HT members come from the ranks of unemployed and uneducated youth. In recent years,

HT has also taken its message to broader groups, including college students, merchants, NGO activists, women's groups, grassroots activists, local leaders, and even educated specialists such as engineers, high school teachers, and government clerks. All these groups are unhappy with the perceived lawlessness in their society, the authorities' inability to deal with economic problems, and officials' increasing reliance on violence to maintain order. Perceived and real discrimination among some ethnic minorities continues to provide new recruits for HT and further undermines the legitimacy of government structures. For example, over 90 percent of HT membership in Kyrgyzstan consists of ethnic Uzbeks.[10] However, local media reports indicate that party membership is crossing ethnic lines. Kyrgyz, Kazakhs, and Tajiks have reportedly joined in recent years.

Reminiscent of Bolshevik strategies in prerevolutionary Russia, Hizb-ut-Tahrir operates in Central Asian republics in small, secretive cells of five to seven people called *doiras* or *halkas,* which make up a large pyramidal structure. Headed by a *mushrif* (group leader), each group member knows only the members of his or her circle and only the *mushrif* knows the next stage superior. This arrangement, for example, makes the attempts of the Uzbek police to plant agents in new HT cells and to penetrate the chain of command nearly impossible.[11]

HT continues to expand its membership by proselytizing among merchants in bazaars, local markets, and during the winter months when farmers and craftsmen are idle. New members are approved to join the party upon the recommendation of an existing member and after carefully studying the program, strategies, and ideology of the group. Then they are encouraged to attract new members by distributing leaflets containing the party's propaganda through traditional social networks and weekly meetings of men.[12] HT has even approached local media outlets by sending them letters requesting cooperation.

Of particular concern are HT's vague future plans in Central Asia. HT members often cannot explain how the caliphate will be achieved, what economic or social policies it will pursue, and what the role of other religious traditions and ethnicities in a truly Islamic society will be.[13] Another major concern is whether the party will remain committed to nonviolent means as it moves to its second and third stages. One prominent example of "changing lanes" is the al-Ikhwan al-Muslimin, the Muslim Brotherhood, in Egypt. The Muslim Brotherhood's activities were relatively peaceful at the outset as the movement concentrated mainly on community development projects. But widespread state repression and radicalization soon led the group to emerge as a major government opponent, and it was later responsible for the assassination of key political figures.[14]

Hizb-ut-Tahrir's pledge to remain nonviolent leaves many local and international observers skeptical. HT members openly admit that they share the longer-term objective of constructing an Islamic state with the IMU. Local authorities and some observers contend that HT rhetoric about its nonviolent nature is simply propaganda. Recent interviews with HT leaders suggest that there are indeed individual members within HT who may become disillusioned by a nonviolent strategy and may react violently to government provocations. Pakistani journalist Ahmed Rashid's recent book discusses HT's ambivalence toward violence. Ali, one of the upper command *mushrifs* of HT-Uzbekistan told Rashid: "Hizb-ut-Tahrir wants a peaceful jihad that will be spread by explanation and conversion not by war. But ultimately there will be war because the repression of the Central Asian states is so strong."[15] Reports of the International Crisis Group (ICG) indicate that despite its alleged cohesion, there are inner confrontations between leaders of the party. According to one recent ICG report, a faction called Hizb-an-Nusra (Party of Victory) branched off from the HT in the Tashkent area, presumably because of disagreements over the party's strategy for political struggle. Some local and international analysts predict further splits within the party and do not exclude the potential for violence.

WHY HIZB-UT-TAHRIR IN CENTRAL ASIA?

Among the political reasons for the resurgence of the Hizb-ut-Tahrir and other Islamic groups are the growing authoritarianism and ineffectualness of authoritarian regimes, the radicalization of politics, and official inability to address long-standing economic and social problems.

The sudden euphoria of independence that engulfed the region in the early 1990s opened up Central Asia to the outside world, ushering in outside brands of Islam with their own agendas. Busy with bolstering their own legitimacy and grappling with new economic challenges, the regional authorities have largely neglected religious affairs and abandoned the Soviet methods of control. As a result, the number of mosques, madrassas, and seminaries in Tajikistan and Kyrgyzstan quadrupled in the first three years of independence, and various religious missionaries flooded into the cities and towns of the region. Some Central Asian leaders exploited public interest in religion to consolidate their grip on power and to promote new national identity building programs. For example, President Islam Karimov of Uzbekistan, shortly after taking office, made a pilgrimage to Mecca in an effort to win the loyalty of local elites. President Nursultan Nazarbaev also initiated the construction of a large mosque in the center of the then capital, Almaty, in 1993.

Growing popular sensitivity over persistent social problems in society are playing into the hands of HT activists. The spread of HIV, drug addiction, and prostitution have emerged as major social problems with the prospect to expand in the next decade. Since the 1991 Soviet collapse, religious leaders in the region have voiced concern over deteriorating social values in their communities, linking the moral decline with the post-Soviet penetration of Western pop culture and vice. They consider the spread of sexually transmitted diseases as a tangible sign of growing modernization and secularization that promote the population's spiritual degeneration. According to some HT members, government campaigns to promote awareness do not address the root causes of the proliferation of infections—the popular drift away from Islamic values.

As economic and industrial output reach their lowest levels and nearly all Central Asian states face the prospect of civil unrest and large-scale violence, HT has effectively cast itself as the promoter of social and economic justice. HT's calls for an end to corruption, greed, and abuse of power resonate with many ordinary people in villages and cities where living standards have fallen drastically over the past decade. By 2002, the national debt of Kyrgyzstan reached approximately $1.5 billion, an amount equal to its annual GDP. In Uzbekistan, the average salary in 2002 was less than $15 per month. Poverty has reached dangerous levels. Kalyk Imankulov, the Kyrgyz security chief, asserts that Hizb-ut-Tahrir's power base is found among the country's vast pool of impoverished citizens. Over 80 percent of Kyrgyz live at or below the poverty line, according to Imankulov, who also stated that the group likely is financed by radical foreign organizations and individuals.[16] Some regional reports indicate that in addition to the regional network in Central Asian republics, HT receives financial support from sympathizers in Jordan, Egypt, Indonesia, and Pakistan.[17]

Together with mass unemployment in certain parts of the region, poverty increases the prospect of localized trouble. An August 2002 incident involving the arrest of a Hizb-ut-Tahrir activist illustrates the extent of the antigovernment mood in south Kyrgyzstan. A mob surrounded police in the town of Arslanbob—in the Jalal-Abad region that was the scene of a March riot—after officers took the Hizb-ut-Tahrir activist into custody. Ultimately police opened fire, wounding one young man. Although the Kyrgyz authorities were able to prevent the escalation of riots, the tension among residents remains high.

The fact that the authorities stifle channels for legitimate civic expression or for securing practical change through democratic means is further empowering HT's campaigns.[18] HT leaflets are quickly becoming the source of information for many who are disillusioned with the propaganda-style state media. For example, Sheikh Sadiq Q. Kamal al-Deen, the director of the Islamic Center of Islamic Cooperation in Osh and the former mufti of Kyrgyzstan, cites the "minimal political participation of the population, the growth of distrust of authority and skepticism about the utility of democratic institutions" as key factors in the growth of Hizb-ut-Tahrir.[19]

Another significant factor in HT's popularity is the party's rejection of violence as political means. Unlike the IMU, Hizb-ut-Tahrir's major appeal is rooted in its commitment to nonviolent means of achieving its ultimate goal. In a region where memories of bloody ethnic clashes between Uzbeks and Meskhetian Turks (in 1989), Uzbeks and Kyrgyz (in 1990) are still fresh, the incursions of the Islamic Movement of Uzbekistan in 1999 and 2000 fueled popular aversion to violent methods. Hizb-ut-Tahrir's call for a supranational Islamic identity and cooperation among all Muslim countries appears attractive to segments of the population in cases where political and social differences between various ethnic communities have created tension in the region.

REGIONAL EFFORTS TO COUNTER HT

Each republic in Central Asia has chosen a different response to counter HT's growing popularity. Republics with more dictatorial regimes and a larger number of practicing Muslims have taken a tough, intolerant stance. Governments with a relative degree of democratic practice have applied less repressive measures. However, the common goal across the region has been the containment and the complete eradication of the group. Uzbekistan and Tajikistan have applied the most repressive measures against Islamic activists through mass arrests and torture. Without distinguishing between moderate believers and radical Islamists, the Uzbek authorities have thrown thousands of suspected extremists into jail, where they languish in deteriorating conditions. According to Human Rights Watch reports, such arrests directly violate practitioners' fundamental right to religious freedom.[20] Annually, dozens of HT activists are sentenced to decades-long imprisonment on fabricated charges of inciting interethnic hatred in Tajikistan. Law enforcement officers often use arbitrary charges and plant narcotics and religious literature on ordinary believers. They also target family members of those who have been arrested by extorting money and exposing them to countless interrogations.

Kyrgyzstan's treatment of HT members is particularly noteworthy. In Kyrgyzstan, the authorities have imposed less repressive measures in the form of fines and suspended prison sentences. In 2001, however, the Kyrgyz authorities arrested about 6,000 people for spreading HT leaflets in the Jalal-Abad region alone.[21] In an effort to explore peaceful options for engaging the party in political process, the Kyrgyz authorities have recently attempted to establish dialogue with members of the group. Discarding the government's overtures as lacking good faith, HT has declined the offer. However, individual HT cell leaders are reported to be in touch with local government officials through informal social links. Largely as the result of Kyrgyzstan's relatively favorable treatment, many HT followers from Uzbekistan have sought refuge in Kyrgyzstan in recent years.[22]

Central Asian governments have also employed local media outlets and state-controlled clergy to counter HT's messages. However, such efforts have not yielded significant results, as both the state-supported clergy and the media lack credibility in public. Meanwhile, those clerics collaborating with the governments appear incapable of presenting credible arguments to counter HT doctrine in mosques. In the Osh region of Kyrgyzstan, 80 percent of imams and mullahs (local clergy) are self-educated individuals with no higher religious education.[23]

Unlike state-supported clergy members and government officials, HT activists enjoy a reputation as honest, incorruptible, and determined individuals. Recent local media reports indicate that increasing numbers of HT members attend local mosques where they continue to spread their message. In the meantime, moderate Islamic leaders who have preserved their independence and criticized the authorities for their inept policies have been suppressed and are kept under strict police surveillance or home arrest.[24] It is these individual leaders who have the authority and capacity to counter the extremist views of HT by reinterpreting Islamic scriptures and sacred texts in a way that promotes ethnic cohesion and religious cooperation.

AVOID DESIGNATING HT A TERRORIST ORGANIZATION

As the example of the Muslim Brotherhood in Egypt demonstrates, lumping Hizb-ut-Tahrir and the IMU together in the same category of terrorist organizations would be a simplistic move that could legitimize the repressive measures of Central Asian governments. Having asserted links to terrorist activity, Central Asian authorities have now banned HT and continuously lobby Western governments to recognize it as a terrorist organization.[25] This suppression is partly rooted in secular leaders' fears that the party's growing appeal for social and political justice challenges their legitimacy in the eyes of the public. Although such fears have a degree of credibility, it is the violent suppression of opposition movements and unwillingness to foster open political debate that are undermining the legitimacy of regional governments.

Branding Hizb-ut-Tahrir a terrorist organization would have serious implications and backlash for regional security. It would further embolden the ongoing official harassment of ordinary believers and lead to widespread public outcry. Such a measure would also be seen by local religious factions as a U.S. effort to support oppressive governments in the war against terrorism. It would undermine U.S.-led efforts to counter Islamic extremism among local populations as well as encourage HT to join forces with terrorist groups such as the IMU or al-Qaeda to press its aims.

EXPLORE OPTIONS FOR INVOLVING HT IN THE POLITICAL PROCESS

In many cases, radical Islamic parties emerged as the result of the denial of their right to participate in political discourse. Such groups as the Muslim Brotherhood and the FIS (Front Islamique du Salut/Algerian Islamist political party) in Algeria competed fairly and nonviolently during their countries' brief openness. But when their anticipated election victories were abolished by secular and military forces, radical factions within these groups adopted terrorist tactics against foreigners and broad segments of society.[26] The United States must reconsider viewing Islamic parties as the enemy and instead encourage their involvement in the political process. Principled support of democracy and human rights in this regard is key to moderating radical Islamists.

The option of political engagement has persuasive historical evidence. Some Islamic parties compete with the respect of law in a relatively open political process in countries like Turkey, Jordan, or Yemen. For instance, the Justice and Development Party in Turkey won about one-third of the votes, and under Turkey's electoral system this has given it almost two-thirds of the seats in the national parliament. Recep Erdogan, its leader, is viewed as the advocate of EU membership for Turkey.

BACK INDEPENDENT AND MODERATE ISLAMIC CLERGY LEADERS

There are many moderate Muslims in all Central Asian republics who believe in a vision of Islam that embraces free thought, free speech, and tolerance. Many of these individuals have condemned the September 11 attacks and have expressed sympathy for American victims. Sadly enough, these moderate voices are under attack by both extremist interpreters of Islam and authoritarian secular leaders. For example, since late 1997, Uzbek police and security forces have arrested thousands of Muslims who did not follow the officially authorized version of Islam or people who attend other places of worship than those approved by the state, according to a report published by the Human Rights Watch. The authorities are targeting other religious groups as well. On September 8, 2002, the internal affairs department of Chirchik, a town in Uzbekistan, raided a Baptist worship service in a private home. All religious literature was confiscated and the identity papers of those in attendance were seized. The group was accused of "inciting religious hostility" because of the content of some Christian materials.[27] Acacia Shields, who heads the Tashkent office for Human Rights Watch, has continuously reported the wide variety of torture practices routinely employed by Uzbek secret services to secure self-incriminating statements against suspects. Officials have also resorted to torture in order to compel defendants to decline legal representation. In addition, authorities have often planted evidence such as illegal religious pamphlets on suspects.[28]

All Central Asian governments must respect the constitutional right of citizens to practice religion in private and public without restriction. While governments should be encouraged to implement the constitutional separation of state and religion, it is important that they also reconsider the Soviet methods of registering religious communities, designating state-sponsored Islamic leaders, and maintaining strict control over religious institutions.

As the authorities stop harassing believers, moderate Islamic clergy leaders will speak out more strongly against Osama bin Laden and other extremist views of Islam. By organizing panel discussions, addressing Muslims in their mosques, and using local media outlets, such leaders can significantly reduce the growing popularity of extremist religious views. These clergy leaders can also benefit from U.S. Department of State–sponsored visitor exchange programs to share views with American Islamic activists and the Muslim community. American Muslim leaders, who are viewed with a degree of respect and admiration among Central Asian Muslims for their bravery and courage (especially after September 11), should be encouraged to visit Central Asia and engage in debate with Muslims there.

CONCLUSION

Many poorer Central Asian citizens have come to equate their countries' political and economic transition with official corruption and the abuse of power. In recent years, Hizb-ut-Tahrir has responded by effectively casting itself as an outlet for those disaffected by political and economic developments over the past decade. The government's reliance on repressive measures in response is actually aiding the radicals' attempts to recruit new members and fan popular discontent. There is a real basis for concern that Hizb-ut-Tahrir's support will continue to grow amid the ongoing political and civil turmoil. The political situation in Central Asian republics is increasingly volatile, and a relatively localized riot like the March confrontation in the Ak-Sui region of Kyrgyzstan can potentially spark much broader unrest. The potential for such riots to be hijacked by extremists groups is also very high.

Such parties as the Hizb-ut-Tahrir and the Islamic Movement of Uzbekistan emerged to fill a vacuum that resulted from the failure of Marxism-Leninism, then Central Asian nationalism. Hizb-ut-Tahrir and other radical Islamic movements, albeit their tactics and ideologies are reprehensible to most Westerners, have potential to become involved in peaceful political process if the "rules of the game" are respected by all sides.

It appears today that the best option for Central Asian governments to combat Islamic radical groups is to pursue economic reforms and political liberalization vigorously. Assistance from the United States is crucial. The new American presence in Central Asia remains a potentially significant lever for an international antiterrorism coalition—if the United States guides its allies toward broader democracy and commitment to the rule of law.

NOTES

1. Ahmed Rashid, *Jihad: The Rise of Militant Islam in Central Asia* (New Haven: Yale University Press, 2002), 119.

2. International Crisis Group (Belgium), Policy Brief on the IMU and HT in Central Asia, 2001.

3. Davron Vali, "Banned Islamic Movement Increasingly Active in Tajikistan," *Eurasianet*, September 5, 2002.

4. Zakir, Osh-based mushrif of HT dai'ra, discussion with author, Osh, Kyrgyzstan, June 2001.

5. See Zamira Eshanova, "Central Asia: Are Radical Groups Joining Forces?" *Eurasianet Partner Post*, October 11, 2002.

6. Rashid, *Jihad,* 133.

7. More information about the goals and objectives of Hizb-ut-Tahrir can be obtained at its official website: www.hizb-ut-tahrir.org.

8. International Crisis Group, Policy Brief on the IMU and HT.

9. Alisher Khamidov, "Islamic Radical Group Steadily Increases Support Base in Kyrgyzstan," *Eurasianet*, September 5, 2002.

10. Igor Grebenshikov, "The Hizb-ut-Tahrir through the eyes of Kyrgyz Journalists," *Media Insight Central Asia,* January 2002.

11. Rashid, *Jihad,* 120.

12. International Crisis Group, Policy Brief on the IMU and HT.

13. International Crisis Group, Policy Brief on the IMU and HT.

14. For more information on the Muslim Brotherhood, see Gilles Kepel, *Muslim Extremism in Egypt: The Prophet and Pharaoh* (Berkeley: University of California Press, 1993).

15. Rashid, *Jihad,* 135–36.

16. Khamidov, "Islamic Radical Group."

17. Tamara Makarenko, "Hizb-ut-Tahrir on the Rise in Central Asia," *Jane's Intelligence Review,* November 12, 2002, www.jir.janes.com.

18. See International Crisis Group, Report on the IMU and Hizb-ut-Tahrir, 2001.

19. International Crisis Group, Report on the IMU and Hizb-ut-Tahrir.

20. Based on information provided by the Human Rights Watch Report for 2002, Uzbekistan has imprisoned about 7,000 practicing Muslims in recent years.

21. Grebenshikov, "Hizb-ut-Tahrir."

22. International Crisis Group, Report on the IMU and Hizb-ut-Tahrir.

23. Grebenshikov, "Hizb-ut-Tahrir."

24. See reports by The Memorial, a humanitarian and human rights organization based in Russia, www.memo.ru/eng.

25. Nikolai Tanaev, prime minister of Kyrgyzstan, recently announced the discovery of a stockpile of guns in the village of Arslanbob, which the authorities claim belonged to HT.

26. Stephen Zunes, "American Policy toward Islam," *Foreign Policy in Focus,* September 12, 2001.

27. International Christian Concern, report, December 2002.

28. "Rights Observers See No End to Religious Persecution in Uzbekistan," *Eurasianet,* September 22, 2000.

7

Islam, Politics, and Security in Central Asia

Aleksei Malashenko

INTERPRETING THE ROLE OF ISLAM

Those who analyze threats stemming from radical Islam tend to indulge in technical discussions involving numerous definitions, such as fundamentalism, neofundamentalism, Wahhabism, neo-Wahhabism, Islamism, and integrationism. Such discussions sometimes acquire an almost theological character, as secular researchers support their arguments with meticulous references to parables and legends from the Qur'an. Not to deny the usefulness of academic research, it should be noted that definitions are open to wide political and ideological interpretation.

Addressing the Soviet Communist Party's twenty-sixth Congress in 1981, general secretary Leonid Brezhnev expressed the official Soviet ideological line that "liberation struggles can be waged under the banner of Islam. This has been shown," he went on to say, "by historical experience, including the most recent one. This experience shows, however, that the same Islamic slogans may be used by reactionary forces for instigating counterrevolutionary uprisings."[1] That statement expresses a pragmatic approach to political Islam, which today is equally characteristic of both President Vladimir Putin of Russia and President Islam Karimov of Uzbekistan, as well as the head of separatist Chechnya, Aslan Maskhadov, or Osama bin Laden, as well as the leader of the Islamic movement of Uzbekistan, Dzhuma Namangani, allegedly killed.

Much water has flowed under the bridge since the above-mentioned communist forum. However, the profound connection between religion and politics remains unchanged. Today secularism is treated in a more "diplomatic" way than before, while religion is regarded as a normal factor of secular life, including its social and political aspects. This is especially evident in the countries of the

Muslim world, where all political forces appeal to Islam and where both a reformist president and his opponent, leader of the Islamic opposition, begin their speeches with a traditional Islamic greeting. Central Asia is no exception to this. Despite its heavy secularization under the Soviet regime, it remains an organic part of the Muslim world—like, for instance, Morocco or Indonesia.

It is not easy to estimate the real strength and influence of Islamists in any given society—even if numerous publications appear on this subject. It is because most books and articles are based on either information provided by the special services, statements of spiritual leaders, or opportunist utterances of politicians and their advisers. Furthermore, radical Islam has long been a tool of secular leaders for their political goals. Also, radical Islam is used by security and law enforcement structures as an excuse for pumping money out of the state budget.

Often analysts portray Islamists as the sole effective opposition force in Central Asia. In some countries—Uzbekistan and Tajikistan, for instance—this is indeed so.[2] In Kyrgyzstan, however, Islamists take part in the political process only occasionally. In Kazakhstan, they remain on the sidelines for the time being. In Turkmenistan, they do not exist as an organized movement. Islamists were not even named by the Turkmenistan special services among the organizers of the assassination attempt on President Saparmurad Niyazov in 2002. At the same time, the possibility of a radical Islamic movement appearing even in the country where the president imposes his own "Rukhnama" ideology cannot be ruled out.

The ruling politicians use a double standard in regard to Islamic movements, whether national or regional nature. Today the "Islamic threat" occupies a prominent place in the press and speeches by politicians. In private discussions, however, local officials refuse to confirm the existence of such danger. Some of the high-ranking politicians in Central Asia admit that they have never even heard of active Islamic organizations operating there and have a difficulty naming their leaders.

At the same time, there is a widespread opinion that if the current trends, like economic crisis, increasing material inequality, and rampant corruption, continue, the Islamists will become a formidable force. Today they seem to constitute a kind of surreal force that is everywhere and nowhere at the same time.

ISLAMIC ACTIVITY IN CENTRAL ASIA

It is important to analyze different stages of Islamic activity in Central Asia. Like any attempt for periodization, this one will look at leading trends and landmarks without pretending to be comprehensive.

Stage one started in the late 1980s and lasted until the early 1990s. Its milestone was 1990, when a national Islamic Rebirth Party was established in the Soviet Union. Before that happened there were parallel Islamic structures in Central Asia, but they were amorphous and few in number and their ambitions were modest.[3]

The branches of the Islamic Rebirth Party, which appeared after 1990, gave an impetus to the formation of similar parties and groups, big and small, on a national and regional scale. Thus in Uzbekistan there appeared in 1991 the famous Adolat (Justice) organization—a cross between Soviet-type vigilante patrols and police vice squads.[4] But even before that two other parties had appeared there: Hezbollah and the Islamic Party of Turkestan (long forgotten and remembered only by experts). It was about the same time that the Party of National Freedom, Alash, emerged in Kazakhstan, and four Islamic groupings (a record for the time) made themselves known in Azerbaijan. In November 1991, the Party of Islamic Rebirth of Tajikistan (PIRT) was officially registered in Dushanbe. Figuratively speaking, a tidal wave of Islamic rebirth swept over the 70 million strong post-Soviet *umma.*

However, the spring of Islamic renaissance was short-lived. As early as December 1991, following the first Tajik elections, a confrontation began between the PIRT and the local Popular Front; starting from 1992 the Adolat Party was persecuted in Uzbekistan; and President Nursultan Nazarbayev of Kazakhstan refused to recognize the Alashists, calling them fascists.

Stage two began around 1992 and was marked by persecution of political Islam. Dozens and then hundreds of mosques belonging to the opposition were closed down, and insubordinate Muslim politicians and clergymen were jailed or sent to labor camps. Radicals who appealed to Islam for achieving their ends joined the extreme opposition and resorted to armed struggle more and more often. In Central Asia and the north Caucasus training camps for Islamic combatants started to appear. A civil war broke out in Tajikistan.

National Islamic "grapes of wrath" were maturing in Tatarstan. And the first president of separatist Chechnya, Major General Dzhokhar Dudayev, declared jihad on Russia.

In the mid-1990s Islamic radicalism became a regular actor on the post-Soviet scene. The main achievement of the Islamic political movement was a 1996 peace agreement between the United Tajik Opposition and the government of Tajikistan and the subsequent formation of a single government coalition, although members of the opposition felt uncomfortable in the corridors of power.

Events in Tajikistan showed, first, that the struggle against Islamic separatists may entail tragic consequences and, second, that it is possible to come to terms with them, turning them from enemies into partners—albeit disagreeable ones.

At the same time, the civil war in Tajikistan, which cost between 60,000 and 200,000 lives, became an important trump card in the hands of Central Asian presidents who were now able to point to their bloodstained neighbor as a weak government that had failed to ensure stability and was forced to make a deal with the "devil's offspring," the fundamentalists.

Similarly, the Khasavyurt agreement that Moscow signed with the Chechen separatists in 1996 was later disavowed as defeatist and described by many as a success of Islamic radicalism. In certain quarters that agreement was regarded as a victory for militant Islam. However, Aslan Maskhadov, who signed the agreement for the Chechen side, opposed the Islamicization of Chechnya and was against the creation of an Islamic state there. The Khasavyurt agreement thus signified the victory of Chechen separatism and not of Islam.

The start of stage three goes back to 1996—the year when the Talibs took power in Afghanistan. By that time, Islamists were organized and consolidated; they had accumulated experience in opposing the ruling establishment, which continued to reject compromise. Having acquired a stable territorial base, Islamic radicals were less vulnerable in their confrontation with the secular authorities. Afghanistan had become a gateway of arms supplies, a territory where Islamic extremists and their allies from different countries could communicate freely and share experiences with each other. In those days Russian newspapers and television scared the man in the street with the possibility of the Talibs appearing in Kazan or holding a parade in Red Square. Becoming increasingly evident were contacts between Central Asian Islamists and Chechen combatants. There were Uzbeks among those taken prisoner in Chechnya, while "natives of the Caucasus" were sighted in the Ferghana Valley.

The emergence of a Taliban state was of enormous symbolic importance: since some had managed to establish a truly Islamic rule in the neighborhood, why not to try to do the same in the Ferghana Valley, for example.

Most of the inhabitants of the Ferghana Valley would have found the rule of the Talibs, who threw TV sets out of windows and closed down public bathhouses, absolutely unacceptable. The popular myth about the just nature of the Talib regime had become widespread as people who visited Afghanistan unanimously reported that the scope of corruption in that country had significantly diminished, unlike the situation in Central Asia.

From 1996 in Uzbekistan the Islamic movement, which had become strong and influential, began to raid the Ferghana Valley regularly, fighting against the Uzbek troops there. The Kyrgyz town of Batken became a kind of symbol of struggle against Islamic combatants when IMU militants made attempts to go into Uzbekistan through Kyrgyzstan. An attempt on the life of

Uzbekistan's President Islam Karimov took place in 1999. Even if the blasts in Tashkent had nothing to do with the Islamic opposition, they coincided with an upsurge in the activity of the Islamists. The Kazakh Alash Party, whose leader, Aron Atabek, returned from emigration and decided to use the original niche of Kazakh Islamic fundamentalism, resumed its activities. There was a reorientation of political Islam in Tajikistan, where the core of the local Islamic Rebirth Party assumed a moderate stand, declaring that the establishment of an Islamic state was something for the very distant future.

The so-called Party of Islamic Liberation (Hizb-ut-Tahrir al-Islamiy, or HT), widely discussed today by analysts, became a prominent political organization. Hizbutchiks (as they call themselves) stand apart from Islamic militants. Having declared their adherence to nonviolent action, they launched a propaganda campaign, distributing leaflets and reaching out to the population in every way. There is no reliable data on the size of the HT membership.[5]

In Uzbekistan the authorities baited the HT. In Kyrgyzstan, the Hizbutchiks were treated less harshly. If arrested they were soon released, and if brought to court, they got off with mild sentences. Whereas in Uzbekistan they work in underground conditions, in Kyrgyzstan they conduct their struggle almost openly. When I visited Bishkek in the autumn of 2002, I was offered the addresses of the local HT leaders to meet and talk with them.

On-and-off efforts to create a caliphate and achieve Islamic-type justice continued until September 11, 2001. That day marked the beginning of stage four in the history of the Islamic movement in Central Asia (and throughout the world). This stage may be described as a lull in what had been until then a religious-political storm. The fall of the Taliban regime and the vigorous attacks against al-Qaeda put local radicals in a difficult position. Their financial revenues had dropped, and they no longer had a reliable Afghan rear. Finally, they sustained losses in their ranks when hundreds of Uzbeks fought staunchly on the side of the Talibs.

An Islamic threat to the ruling regimes in Central Asia has been nonexistent since September 11, 2001. The Islamists are not prepared to take risks now. Despite the lull, the ground for radical protest actions remains, as has the possibility of old Islamic organizations continuing and new ones entering the stage.

In the north Caucasus, however, the post-September lull has long been over. In a sense, the active character of the Chechen resistance and the spreading of the Chechen conflict to neighboring regions (e.g., Ingushetia) in the autumn of 2002 has shown that this resistance is, to a certain extent, independent of al-Qaeda and other international Islamic organizations. In the Middle East, there has been no lull at all. The war there has been going on as before in spite of the strikes delivered against international terrorism.

ISLAMIC ALTERNATIVE

People who see social change in the light of Islam continue to insist on their alternative, albeit a utopian one. The significance of an Islamic alternative for Central Asia must not be exaggerated or underestimated. Although its leaders are not capable of destabilizing society in that region on their own, their chances of becoming involved in any crisis situation are high.

Crisis events, whether in democratic Kyrgyzstan or in authoritarian Uzbekistan, can occur wherever the ruling regime fails to raise the people's standard of living appreciably.

Islamists may well cooperate with political organizations far removed from the idea of pure Islam. Indicative in this respect is the situation in regard to the political elite in Kyrgyzstan. In 2002 President Askar Akayev's position was noticeably weakened, and people began to express displeasure with his presidency. Some clashes occurred in the country (e.g., the "Aksy events") during which people were killed and some opposition politicians were arrested.[6] In the middle of October 2002, the opposition in Bishkek tried to hold its own session of Kurultai (Grand Assembly), which in the opinion of its organizers (from communists to radical democrats) would reveal the failure of President Askar Akayev's domestic policy.

The secular opposition in Kyrgyzstan did not list Islamic radicals among their allies. They are certain, however, that the Islamists will use the growing tensions to affirm their influence. In such a case, the ruling establishment may try to exploit political Islam for curtailing the democratic rights and fanning interethnic discord (between the Kyrgyz and Uzbek). At the same time, the ruling quarters do not exclude the possibility of the Islamists cooperating with the secular opposition.

Tentative comparisons could be made between the situation in Kyrgyzstan and Kazakhstan. Such comparisons are possible because the ruling establishment in Kazakhstan, despite the widespread view that it has achieved an "economic miracle," has failed to achieve a real breakthrough in the economic situation. Many impartial experts have expressed doubt as to the effectiveness of the economic policy pursued, let alone success in building a civil society there. Symbolically, American analyst Martha Brill Olcott, an expert on the history of Kazakhstan and its present-day situation, has written a book entitled *Kazakhstan: Unfulfilled Promise*.[7]

Both in Kyrgyzstan and Kazakhstan there is an active secular opposition. For a number of reasons, including the possibility of realizing dissenting ideas and circumventing religion, it is doubtful that Islam will become an essential factor in the inner political life of Kazakhstan. However, its role as a participant in the political process, as a secret partner in some factions, cannot be ruled out completely.

ETHNIC FACTOR

Interethnic relations have always influenced, and will continue to influence, the situation in that republic and are far from ideal. Islamic adepts are most numerous among the Uzbeks and Uyghurs, among whom Islamic and separatist organizations are the most popular. Meanwhile, in the opinion of Kazakh analysts, it is these organizations that threaten stability in the republic.

The HT party and the Islamic Movement of Uzbekistan have a certain influence among the people living in the southern part of Kazakhstan. Both Tashkent and Almaty have repeatedly declared their readiness to cooperate (and they are in fact cooperating) in persecuting Islamists. At the same time, certain sections of Kazakhstan's elite are concerned that in some cases the Uzbek leadership is capable of using the Uzbek Islamists as a means of exerting pressure on its neighbor.

As for Uyghur Islamism, it is of secondary importance, being subordinate to the separatist movement in the Xinjiang Uyghur Autonomous Region of China. The main goal of the National Front for the Liberation of Eastern Turkestan and of the Organization for the Liberation of Uyghurstan is the establishment of an independent Uyghur state. Uyghur separatism is akin to Chechen separatism in that both movements aim to form a national, not an Islamic, state. At the same time, both separatist movements feature an Islamic element, which helps them obtain outside assistance and turn ethnic separatism into a component of the world Islamic movement.

The struggle against the Uyghur Islamic separatists forms the strategic basis of military and political cooperation between Kazakhstan and China. Both states realize the danger of outside interference and both are interested in maintaining internal stability. In the foreseeable future, neither Beijing nor Almaty is likely to use separatism or Islamism as a means of exerting pressure on each other.

ISLAM AND POLITICAL OPPOSITION

In Uzbekistan, certain forces within the ruling establishment, rather than some hypothetical but nonexistent official opposition, could become a potential ally of the Islamic movement. It is not possible, if only for ethical reasons, to name any particular factions or concrete persons. However, it is believed in Tashkent, and even more so in the provinces, that, in a certain situation, the opponents of Islam Karimov are capable of forming an alliance with the Islamic opposition.

The authorities suspected a number of groups of organizing the attempt on Islam Karimov's life in February 1999, including some that are close to the Uzbek president. Karimov himself does not exclude the possibility of such an alliance. If another reform campaign should fail, it will surely result in people's utter disillusionment with the ability of the local ruling elites to extricate the society from a permanent crisis. "The spirit of an Islamic alternative" will then dominate the feeling of general hopelessness and may provoke a conflict—with unpredictable consequences.

Curiously, like the Chechen separatists, some Islamists in Central Asia, including those who belong to the Islamic Movement of Uzbekistan, compare themselves to wolves. There is truth in that simile. Both Chechen and Uzbek extremists, who capitalize on the social ills of the political establishment—incompetence, corruption, and so on—resemble the "sanitation workers of the forest," the wolves.

The tragically paradoxical character of the situation in Central Asia does not guarantee the failure of a new reform campaign. There may be a social explosion even if the campaign is successful. In fact, the reform must be conducted, more or less, in the manner of shock therapy; otherwise economic stagnation will be perpetuated. Suffice it to say that the introduction (necessary and unavoidable) of a "normal" dollar exchange rate of the local som in Uzbekistan may negatively affect the people's standard of living, which is already low. And this may provoke mass protest actions.

On the macro level, a successful reform campaign may result in a total polarization of society, the crash of the traditional economic sector, and soaring unemployment. The consequences of such reforms are well-known from the experience of other Muslim countries. Modernization usually entails a traditionalist reaction, which in its extreme forms has led to an Islamic revolution in Iran and an unending civil war in Algeria.

The process of "archaization" in Central Asia started right after the disintegration of the Soviet Union and is now developing—not as an opposite of modernization and reform but for the sake of the basic survival of the greater part of society. In other words, the role of tradition as a regulator of social relations is bound to increase, the traditional economic sector will keep reproducing itself, and all that taken together will be a prerequisite for the politicization of Islam and the activity of religious radicals.

Such a course of events will not necessarily culminate in an Islamic revolution followed by the establishment of a caliphate. The power structure still has levers for relieving the situation, from direct pressure to compromise. Besides, not all of society is prepared to rely on the Islamic model as a panacea for present and future misfortunes. In the first place, the administrative resource is not limitless and in the second, it is the radical Muslims who play the prime mover in the course of social upheavals, while the moderate Muslims, skeptical in regard to a caliphate, often yield the initiative to the Islamists and become their victims too. One day the Central Asian ruling elites will have to recognize the legitimacy of political Islam and determine its role and place in the political system. In any case, as mentioned above, the overall situation in Central Asia (with the possible exception of Kazakhstan) is conducive to the spread of religious radicalism; some adherents are still in favor of employing terrorist methods to attain their ends.

ISLAM AND TERRORISM

The events of September 11, 2001, showed that Muslims generally censure acts of terrorism that entail loss of human life. At the same time, some of them try to justify the terrorists, regarding their acts as a reaction to the negative aspects of social life, tension between states and confessions, and so on. As a result, terrorist activity has acquired broad support—overt and covert. As Maxime Rodinson, a French expert on Islam, has justly observed, "Terrorists move about in populous places like fish in the water, and some people around them understand their aims, while others, who disapprove of their methods, are incapable of disavowing their movement and, in the long run, are compelled to support it."[8]

In Central Asia it is not easy to distinguish between religious-political radicalism and terrorism. Despite the efforts of many, the notion of terror has not been given a precise, scholarly definition.[9] Terrorist methods of struggle have always been characteristic of the proponents of most diverse ideological and political views—not only of Islamists but also of communists. In the future, terror is unlikely to remain the "privilege" of Muslim radicals only.

The imprecise definition of terror makes it possible to describe as "Islamic terrorists" any opposition force that appeals to Islam. That is what the Russian and Central Asian presidents as well as the leaders of China and India do. The current global antiterrorist campaign has not led to a consensus definition of terrorism between Russia and many Western states, which still refuse to identify international extremism as the main cause of the Chechen conflict. The correlation between the real and virtual threat of Islamic terrorism is still not clear. After September 11, when military actions by Islamists in Central Asia practically ceased and their political activity limited to cautious propaganda, the struggle against Islamic terrorism has become one of the main instruments of conducting domestic policy by Central Asian regimes and at the same time attracting the attention of foreign powers, above all the United States.

During 2002, terrorists were active in Europe and Southeast Asia. But in Central Asia there has not been a single act of terrorism. Today there is hardly a single organization in Central Asia capable of carrying out a large-scale terrorist act. Even the most prominent of them, Hizb-ut-Tahrir, which after the start of the military operation in Afghanistan began calling for self-sacrifice among those following the road of jihad, is incapable of this.

During what might be called an Islamic pause in Central Asia, the local propaganda became quite inventive. In the autumn of 2002 some Central Asian periodicals reported on the activity of an extremist organization called the Islamic Movement of Central Asia. However, based on available information, the organization is fictitious.

According to some sources, the reference to a fictitious organization was intended to remind people about the existence of the Islamic Movement of Uzbekistan, which despite keeping a low profile was still popular. In the opinion of some local analysts, the IMU, though deprived of external financial sources, can still count on internal financial support from various segments of the population, including the underprivileged ones. So the local ruling elites have good reason to be worried—even if their show of anxiety is intended primarily for the public abroad.

CONCLUSION

It looks like Central Asia is living in anticipation of the fifth stage of Islamic political activity. But nobody knows when and how this new stage will come about. Everybody agrees, however, that it will arrive. Terrorism can be eliminated from political life only through sustained effort. Everybody also agrees that terrorism can be eradicated mainly through the solution of socioeconomic problems, which will diminish or even destroy its breeding ground. Nobody questions the need for destroying such international terrorist structures as al-Qaeda. The problems lie elsewhere. First, in what way and how soon can the vital problems of traditional societies, including those of Central Asia, be solved? Second, is it correct to equate terrorists with separatists and with opposition movements in general? Third, what are the proportions of people from the underprivileged and marginal sections of the population and from the middle classes, including technocrats, among the terrorists? Fourth, is terrorism merely a chain of actions (even if planned actions) that have a more or less definite source (Palestinian, Chechen, or Uzbek), or does it represent a new global phenomenon? And fifth, is it correct to consider the activity of Muslim terrorists in the context of the civilizational conflict?

Alexei Bogaturov, a Russian political analyst, believes that "terrorism cannot be destroyed as a world transnational network" in general. In his opinion, terrorism is a consequence of the cardinal geopolitical changes that have occurred lately, "an ill-begotten, illegitimate child of globalization."[10] Since this chapter is not intended to critique that premise, I will leave it without comment. However, analysis of the situation in Central Asia shows how the "transnational network" adapts to the regional situation while the local Islamic forces adapt themselves to it.

By summarily rejecting the Islamic opposition, by closing down hundreds of mosques and persecuting anyone who utters the word "caliphate," the Central Asian regimes not only restrict freedom of political maneuver for themselves but also push the opposition into the fold of the above-mentioned transnational network.[11]

Achieving better security in Central Asia presupposes ridding that region of terrorism. For a number of reasons, this cannot be done only by the regional ruling elites relying on the local resources. Terrorism can only be eliminated through concerted, well-coordinated efforts on a global scale. This was declared back in the mid-1990s and began to be effected after September 11, 2001.

Getting rid of terrorism presupposes not only systematic military and police actions and the stepped-up efforts of the special services, but also continuous efforts to eradicate the basic causes of terrorism and change the mentality of the part of society that views extremism with a degree of sympathy. Hence the need for preventive measures, including contacts with certain radical politicians—not excluding those who support the Islamic alternative. Elimination of terrorism is by no means the same thing as eradication of Islamic opposition ideas. Security and stability in the Muslim world can only be achieved on the basis of a consensus among the broad spectrum of political forces.

NOTES

1. Documents and Records of the 26th CPSU Congress, Moscow, 1981, 13.

2. The political process in Tajikistan is not limited to a standoff between the Islamists and the secular forces.

3. Bakhtyar Babadjanov, a noted Uzbek scholar, considers Muhammadjan Hindustani, the well-known religious authority who was active in the 1970s, to be the spiritual father of the Islamic renaissance in Central Asia. See Bakhtyar Babadjanov and Muzaffar Kamilov, "Muhammadjan Hindustani (1892–1989) and the Beginning of the 'Great Schism' among Muslims of Uzbekistan," in Stephane A. Dudoignon and

Kamatsu Hisao, eds., *Islam in Politics in Russia and Central Asia (Early Eighteenth to Twentieth Centuries)* (Tokyo: University of Tokyo, 2001), 195–219.

4. Officially organized citizen volunteer groups that helped maintain public order.

5. The absence of precise data on the size of the HT membership is exemplified by the fact that according to the well-informed experts at Radio Liberty it ranges from a few thousand to a hundred thousand, www.religioscope.com/articles/2002/002_hizb_b.htm.

6. Formally, what touched off the "Aksy events" was an agreement on the demarcation of the Kirghiz-Chinese border that favored China and was criticized by MP Beknazarov. However, some local politicians believe that the real reason for the unrest was the people's dissatisfaction with their living standard. Furthermore, in March 2002 the authorities stopped Nurlan Sydykov, a popular politician they did not like, from running for Zhogorku Kenesh (Kirghiz parliament). This led to a confrontation between the authorities and the people of the Osh region, who had shown signs of insubordination before.

7. Martha Brill Olcott, *Kazakhstan: Unfulfilled Promise* (Washington, D.C.: Carnegie Endowment for International Peace, 2002).

8. Maxime Rodinson, *L'Islam politique et croyance* (Paris: Fayard, 1993), 299–300.

9. There are several typological paradigms of terror. Thus it may be international, political, military, nationalist, religious, ideological, and psychological.

10. Alexei Bogaturov, "A Three-Headed Monster," *Nezavisimaya Gazeta*, December 25, 2002, 2.

11. Incidentally, some members of the Islamic Movement of Uzbekistan use different terms: the Great Kokand Khanate and Great Khoresm. A few years ago I was shown a map of the Great Khoresm.

II

ENERGY SECURITY

8

Central Asia's Energy Resources: Japan's Energy Interests

Manabu Shimizu

Japan's energy situation is distinguishable from that of other developed countries by high dependence on oil as its primary energy source. In FY2001, the rate of dependence on oil as primary energy was 49.4 percent, having declined from 77 percent in 1970 to the present level.[1] Although natural gas and atomic energy accounted for 13 percent each of total supply of primary energy in FY2001, the importance of oil is undeniable. Another characteristic of Japan's energy situation is that Japan has to import as much as 100 percent of its oil from abroad, since it is not endowed with oil resources. This fact reveals Japan's vulnerability to oil suppliers abroad; energy policy is one of the most serious issues facing Japan.

Natural gas supplies about 13 percent of Japan's energy needs, similar to the share of nuclear energy. As the world's largest importer of natural gas, Japan acquires as much as 97 percent of its total natural gas demand in the form of liquefied natural gas (LNG). In contrast to oil producers, countries that supply natural gas are more geographically diversified. Japan's dependence on the Middle East is limited to about 22 percent. In 2001, out of the total import of 4.25 billion LNG ton equivalent, Indonesia occupies the leading share with 30.2 percent, followed by Malaysia (20.8 percent), Australia (13.8 percent), Qatar (11.7 percent), Brunei (11.0 percent), Abu Dhabi (8.9 percent), Alaska (2.3 percent), and Oman (1.2 percent). The Asia Pacific region imports 78 percent of its natural gas.

However, since the first oil crisis in 1973 and the second oil crisis at the Iranian revolution, Japan concentrated its effort to reduce energy consumption and has developed energy-saving technology that is competitive in the world market. At present, suppose the primary energy consumption per real

GDP is at 1 in case of Japan, then the United States is 2.74, while Germany is 1.41.

JAPAN'S OVERDEPENDENCE ON GULF OIL

Japan suffers from an overdependence on the Middle East, which is geographically distant. It takes at least two weeks for an oil tanker to cover the distance from the Persian Gulf to Japan, which induces potential security issues on the way. A concerted effort by the government and the private sector to diversify its sources of oil for the past three decades achieved some success as in the middle of 1980s the rate of dependence on the Gulf came down to 67 percent. However, the reversal began again and in 2002 Japan again depended on the Gulf for 87 percent of its oil imports. In 2004, Saudi Arabia became the biggest supplier of oil to Japan with 26.2 percent of the total imports, followed by the UAE with 25.0 percent. The anxiety Japan has now is expected to continue with its dependency on the Gulf in the near future unless Japan takes drastic measures to reverse the trend.

Since the first oil crisis in 1973, Japan has tried to explore oil abroad by investing capital and increasing the percentage of oil imports produced by Japanese companies. Japan set the target of oil imports by Japanese companies at 30 percent of total imports. Japan tried to support efforts by oil exploration companies in the private sector through huge investment and credits by the semigovernmental institution JNOC (Japan National Oil Cooperation). The idea was to develop these Japanese companies into Japan's oil majors such as ENI in Italy or Total in France. However, Japan's target to raise the ratio of import from Japan's oil companies to 40 percent of the total import was not realized, as the highest level was only 12 percent. While French TotalFinaElf is ranked as the fourth major oil company in the world after Exxon Mobil, Royal Dutch Shell, and BP, Japan lagged far behind in spite of the total expenditure of approximately US$40 billion through the JNOC. The JNOC was an institution mostly financed and supported by the Japanese government.

FAILED EXTENSION OF EXPLOITATION CONCESSIONS

The major reason behind the failure to develop Japan's oil companies is government funding distributed to more than 200 oil-exploring companies, most of which failed to find oil or gas reserves. The criteria for giving credit to those companies were not strict enough, and the companies were not required to pay back the credit they got to the JNOC when they failed to find reserves large enough to be exploited commercially.

In Japan, government control over the petroleum industry as a whole, including refining, was strong. Refineries were regulated through the petroleum law. In the early 1990s, however, the regulation over major aspects of refinery was discontinued. As a result, government guidelines on developing its oil majors were not strong enough to meet the target, and the JNOC was forced to reorganize in 2004. Japan should draw lessons from its experience. Most probably it played a leading role when it should have deregulated, in the case of refineries. Japan should have established its oil strategy on a firmer base. We have observed fluctuation of fundamental strategy in the formation of policy.

In February 2000, the Arabian Oil Company of Japan (AOC) failed to renew its concession agreement with Saudi Arabia on the oil exploitation project, which is situated in the neutral zone straddling Kuwait and Saudi Arabia. The AOC was the first success story in Japan's effort to explore for oil abroad. Therefore the failure to extend the concession agreement raised arguments about energy security in Japan. The story behind the failure has not been disclosed fully. However, it is certain that there was a misunderstanding between Japan and Saudi Arabia concerning Japan's commitment to establish the railway to the seashore. At the same time, the failure reflected to some extent the fluctuations in Japan's oil policies, as indicated below. The AOC agreed to downgrade its operations in Kuwait from a concession-type arrangement that expired on January 4, 2003, to a technical services agreement considered less attractive by the industry.[2] It was the only foreign oil concession in Kuwait, agreed on in 1958 and sustained after the 1962 constitution, which outlawed concessions and production-sharing agreements. It also survived the nationalization of Kuwait Petroleum Company in the 1970s. Foreign ownership of oil reserves has been highly controversial in Kuwait. Under the new five-year agreement, AOC provides technical services and helps arrange $750 million in soft loans in exchange for guaranteed oil sales to AOC for twenty years of up to 170,000 barrels per day. Concessions and production-sharing agreements are considered attractive by oil companies because they allow them to control prices and "book" reserves on their balance sheets. Arabian Oil and Fuji Oil, a midsize oil refiner, established AOC Holdings as a joint-holding company.

Nonetheless there are some success stories in the effort to explore new oil fields such as the Abu Dhabi Oil Co., a subsidiary of Cosmo Oil Company, or Japan Petroleum Ltd., or Indonesian Oil by INPEX, (founded in 1966 and renamed in 2001 the INPEX Cooperation Ltd.). In spite of those efforts, the results of Japan's efforts to explore for oil abroad did not meet expectations.

IS OIL A STRATEGIC COMMODITY OR
AN ORDINARY COMMODITY?

It is important for Japan to draw lessons from earlier policies on energy security. Japan failed to develop a comprehensive strategy to promote its energy security. However, Japan tried to shift to natural gas and nuclear energy while developing new energy such as fuel cells. Japan's policy on nuclear power, such as pluthermal utilization or nuclear fusion, faces some problems because of technical accidents and anti–nuclear power movements during the past decade. Japan's rate of dependence on nuclear power as a primary energy source in 2000 was around 13 percent. According to some estimations, by 2010, Japan's energy demand will increase by 17 percent over 1990 levels. To realize the Kyoto Protocol's environmental targets, Japan will have to build thirteen new nuclear power units in addition to existing nuclear power plants. Even given this, Japan cannot evade its dependence on oil in the near future. Japan should maintain contacts with the leaders in the oil- and gas-exporting countries, combined with economic or technical assistance and dynamic intelligence activities, in order to have a wider and longer perspective on the oil market. Japan can boast of superior technology in the field of downstream and also energy-saving technologies that could be the best in the world. The technological level in the downstream is a big asset for energy diplomacy for Japan.

Japan's understanding of energy security helps generate its policies on energy. Japan has not had a clear, consistent idea about energy security in regard to oil. Since the middle of the 1980s there has been confusion concerning oil commodities. Japan has accepted to some extent the theory that oil has changed from a strategic commodity to an ordinary commodity in the world market. In other words, if any country is ready to pay market prices for oil, it is not difficult to get the necessary amount of oil even in the absence of strategic relations with the oil-exporting countries. There is some truth in the theory if one takes into account OPEC's weakened control on the market and newly emerged futures trading in oil in New York and London. The oil market is now connected all over the world as a common market.

On the surface, this theory seems to be relevant in the new international economic framework. However, there is no denying the fact that procurement of oil is related to wider international political relations. Another period of politicization of oil could occur due to a realignment of international relations after September 11. Any part of the world, particularly the Middle East, could have a negative impact on the supply and price of oil all over the world. One of the most conspicuous developments is a possible change in relations between the United States and Saudi Arabia as well as U.S. involvement in Iraq.

Relations between exporters and importers of natural gas are more mutually dependent, and strategic consideration is required to lay pipelines for natural gas as well as oil.

Another factor to be taken into account is an emergence of new economic centers such as Brazil, and Russia, India, and China, the so-called BRIC countries. China and India have begun to suffer from constraints on the supply of oil and natural gas. Both countries expect a deficit of energy resources required for sustainable economic development in the near future. These new developments have shaken the former strategy, which depended on the conception of oil as an ordinary commodity.

JAPAN'S NEW EURASIAN INITIATIVE

Japan's stance toward the Central Asian republics was positive after the Soviet Union dissolved. Japan took the lead in persuading other members of the Organization for Economic Cooperation and Development (OECD) to include the Central Asian republics as recipient countries of official development assistance (ODA). As of 2000, Japan is the biggest ODA donor to Kazakhstan, Uzbekistan, and Kyrgyzstan.

Japan's first proclaimed government initiative was the so-called New Eurasian Initiative. In July 1997, the prime minister of Japan, Mr. Ryutaro Hashimoto, proposed a "new Silk Road policy or new Eurasian policy," which emphasized Japan's role in developing Central Asia as well as the Caucasus in the former Soviet Union. It was explicitly and implicitly accepted in the proposal that Central Asia and the Caucasus were strategically important to Japan. However, the policy was not fully concretized and allowed for a wider understanding and explication. On the one hand, the historic dream of the Silk Road appeals psychologically to the Japanese people in general and the older generation in particular as one of the important sources of Japanese culture. On the other hand, stability in Central Asia and the Caucasus was taken as one of the prerequisites for wider Asian stability, including China and South Asia. In this context Central Asia was given priority in Japanese foreign policy. The coordination of Japan's new Eurasian policy with Japan's policy toward Russia remained to be elucidated afterward. Hashimoto's initiative tried to rationalize Japan's policy toward Central Asia and broadened Japan's perspective of foreign policy by including the Caucasus countries in the framework of this new Eurasian policy.

Japan's initiative did not neglect oil and gas energy resources but did not assign them any special priority either. Central Asia has acquired importance in Japanese foreign policy as a significant additional source of energy, particularly oil and gas. However, Japan's dilemma was that promising oil or gas fields in the Caspian Sea area, on land as well as offshore, were already under the control of Western oil majors, and there was limited room for Japanese participation. Japanese businesses sent their missions mainly to oil-rich countries in Central Asia and the Caucasus, such as Kazakhstan, Uzbekistan, Turkmenistan, and Azerbaijan. However, Japan's government did not ignore other countries in the area, including Kyrgyzstan, Tajikistan, Georgia, and Armenia. The government's understanding is that Central Asia and the Caucasus should be taken as one region in the sense that any instability would inevitably spill over to the neighboring countries and destabilize those countries with rich natural resources also. For example, in 1999, four Japanese were taken hostage by the IMU (Islamic Movement of Uzbekistan) in Kyrgyzstan and were ultimately released with the help of the Tajik government. Japan's policy framework was that it should not neglect those countries and should take into account social and political as well as humanitarian considerations. Japan's resources to realize targets of foreign policies are limited to the ODA, governmental economic and technical assistance.

ASIAN DEPENDENCE ON MIDDLE EAST OIL

Japan's interest in Central Asia and the Caucasus should not be understood only in the bilateral framework of interest between the region and Japan. Japan is obliged to take into account Asian oil- and gas-consuming countries as a whole when it plans energy strategy. In this regard new developments in the economic situation in Asia for the past three decades should be considered. In 1973 Japan imported oil at the rate of 4.9 million barrels per day, while South Korea imported 0.28 million barrels per day, Taiwan imported 0.18 million barrels per day, and China imported none. At the time, Japan was the only country in the area importing a huge amount of oil.

However, by 2000 the oil situation in Asia had changed drastically. Each day on average Japan imported 4.3 million barrels, while South Korea imported 2.8 million barrels. Taiwan each day imported 0.8 million barrels while China imported 1.4–1.5 million barrels. Except for Japan, the economies in the area increased their imports of oil tremendously. South Korea, Taiwan, and China combined surpassed the volume of oil imported by Japan. On average each country imported about 77–78 percent of its oil demand from abroad.[3] Major suppliers of oil to those Asian countries are situated in the Middle East. Asian economies now compete among themselves to get oil from the Middle East. India also came to the fore as a big oil importer since its rapid economic growth in the 1990s.

Among the Asian countries, Japan is conspicuous in its degree of dependence on Middle East oil, although Asian economies in general increased their overall dependence on the Middle East. Japan developed its petroleum refining capacity, despite severe environmental regulations, to cope with oil with heavy sulfur imported from the Middle East. China and other economies are not prepared to refine this heavy sulfur oil and thus prefer light oil from western Africa and Indonesia.

Among the Asian economies, China became a net importer of oil in 1993 and has increased its annual oil imports due to rapid economic growth. China has been very eager to participate in the "upper stream" in the oil industry wherever possible, particularly in Iran, Iraq, Saudi Arabia, and Sudan. China's behavior appears to be motivated by traditional strategic concepts of encircling its own oil fields. At the same time China pursued a strategy to develop its state oil majors by restructuring PetroChina and Sinopec.

JAPAN AND THE SURROUNDING ASIAN COUNTRIES

Japan's policy in energy security has to take into account neighboring Asian economies, namely, South Korea, Mainland China, Taiwan, and India, as their increasing dependence on imported oil poses a serious challenge to the region in the future. Those economies mainly look to the Middle East for oil, as it has the biggest potential future energy resources. Therefore, energy security in the region faces two challenges. The first involves coping with emergencies such as interrupted oil imports or an abnormal rise in oil prices caused by wars or other unexpected political developments, such as in Iraq. The other challenge is to establish a long-term, sustainable oil supply. Both challenges require international cooperation among the countries concerned, although competition is expected to increase.

The first challenge could be dealt with through international cooperation in regard to national oil stockpiles. However, only Japan currently achieves its national stockpile target, although South Korea has a similar system. Japanese stockpiling of oil is implemented in the private sector as well as in the public sector. In Japan, the private sector is obliged by law to stock more than seventy days' consumption. State stockpiling of oil began in 1978 to supplement private sector stockpiles. The total state oil stockpile was gradually raised to 50 million kiloliters in 1998 and remains at that level. In January 2003, the Japanese government decided to release state oil stockpiles in case of oil deficit, which occurred in the 1991 Gulf crisis, when the private sector was reluctant to release its oil stockpiles as demanded by the government and failed to supply enough oil because the release was not obligatory.

The International Energy Agency (IEA) decided on the release of 2.5 million barrels per day by all member states at that time. The private sector sometimes engages in speculation in future trade, to the detriment of consumers.

China is also considering oil stockpiling against emergencies. However, the cost is great, and the three state oil companies face cost constraints. Alleviating stiff competition for crude oil among the major Asian consuming countries should be an imperative target for Japan's energy strategy. China has increased its imports every year since it became a net oil importer in 1993. China's oil consumption is expected to equal Japan's in ten years. Additionally, South Korea depends totally on imports for oil, and India increased its oil imports from the Gulf as its rate of economic growth grew in the 1990s. India's domestic supply of oil can only supply 30 percent of its demand.

JAPAN'S ENERGY STRATEGY IN CENTRAL ASIA AND THE CAUCASUS

Japan's policy toward Central Asia is influenced by energy issues in Japan and Asia as a whole. At present, the quandary is how to coordinate the Asian countries' interests in the energy and how to develop mutual cooperation in energy supply in the future. While we observe multiple clashes of interests among the Asian oil consuming economies, there are also conflicts between oil exporting countries and oil importing countries concerning oil and natural gas prices.

In July 2002, Japan sent an energy mission to Central Asia. The membership was composed of government officials, representatives of the private sector, and academic figures. The main purpose of the mission to Central Asia and the Caucasus (Kazakhstan, Uzbekistan, Turkmenistan, and Azerbaijan) was to promote cooperation between Japan and the host countries, not only in energy but also in other fields.

Japan is sometimes mistakenly thought to be interested in securing oil and gas from Central Asia. However, Japan does not expect to import oil and gas directly from the Caspian region in the near future because the geographical distance is so great and there are no viable and economical methods of transportation. Japan expects that Caspian oil will contribute, even if indirectly, to easing the oil crunch in the market by injecting a new supply of oil and gas. Except for anticipated profits by Japanese companies that invest in a variety of oil and gas exploiting projects, any direct connection through supply and demand is not expected. Japan tries to locate Central Asia within the framework of supply and demand of oil in the world market and thus to get positive results indirectly from Asia and the Caucasus.

THE RUSSIAN FACTOR IN JAPAN'S ENERGY SUPPLY

Russian oil and gas might be a more viable alternative source for Japanese energy needs. Japan, in cooperation with the majors and other international partners, invests in Sakhalin projects, which are expected to supply oil and gas to Japan. India's ONGC (Oil and Natural Gas Commission) also participates in Sakhalin, illustrating India's keen strategic interest in obtaining oil and gas. There are six projects in Sakhalin. Unfortunately, Japanese consumers or companies have been reluctant to purchase oil and gas from Sakhalin, diminishing any prospect of laying a natural gas pipeline to Japan. Its hesitation was related to the absence of a peace agreement between the two states. However, new indicators suggest that Sakhalin reserves could be even greater than those in Kazakhstan.

The triangular geopolitics among Russia, China, and Japan must be taken into account when we consider Russian oil and gas exports. An oil pipeline from the Thumeni oil fields in western Siberia to Nakhodka along the coast overlooking the Japan Sea was proposed by the Soviet Union to Japan in 1972. Japan tried to respond to the proposal positively after the shock of the 1973 oil crisis, but did not follow up on the proposal because of strong Chinese objections. Twenty years later, in October 2002, Noriko Kawaguchi, foreign minister of Japan, talked about the possibility of energy development cooperation in eastern Siberia. However, it was the gas project in Sakhalin that was emphasized in this instance.

In 2003 Japan emphasized anew its interest in a pipeline project from Angarsk in eastern Siberia. Transnefti, the Russian state pipeline monopoly, proposed the Angarsk pipeline, with a total length of a little less than 3,900 kilometers, with expected construction costs of US$5.2 billion and with the capacity of transporting a million barrels per day. China proposed laying another pipeline from eastern Siberia to Daqing. The Daqing pipeline was supported by the Russian oil company, Yukos, with a length of 2,200 kilometers, an expected construction cost of US$2.5 billion, and a capacity of transporting 600,000 barrels per day. A problem was that the potential production was not enough to supply both proposed pipelines at the same time. The Nakhodka pipeline requires more investment per barrel of oil to be transported with an unspecified supplier and unspecified final consumers, which would most probably include Japan. The Daqing pipeline has the specified consumer in China on a long-term basis but might give China a strategic lever on Russia as the sole consumer of oil through the pipeline. The pipeline issue has become a triangular struggle over Siberian oil by Russia, China, and Japan.

Japan's Prime Minister Junichiro Koizumi paid an official visit to Russia in January 2003. One of the important issues he discussed with President

Vladimir Putin was cooperation in the field of energy development. They discussed the development of oil and gas in eastern Siberia and the Russian far east, including supply routes of oil through pipelines. Taking into account the new relations between Russia and the United States, including their cooperation in the field of oil and natural gas, Japan envisions positive potential cooperation with Russia regarding Siberian energy development.

Since then, Russia's stance on the pipelines has changed time and again. In May 2005 Mr. Shoichi Nakagawa, minister of economy, international trade, and industry, told the *Financial Times* that Russia would build pipelines in two stages and indicated that the first stage would connect Skovorodino in eastern Siberia with China, although the second stage would join Skovorodino with the Pacific.[4] Japan had to recede to the second position in the struggle with China for oil in eastern Siberia.

JAPAN'S NEW ENERGY POLICY ORIENTATION

Japan's Basic Law on Energy Policy Making, enacted in June 2002, specifies the three principles of supply and demand of energy: a steady and assured supply of energy, an adaptation to environmental requirements, and an active use of market mechanisms. It is noteworthy that market mechanism is now ranked as a priority.

The JNOC was dissolved in March 2005. It was a public sector organization designed to function on two fronts. The first function was to promote exploration of oil and gas through subsidized credit and investment in oil exploration companies, mainly in the private sector. The second function was to stockpile petroleum against expected emergencies. However, the issue of bad performing credit by the JNOC to oil exploring companies has been discussed for a couple of years, and the cost-benefit principle of the JNOC was put in doubt. It was decided finally to reorganize it. Oil stockpiling was assumed by the state. However, exploring new oil fields remains important for Japan. The former JNOC invested in the Kashgan oil and gas fields in the Caspian Sea, the Asadegan oil field in Iran, and the Sakhalin projects. The new organization is expected to be more cost oriented when it extends credit to exploration companies.

CASPIAN OIL EXPLORATION AND PIPELINE PROJECTS

Japan is a latecomer and minor partner in the exploration of the Caspian region. Japan's interest in the Caspian oil project is represented by two Japanese companies—ITOCHU Oil Exploration in Azerbaijan and INPEX (International Petroleum Exploration Co. Ltd.) in the ACG, Kashgan and BTC pipeline projects. Although their participation percentages are small compared with the Western oil majors, they represent Japan's desire to be a partner in the development of the oil industry in the Caspian region. The Caspian Sea region could be a major source of "upstream" in the supply of oil and gas to the world market and indirectly beneficial to the Japanese oil market. For the moment, most of the existing or expected market for oil in the Caspian region is in Europe, as it is not profitable to transport Caspian oil to the Asia Pacific. However, this new North Sea supply could ease market conditions. At the same time, Japanese companies in these projects can learn oil exploration techniques from their Western partners. The majors made huge strides in oil exploration technology in the 1990s through the use of information technology, thus reducing the cost of exploration drastically. Additionally, these ventures reflect Japanese efforts to diversify oil resources outside the Middle East. Although Japan will not be a direct market for oil and gas in the region and shows a comparatively low profile, participation is in Japan's national interest, and any huge future pipeline projects that connect Kazakhstan or Turkmenistan with China need Japan's financial participation.

ACG PROJECT

CIECO (Itochu Oil Exploration Co. Ltd.) is a subsidiary company of C. Itoh & Co., one of the leading *sogoshoshas* (general trading companies) of Japan. Itochu Oil participated in the ACG (the Azeri and Chirag fields and the deep water portion of the Gunashli field) project off the coast of Baku as a small partner from the beginning. The ACG project in Azerbaijan is the most promising one for the moment, with an expected reserve of 5.3 billion barrels of oil. The contract period is between 1994 and 2024 on PSA (production sharing agreement). The operating international consortium AIOC (Azerbaijan International Operating Company) is composed of ten companies from seven countries. AIOC was led by BP and Amoco with 17 percent each; other major partners are Unocal (10 percent), SOCAR (10 percent), Statoil (8.6 percent), Exxon Mobil (8 percent), TPAO (6.8 percent), Devon (5.6 percent), and Delta Hess (2.7 percent). Japan's CIECO got a share of 3.9 percent.[5] Later, BP and Amoco merged into one company as BPAmoco (now BP) with 34 percent of share in the AIOC.

In the initial stage, the leading Russian oil company, Luk Oil, also participated in the project with a 10 percent share, as one of the major partners. However, Japan's INPEX attracted international attention by buying 10 percent interest in the ACG project from Russia's Luk Oil. On December 20, 2002, Luk Oil and INPEX agreed to transfer Luk Oil's share of 10 percent of the ACG project to INPEX. Japan's companies' share was enhanced to 14 percent of the project by the agreement. Although INPEX is a latecomer, the company actively participates in various projects in the Caspian region, including ACG and the BTC pipeline. INPEX's original Japanese name was Indonesian Petroleum Exploration Co., and it has a successful record in oil exploration projects in Indonesia.

KASHGAN PROJECT

INPEX also participated in the so-called Kashgan project in the northern Caspian region. The Kashgan project is led by the Italian Agip Oil as the operator. Each of the five companies—Agip, British Gas, Royal Dutch Shell, Exxon Mobil, and TotalFinaElf—has an equal participation of one-sixth of the total share of the project, 16.6 percent, while Japan's INPEX share is one-twelfth at 8.33 percent as a minor partner. INPEX's interest is represented by the INPEX North Caspian Oil Co., whose shares are divided into INPEX (45 percent), Oil Resources Exploration Co. (2.5 percent), Mitsubishi Corp. (2.5 percent), and JNOC (50 percent).[6]

According to an estimate by the Wood Mackenzie Co., the remaining reserve of oil in Kazakhstan is 29 billion barrels while that of natural gas is 90 trillion cubic feet. Those resources are held by the Kazakh government or state oil companies, 30 percent; Chevron Texaco, 13 percent; Exxon Mobil, 11 percent; British Gas, 9 percent; Agip, 9 percent; TotalFinaElf, 5 percent; Royal Dutch Shell, 5 percent; INPEX, 3 percent; Conoco Philips, 3 percent; Luk Oil, 2 percent; and others, 10 percent. The Western oil majors are conspicuously present in Kazakhstan. Japan's interests as a minority are represented by the INPEX Corporation.[7]

BTC PIPELINE PROJECT

The BakuTbilisiceyhan (BTC) oil pipeline project was a hot issue among the countries concerned. The pipeline construction was completed in May 2005. BakuTbilisiceyhan Pipeline Company is led by BP (32.60 percent) and SOCAR (25 percent), while other partners are Unocal (8.9 percent), Statoil (8.71), TRAO (6.53), ENI (5 percent), TotalFinaElf (5 percent), C. Ito. Co. (3.4 percent), INPEX (2.5 percent), and Delta Hess (2.36 percent). The two Japanese companies, C. Ito. Co. and IMPEX, hold 5.9 percent of total shares.

IMPEX bought its shares from the original shareholders, BP and TRAO.[8] The pipeline has the strategic implication of not depending on Iran and Russia for transportation. Therefore at the inauguration of the pipeline, Fikret Yusifov, Russian minister of Caspian affairs, was conspicuously absent in spite of the fact that the presidents of Azerbaijan, Georgia, Kazakhstan, and Turkey attended. The United States sent its energy secretary. It is expected that in 2008 the full capacity of one million barrels per day will be utilized.[9]

JAPAN'S NEW INITIATIVE: CENTRAL ASIA PLUS JAPAN

In August 2004, then Foreign Minister Yoriko Kawaguchi paid an official visit to Central Asia and proposed a new Japanese initiative concerning Central Asia, which was called Central Asia and Japan.[10] The new initiative indicated to five Central Asian republics Japan's commitment to give continuous help. The initiative tried to show Japan's option side-by-side with the Russian option, the Chinese option and other options. Although the energy issue is not excluded, Japan does not expect a direct supply of oil from the Caspian area for the moment. Japan is interested in increasing overall influence in the area by giving bilateral and multilateral aid. Japan's clear message in the new initiative or forum is that Japan has an interest in developing regional cooperation in various fields, as any separate development among the five countries is not productive from an economic point of view. Therefore Japan is expected to express a favorable opinion on any economic project that can enhance cooperation among the concerned countries.

CONCLUSION

Japan's energy interests in Central Asia and the Caucasus are strategically important. The region's energy potential should not be neglected. Although Japanese companies cannot take exploration initiatives, they consider it important to participate in projects seeking new energy sources. Japanese companies are taking part in the ACG, Kashgan, and BTC projects. It is also important to cooperate in the region to realize economic, social, and political stability in Central Asia, which is essential for the stability in the surrounding Asian countries such as China, South Asia, and West Asia.

Japan does not expect to import oil and gas from the Caspian region because of the geographical distance. However, Japan does not exclude the possibility of swapping oil in the Gulf with oil in the Caspian region if conditions allow. However, any additional supply of oil to the world market from the region would be welcomed, as it could ease tensions in the market. Many Asian countries are expected to rush to the Middle East, particularly to the Gulf for additional supplies of oil. Japan must promote mutual cooperation against emergencies so that Asian countries can cooperate to overcome difficulties in the future. Any pipeline projects destined for East Asia attract Japan if they are economically viable. At the same time any oil and gas reserves that are attractive from an economic point of view are taken more seriously than before by Japan. The reason lies in China's increasingly aggressive posture toward oil reserves all over the world. Japan seems uneasy about depending on the theory that oil is an ordinary commodity. There are some contradictions even among the oil policies of Japan. However, as far as oil and gas reserves in Central Asia are concerned, Japanese demand is limited.

Japan expects there is scope for cooperation between Central Asian and Caucasian republics in various fields, including refineries and power generation. For the moment, ODA plays a major role for Japan. However, Japan should explore more fields of economic activity with initiatives by the private sector in the future.

A transition to a market economy is not an easy task because this is an experiment Japan has never tried before. After ten years of experiments, there are many forms of market economy among the Central Asian and Caucasian republics. Various challenges loom. Oil and gas exporting countries enjoy current higher prices and new production. However, the final result of development remains unknown because some OPEC countries have failed to establish stable and prosperous economies, even with enormous wealth from oil and gas.

NOTES

1. Agency for Natural Resources and Energy, Government of Japan, "Natural Resources and Energy," www.enecho.meti.go.jp/energy/index_energy02.htm (June 25, 2005). The figures related to Japan in this article are cited from the same source.

2. Arabian Oil Co., "Bridge between Japan and Oil Producing Countries," *Arabian Oil Co,* www.aoc.co.jp/pro/khafji (June 25, 2005). For the new agreement with Kuwait, see Arabian Oil Co., "New Agreements with Kuwait," *Arabian Oil Co.,* www.aoc.co.jp/pro/agreement.html (June 25, 2005).

3. "Natural Resources and Energy."

4. "Russian Pipeline Operator Assures China, Japan Will Both Get Adequate Supplies," *Financial Times,* May 3, 2005, 1.

5. Figures are as cited on the Itochu Corp. web page at Itochu Corp., www.itochu.co.jp.

6. Inpex Corp., www.inpex.co.jp (June 16, 2005).

7. Inpex Corp.

8. JNOC, *Sekiyu-tennengasu-rebyu* (Oil and Natural Gas Review), July 2003, 19.

9. *Daily Mainichi*, May 26, 2005, 1.

10. Government of Japan, Ministry of Foreign Affairs, "Central Asia Plus Japan," www.mofa.go.jp/mofaj/gaiko/bluebook/2005/hakusho/h17/index.html (August 24, 2004).

9

China's Energy Interests and Quest for Energy Security

Kang Wu

China has a huge energy sector and a large energy market. The world's most populous country ranks second in both total primary commercial energy consumption and primary commercial energy production after the United States.[1]

The Chinese economy has expanded substantially since the late 1970s. While the economy is facing many problems, it is expected to continue to grow strongly. Rapid economic growth in China will require massive amounts of additional energy in the coming decades, creating challenges for both China and the rest of the world.

The main objective of this chapter is to discuss China's energy interests in the context of domestic developments and global energy supply. In addition to the continuous growth in energy demand, critical issues facing China include the changing structure of energy consumption (higher demand for lighter and cleaner energy products), shortages of domestic oil and gas supply, and rising imports of energy—particularly imports of oil and later natural gas.

The chapter is organized as follows. First, the chapter examines the overall structure of primary commercial energy consumption in China and its future growth. Next, the chapter reviews China's changing energy policy for coping with rising energy demands since the 1980s. China's rising energy import dependence at present and in the future is discussed next. Finally, China's quest for energy security and the role of Central Asia are examined, followed by concluding remarks.

THE CHANGING STRUCTURE OF PRIMARY ENERGY CONSUMPTION

In 2004, China consumed 25.2 million barrels of oil equivalent per day (boe/d) of primary energy, behind America's 46.6 million boe/d but ahead of Russia's 13.4 million boe/d and Japan's 10.3 million boe/d.[2] On a per capita basis, however, China's primary energy consumption is about 70 percent of the world average.

Coal dominates China's primary energy consumption. Oil is the second largest source of primary energy consumption in China. Growing dependence on imported oil since the early 1990s has increasingly been a concern to the Chinese government, leading to a hot debate over China's energy security. Natural gas currently has a minor share in total primary energy consumption in China, but its importance is growing. Nuclear power was a late starter in China's energy development, but its expansion has been rapid since the 1990s. Hydropower has traditionally been given a priority status, and thus construction of hydropower plants has proceeded briskly in the past several decades.

China's primary energy consumption declined for two consecutive years in 1997 and 1998, mainly because of the drop in coal consumption. Although coal consumption continued to decline for 1999 and 2000, the growth of total primary energy use was positive between 1998 and 2001, thanks to the strong demand for oil and natural gas. Driven by rapid economic growth, increasing automobile sales, and strong demand for electric power, China's primary energy consumption soured at double-digit rates in 2003 and 2004. As a result, the overall level of primary energy consumption has gone up substantially (figure 9.1).

Coal

Coal is the leading fuel in China's primary energy consumption, although its share is declining notably. In 2004, coal accounted for nearly 70 percent of primary energy consumption, down from 76 percent in 1980 and 79 percent in 1990 but up from 68 percent in 2001 (figure 9.2). Back in the 1950s and early 1960s, the share of coal in total primary energy consumption was in the range of 85 to 96 percent.

China claims to have vast coal deposits and resource potential. According to the latest coal resource appraisal, China's total coal resources are 5.1 trillion metric tons; resources at depths of 1,000 meters or less are estimated at 2.6 trillion tons.[3] Despite the huge coal resources in China, the proven part is only a fraction of the total. For instance, BP estimates that China has 114.5

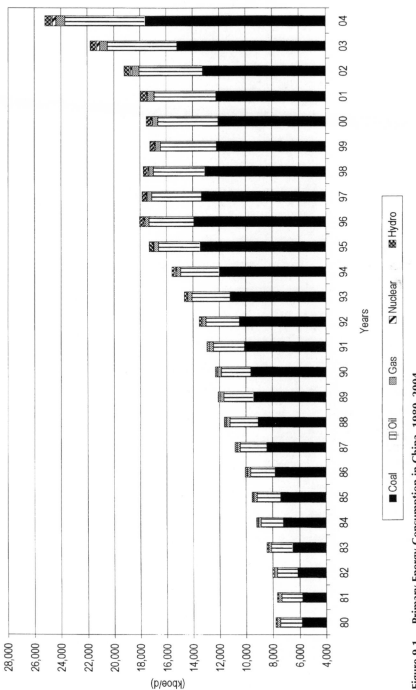

Figure 9.1. Primary Energy Consumption in China, 1980–2004

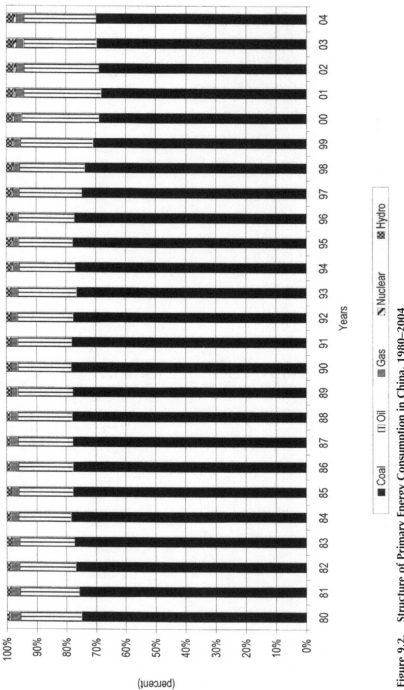

Figure 9.2. Structure of Primary Energy Consumption in China, 1980–2004

billion tons of proven coal reserves, ranking third after the United States and Russia and accounting for 11.6 percent of the world total.[4]

China's coal consumption in 2004 was over 1.8 billion tons, up notably from 1.2 billion tons in 2000 and the previous peak consumption of 1.5 billion tons in 1996. The decline in coal consumption occurred first in the industrial sector. Between 1996 and 2001, China closed down over 20,000 high–energy consumption and high-polluting enterprises, which led to a huge reduction of coal consumption. Further reduction in coal use was achieved by lower consumption in the residential sector. The surge in coal use since 2002 has also been unprecedented in China, driven exclusively by the use of coal in the power sector.

Between 1980 and 2004, coal consumption in China increased at an average annual rate of 4.7 percent a year. The growth rate was slightly slower than the average rate of 5.0 percent a year for total primary commercial energy consumption during the same period. For the coming ten years, because of the government's efforts to promote the use of natural gas, nuclear power, and hydroelectricity, the share of coal in the country's total primary energy consumption is expected to decline, though the absolute amount of use will continue to grow.

Oil

Like coal, oil resources claimed by China are huge. Based on the most recent nationwide oil and gas appraisal, China has put its total oil resources at 730 billion barrels or 1 trillion billion tons. BP, however, listed China's proven oil reserves at 17.1 billion barrels for the start of 2005, only 1.4 percent of the world total. The proven reserves could change, however, as more exploration and production activities are conducted.

Oil demand growth has been strong in China since the early 1990s. Total petroleum product consumption, including direct burning of crude oil, amounted to 6.1 million barrels per day (b/d) in 2004, up from 1.6 million b/d in 1980 and 2.2 million b/d in 1990. Although the annual growth rate of consumption in China was only 3.2 percent during the 1980s, the growth accelerated dramatically to 7.5 percent per annum on average between 1990 and 2004.

China's total petroleum product consumption is expected to increase to 8.6 million b/d by 2010 and 10.4 million b/d by 2015 under this base-case scenario.

Natural Gas

In 2004, natural gas accounted for 2.7 percent of China's primary commercial energy consumption, up from 2.3 percent in 1990. This share of gas in China is still low compared with the gas share in total primary energy consumption for the rest of the Asia Pacific region (16 percent) and in rest of the world (27 percent).

In its latest appraisal, the Chinese government reports that total natural gas resources in China amount to 1,343 trillion cubic feet (tcf), or 38 trillion cubic meters (m³). The proven part, however, is far lower. For instance, BP listed 78.7 tcf (2.2 trillion m³) as China's proven natural gas reserves for the start of 2005, accounting for 1.2 percent of the world total. The difference suggests that China has to make a greater effort to convince international investors that it has more proven gas reserves than what has been independently estimated.

Despite its minor role in China's overall primary energy consumption, natural gas consumption has been growing fast since the mid-1990s, averaging 8.6 percent per annum between 1995 and 2004. With efforts to develop its own resources and bring in imports in the form of liquefied natural gas (LNG) starting as early as 2006 and by pipeline in the future, this growth is expected to accelerate over the coming decade and beyond.

Hydroelectricity and Nuclear Power

China's electric power generating capacity and electric power generation are the second largest in the world after the United States, although China's per capita electricity consumption remains low. The country's gross power generation reached 2,103 terawatt hours (TWh) in 2004, up from 301 TWh in 1980 and 621 TWh in 1990. Hydropower and nuclear power are two primary commercial energy sources for power generation.

China's hydroenergy resources (potential power generation) are claimed to be 5,922 TWh. The actual hydroelectricity generation in 2004, however, was 340 TWh, indicating a low utilization of the resource potential. The Chinese government has vowed to continue building hydropower plants in the country. The huge, controversial Three Gorges hydroelectric project on the Yangtze River is an example. When the project is completed in 2009, it will be the world's largest and perhaps most expensive hydropower plant—with a capacity of 18,200 megawatts (MW), and consisting of twenty-six generators (700 MW each). Now the gigantic power plant is partially operational, where twelve of a planned total of twenty-six generators were completed as of mid-2005, with a combined capacity of 8,400 MW. In 2004, the Three Gorges power plant generated 39.2 TWh of power. The power was sent to Guangdong, Guangxi, Yunnan, Guizhou, and Hainan Provinces.

In addition, China recently launched grand west-east power supply schemes with several mega-hydro projects in southwest and northwest China.

Electricity produced there will be sent to fast-growing eastern and southern China, through massive west-to-east power transmission grids. In the meantime, China has vowed to develop small hydropower plants throughout the country, while admitting that environmental and ecological consequences for rivers are a growing concern in its nationwide hydro plan.

Over the next ten to fifteen years, the Chinese government's target is to increase or at least maintain the hydropower share in the country's total installed power generating capacity. As such, the share of hydroelectricity in China's primary energy consumption is expected to go up.

Until 1982, China did not elect to build any nuclear power plants, in spite of the country's long development of indigenous nuclear technology. Between 1982 and 1993, nuclear power construction proceeded rather slowly. The country's first nuclear power plant, at Qinshan in Zhejiang Province, with a capacity of 300 MW, started commercial production in May 1993. Commercial production started for the two 900-MW nuclear power units at Daya Bay, Guangdong Province, in February and May 1994. By early 2005, China had an installed nuclear power capacity of 6,856 MW, up from 2,100 MW a year ago. When another project is completed in Jiangsu Province, China is expected to have a total installed capacity of 8,976 MW.

The Chinese government has recently pushed hard to build more nuclear power plants in the country. The government's ambitious target is to have 36 GW of installed nuclear power capacity by 2020. More nuclear power plants are certain to be built, since additional projects are being approved. As a result, the share of nuclear power in China's primary energy consumption will increase significantly, though starting from a base of only 1 percent at present.

AN OVERVIEW OF CHINA'S ENERGY POLICY

Before the open-door policy was introduced by the Chinese government in 1978, energy policy was part of China's overall planning economy. The energy policy was patterned after the Soviet-style central planning system, which was adopted in the early 1950s, and "self-reliant" development, which lasted from 1960 to the late 1970s.

Since the late 1970s, China has pursued sweeping economic reforms and achieved rapid economic growth. The huge energy production required for China to realize its ambitious economic target led the government to recognize energy as one of the most critical issues in Chinese development and to begin energy sector reforms in the early 1980s.

During the reform era of the 1980s, 1990s, and 2000s, the Chinese economy evolved from a "socialist commodity economy" to a "socialist market economy." The latter assumes that state corporations can act as profit-making entities under loose government guidelines. Since the mid-1980s, this policy has led to the transformation of state energy corporations from pure government plan implementers to active market participants. This process has been accelerated by China's entry into the World Trade Organization (WTO) in late 2001.

Following the abolition of the Ministry of Coal Industry in 1998, China's coal industry was decentralized. Today, coal producers in China are spread throughout the country, which include over 2,000 state-owned coal mines (dozens of which are large ones) and tens of thousands of smaller coal mines owned by local towns and villages. The Ministry of Power Industry was also abolished in early 1998, following the establishment of the State Power Company (SPC) in 1997. A massive new power sector reform has unfolded since the end of 2002, where the state-owned State Power Company was broken up to form five regional power generating companies and a national network (grid) company, which now coexist with many other power producers, including independents.[5]

Despite numerous reforms and the abolition of the Ministry of Petroleum Industry in 1993, China's upstream oil sector and downstream refining industry are still monopolized by three large state oil companies. However, as a concession China made to enter the WTO, the monopoly held by state oil companies will be weakened gradually.[6] All three state oil companies— CNPC (China National Petroleum Corp.), Sinopec (China Petrochemical Corp.), and CNOOC (China National Offshore Oil Corp.)—have been partially privatized by forming publicly listed companies and launching initial public offerings in 2000 and 2001.

In March 2003 the Energy Administration within the National Development and Reform Commission (NDRC) was established. NDRC is renamed and reorganized from the previous State Development Planning Commission (SDPC), which also assumed some of the functions of the now defunct State Economic and Trade Commission (SETC). Establishing the Energy Administration reflected the government's desire to have a government agency supervising all energy activities, ranging from coal and power to oil and gas. The importance of energy was further demonstrated when the State Council— China's cabinet—formed the State Energy Leading Group (SELG) in June 2005, led by Premier Wen Jiabao. SELG has its own energy office within NDRC, which is directly headed by the NDRC chairman. Through the multilayer organizations, the Chinese government hopes that important energy policy issues can be dealt with at the highest level.

China's energy planning is reflected in its five-year plans and long-term social and economic development plans. In March 2001, the National People's

Congress—China's parliament—passed a resolution on the Program of the Tenth Five-Year Plan for China's National Economic and Social Development. Under this national program, energy development is selected as one of the key areas important enough to have a national plan. The major components of the overall strategy for energy development defined under the tenth FYP are (1) to optimize energy mix while ensuring the overall energy security; (2) to improve energy efficiency and energy conservation; (3) to protect the ecological environment; and (4) to develop western China.[7] The year 2005 was the last year of China's tenth FYP. Plans are now being made and targets being set for the eleventh FYP, which covers the years 2006 to 2010.

In the government's view, ensuring energy supply security is a precondition for implementing the overall energy strategy. The government continues to make it a priority for relying on domestic energy supply and stresses that coal will be the major fuel for China over the next five years. The government also calls for increasing links with international energy markets, establishing national petroleum storage, diversifying sources of energy imports, developing alternative fuels to oil, and adopting energy conservation technologies.

To optimize the energy consumption mix, the government calls for increased use of natural gas, hydroelectricity, and other clean fuels and for reduction in coal consumption by end users. Associated with the future of the coal sector development, the government will continue its policy for limiting the production of small coal mines, promoting the production of large coal mines, upgrading coal processing, and limiting the production of coal with high sulfur and ashes. The government intends to adopt an active policy for developing hydropower and calls for reasonable development of nuclear power.

Among other things, the government calls for greater use of advanced technologies and expanding the role of marketing in the energy sector in order to improve energy efficiency. Despite the low per capita consumption of energy, it is widely believed that the use of energy in China is very inefficient. The government also pledges to give the development of clean technologies—especially clean coal technologies—a high priority to protect the environment.

Finally, the government has made development of western China an important part of the energy development strategy. Under this strategy, west-to-east gas transportation and power supply have been initialized to stimulate economic development in western China.

For individual sectors, coal remains the cornerstone of China's energy policy. The government attaches great importance to integrated production, transportation, and consumption plans for the coal industry, with emphasis on the production of clean, premium-quality coal and the improvement of the efficiency and management structures of coal mines. The government has also taken massive steps to close the inefficient, unsafe small mines that cause many environmental problems.

In the oil and gas sector, China's current strategy is to increase domestic exploration and production activities, reduce costs, enhance upstream natural gas exploration and production activities, promote overseas oil and gas investment, and establish China's own strategic or government petroleum storage. The last two are closely related to China's rising concern on energy security. For domestic oil and gas, the specific strategy for the Chinese oil companies is to "stabilize the eastern fields, develop the western fields, lay equal emphasis on oil and gas, and further open up the industry." This strategy reflects the reality that oil fields in eastern China have largely reached the mature stage and China's gas exploration was neglected in the past.

In other areas, the development of hydropower is the traditional focus of China and exemplified by the construction of the Three Gorges hydropower plant and the launch of the west-east power supply plans. For nuclear power, it has recently been reemphasized. Additional nuclear power plants are certain to be built over the next ten to fifteen years. Another traditional area of government emphasis is rural energy, including biomass, and is expected to continue.

China's energy policy objectives include developing new energy resources such as solar, wind, and geothermal energy. But given the limitations of Chinese investment in energy and the constraints of indigenous technologies, large-scale development of these new sources is unlikely in the foreseeable future.

The future direction of China's energy policy centers on the government's plan for an integrated energy policy. This work is still preliminary as important targets are more or less set along the line of individual sectors. Compared to previous energy policies, the issues of energy supply security, optimal energy mix, energy efficiency, protection of ecological environment, and western China development are either new or have been given higher priority. In the petroleum sector, the policy change for oil is less dramatic with few new initiatives except for the government's call for increasing overseas oil investment. However, the expansion of the gas sector is firmly laid out in the plan. Strategic petroleum stockpiling is a new task and has been under construction since 2004.

RISING ENERGY IMPORT DEPENDENCE

In the past, China managed to produce nearly all the energy it needed. Since the late 1980s, however, the country's energy imports, primarily oil, have increased significantly, while oil exports have been declining. Currently China is a net energy importer, owing to the fact that net oil imports have outweighed net coal exports in the recent past.

China has long been a net coal exporter, but increasing amounts of coal are being imported to meet the booming demand in southern China. In 2004, China exported 87 million tons of raw coal, up from 17 million tons in 1990, and 29 million tons in 1995, but down from 94 million tons in 2003. The country also imported 19 million tons of coal in 2004, up sharply from 2 million tons 2000 and 11 million tons in 2003. Over the next ten to fifteen years, China's coal exports are expected to continue but will likely decline in volume.

Currently, China is not a natural gas importer. However, two LNG projects are under construction, one in Guangdong Province and one in Fujian Province. Completion of the Guangdong LNG is expected for 2006 and the Fujian LNG two years later. Beyond 2007, more LNG imports are forthcoming, coupled with possible pipeline gas imports from Russia and Central Asia over a longer period of time.

China is a net energy importer today only because of rising oil imports. In the future, natural gas will add to China's growing energy import dependence while the gap between oil demand and supply widens continuously.

CHINA'S OIL PRODUCTION

The majority of China's crude oil is produced onshore, but offshore production has been increasing rapidly. The share of offshore production in the country's total crude output increased from 1.0 percent in 1990 to 5.7 percent in 1995 and 13.8 percent in 2004. The offshore crude production accounted for about two-thirds of the country's net incremental output between 1990 and 2004.

About 27 percent of the 2004 crude production was from the Daqing oil field. The second largest oil field at the present time is the Shengli oil field and the third largest is the Liaohe oil field. Output from these three fields accounted for 49 percent of China's total oil production in 2004, down from 74 percent in 1990.

Crude output from Xinjiang Autonomous Region in the West, which includes production from three major basins—Tarim, Junggar, and Turpan-Hami—increased from 139 kb/d in 1990 to 374 kb/d in 2004. In fact, Xinjiang was the largest contributor to China's incremental onshore production during this period, followed by the Ordos basin in the northwest.

Petroleum Product Demand

Petroleum product demand in China is characterized by spectacular growth—especially since the early 1990s—and a radical transformation of the demand pattern (figure 9.3). Second largest in the Asia Pacific region after Japan, China's petroleum product demand was 6.1 million b/d in 2004, including direct use of crude oil for industrial sectors and power generation. Between 1980 and 2004, the petroleum product demand growth averaged 5.7 percent per annum, in which the growth accelerated to 7.5 percent per year on average since the 1990s.

China's large appetite for petroleum products has been an outcome of, as well as a fuel for, the rapid economic development arising from the country's successful reformist policies. The potential impact of an acute energy shortage on a rapidly growing economy was partially responsible for a shift in the long-standing national oil policies of self-sufficiency and export maximization. Since 1986, restrictions on oil product imports have been relaxed, and oil exports were reduced to alleviate the shortage of petroleum products in the country. During the 1990s, the government swung between liberalization and attempts to regulate the petroleum market as well as oil imports and exports. Since 1998 and particularly after its entry into WTO, China has been moving gradually toward further liberalization of the oil markets, ranging from oil prices to foreign trade. These policy changes, coupled with changes in the international oil market and regional and global economic developments, have impacted China's demand growth a great deal.

While total petroleum product growth remained strong during the 1990s, the same cannot be said for individual products. China's product demand pattern has undergone a radical transformation in response to the country's past economic and energy policies. China's product demand slate in the early 1980s was heavily oriented toward bottom-of-the-barrel products, with heavy distillates (including fuel oil, crude oil for direct burning, and other products) accounting for 43 percent of the total demand in 1985. This share has fallen steadily, owing to the government's policy of minimization and eventual substitution of fuel oil use in power plants by coal. In 2004, heavy distillates constituted 23 percent of China's total product demand. As the share of heavy distillates declines, the share of light to medium distillates is on the rise. The strong demand growth for transportation fuels, as well as for feedstock for China's growing petrochemical production capacity, has also contributed to lightening the country's product demand barrel.

Changing Oil Trade Pattern

China's crude and product exports peaked in the mid-1980s at 600 kb/d and 125 kb/d, respectively, but have since declined. In the meantime, imports of

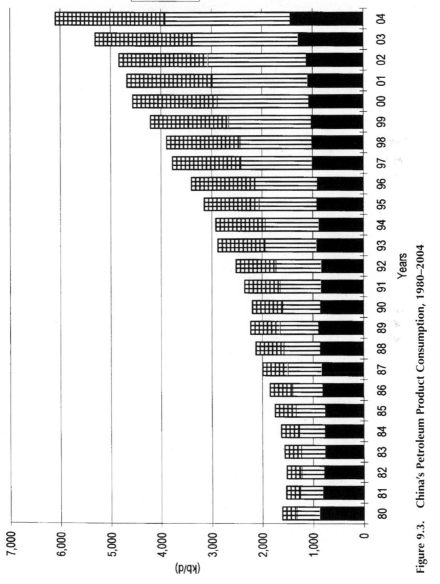

Figure 9.3. China's Petroleum Product Consumption, 1980–2004

crude, and to a lesser extent products, have increased rapidly. China has become a net overall oil importer since 1993. In 2000, the net imports reached just under 1.5 million b/d, declined to 1.4 million b/d in 2001, but rose again in the subsequent years to an unprecedented level of over 3 million b/d in 2004 (figure 9.4).

China is still a crude exporter, but the volume is much smaller today than a decade ago. In 2004, China's crude exports were 110 kb/d, down from 601 kb/d in 1985 and 377 kb/d in 1995. Daqing is the only onshore crude that is still being exported; the rest of China exports crude from the offshore fields.

China's product trade has been undergoing dramatic changes since the early 1980s. Prior to the policy shift that relaxed petroleum product import restrictions in 1986, China's product consumption was supplied almost entirely through domestic production. Between 1980 and 1985, China exported an average of about 110 kb/d of refined products and imported just under 30 kb/d each year. Since then, China's product imports have risen from a low of 18 kb/d in 1986 to 364 kb/d in 1995 and an all-time high of just under 1 million b/d in 2004.

FUTURE OUTLOOK

China's petroleum sector and oil markets are expected to change continuously over the next ten to fifteen years. On the supply side, crude production growth inside China is expected to be flat. For petroleum product demand, the growth is likely to be strong. The results are a continuously rising import requirement for oil over the long term.

In the best-case scenario, total oil consumption (petroleum product demand plus direct use of crude) in China is projected to reach 8.6 million b/d in 2010 and 10.4 million b/d by 2015 (figure 9.5). These projections are very sensitive to alternative assumptions under different scenarios.

On the supply side, China's upstream oil industry faces a precarious situation, as production from Daqing and Shengli oil fields is stagnating, Huabei oil production is declining, and Liaohe field production is increasing slowly. The hope for incremental production is likely to come from the west, offshore, and other marginal fields in the south. On an overall basis, China's crude production is projected to grow steadily but slowly, reaching 3.6 million b/d in both 2010 and 2015. The Paris-based International Energy Agency is pessimistic about future oil production growth in China, predicting that the oil production will soon decline, albeit gradually.[8]

As domestic production continues to lag behind demand, China's net oil (including both oil and products) import requirements are expected to surge

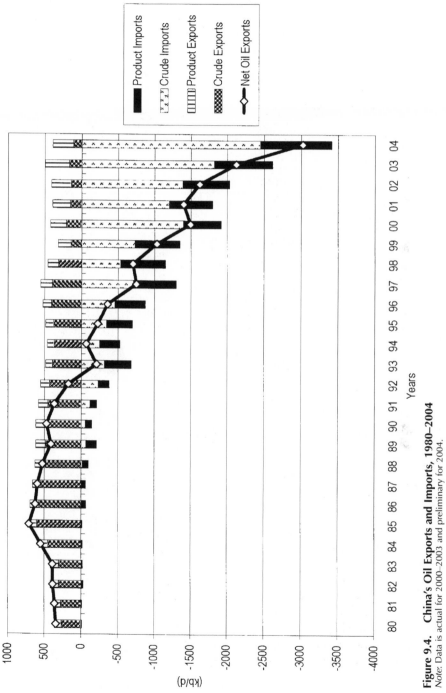

Figure 9.4.   China's Oil Exports and Imports, 1980–2004
Note: Data is actual for 2000–2003 and preliminary for 2004.

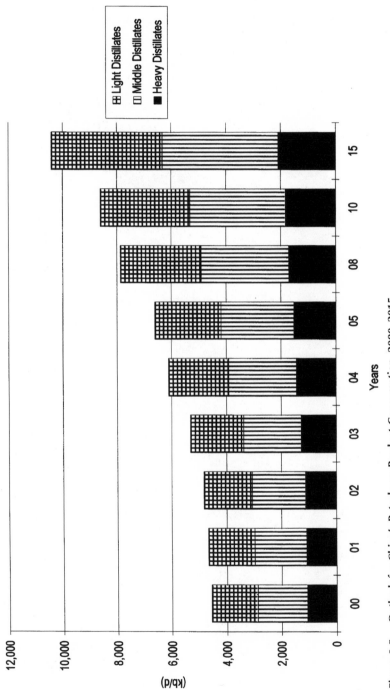

Figure 9.5. Outlook for China's Petroleum Product Consumption, 2000–2015

to 5.5 million b/d in 2010 and 6.9 million b/d by 2015 (figure 9.6). Between 70 and 85 percent of these imports are likely to be crude, while the rest will be refined products. Out of these imports, the role of the Middle East, which is already important, will grow steadily.

CHINA'S QUEST FOR ENERGY SECURITY AND THE ROLE OF CENTRAL ASIA

Because of the continuous rise in oil imports and price volatility in the global oil markets, energy security has increasingly become a big concern for the Chinese energy policy makers. At present, China's emerging energy security policy has the following elements and objectives:[9]

- To enhance domestic oil and gas exploration and production activities and maximize oil and gas production
- To diversify the sources of oil and gas imports, increasing the share of oil and gas imports from Russia and Central Asia
- To strengthen the overseas investment by state oil companies, particularly in the Middle East, Asia Pacific, Russia, and Central Asia
- To undertake different ways of trade to avoid transactions risk
- To increase the investment in oil and gas infrastructure and open more channels to imports
- To establish strategic petroleum stockpiling (SPS)

The construction of SPS system is now under way in China. NDRC is in charge of the work. The NDRC Energy Administration (EA) is home to the national office of SPS. Currently, phase 1 of the SPS is under construction. The target for phase 1 is to build around 100 million bbl. Target for phase 2 is to build an additional 90 million bbl of strategic stockpiling by 2010. The four selected sites for phase 1 are Zhenhai (Zhejiang Province) with Sinopec, Aoshan (Zhejiang Province) with Sinochem, Huangdao (Shandong Province) with Sinopec, and Dalian (Liaoning Province) with PetroChina.

Among all the elements for China's energy security, diversification of petroleum imports has been particularly emphasized to reduce the overall risk of supply interruptions. Given the fact that Central Asia is adjacent to China and has become a rising energy exporter, one natural question to ask is, Can Central Asia be a viable alternative energy supplier to China? To answer this question, it is important to examine, among other things, the energy linkage between China and Central Asia and the structure of China oil imports, at present and in the future.

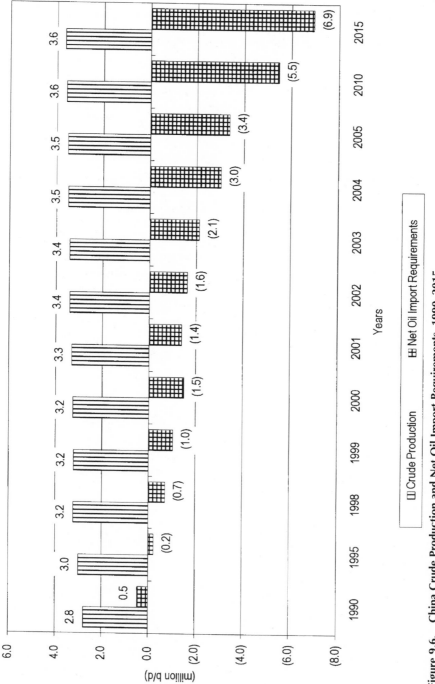

Figure 9.6. China Crude Production and Net Oil Import Requirements, 1990–2015

China's overseas oil investment in Central Asia is led by the state-owned CNPC and has focused almost exclusively on Kazakhstan. Other Central Asian countries with Chinese interest are Azerbaijan, Turkmenistan, and Uzbekistan.

Since early 1997, CNPC has invested nearly US$10 billion in Kazakhstan. CNPC bought a 60 percent equity share in CNPC Aktobemunaygaz (Aktobe Oil and Gas) in 1997, turning the company into a subsidiary of CNPC. Also in 1997, CNPC took a 60 percent stake in a joint venture formed with another Kazakh oil company, Uzenmunaigas, to invest in the Uzen oil field. As part of the agreement, a 156-mile pipeline from the Uzen oil field to the Turkmen border was completed in 2001, connecting to pipelines to Iran, as part of the Swap Project among these Caspian Sea countries. In March 2003, CNPC completed the 449-km (279-mile) Atyrau-Kenkijak oil pipeline with a total investment of US$160 million, so oil can be transported out of the Kenkijak field to the Caspian Sea. The initial capacity of the pipeline was 120 kb/d and is expected to increase to 180 kb/d in 2004 and 240 kb/d by 2006. In the meantime, China and Kazakhstan is building the longer pipeline to connect the two countries. At present, the construction of the pipeline has been under way since late September 2004. The Kazakh-China pipelines are divided into several sections: the above-mentioned Atyrau-Kenkijak pipeline is actually considered the first section of the plan; the second section, which is now being constructed, stretches from the central Kazakh site of Atasu to the Chinese border town of Alashankou. The cost of the Atasu-Alashankou line is estimated at US$700–$800 million, and is divided equally between China and Kazakhstan. The pipeline project for this segment is expected to be completed by the end of 2005. Within China, the pipeline will extend from Alashankou to Dushanzi. The Atasu-Dushanzi pipeline is 1,300 kilometers (809 miles) long, of which the length in China is 270 kilometers (168 miles). The next section is to connect Kenkijak with Atasu, and the length is 1,340 kilometers (834 miles). The total length from the Caspian Sea's Atyrau to Dushanzi will be 3,089 kilometers (1,922 miles). The volume of Kazakh crude exports to China, via these pipelines, is initially set at 200 kb/d and is expected to go up to 400 kb/d. CNPC/PetroChina is now looking for more upstream projects in Kazakhstan in order to fill the long distance oil pipeline, where Caspian crudes will eventually be exported to China.[10]

China's attitudes toward the crude pipeline from Kazakhstan and the overall investment toward the Central Asian country have changed dramatically and become more positive as well as active since 2004, after China suffered a series of setbacks in its attempt to invest and secure an oil supply from Russia. First in December 2002, PetroChina, CNPC's publicly listed subsidiary, had to withdraw from the bid on Russia's state-owned Slavneft because of strong resistance from Russian nationalists. Then in 2003 and 2004, the original plan between CNPC and Yukos for building an oil pipeline from the Angarsk field in Russia to China's Daqing was aborted. The setbacks have forced the Chinese state oil company and China as a whole to reexamine its overall Russia and Central Asia energy strategies and have helped to rekindle the Kazakhstan-China oil pipeline project.

At present, Kazakhstan is the only Central Asian country exporting oil to China, which is transported by rail, and the share in China's total imports is tiny. In 2004, China imported nearly 2.4 million b/d of crude oil, of which 45 percent came from the Middle East, while the share of Central Asia was only 1 percent. Although Russian oil exports to China are also transported primarily by rail, the volume was nearly eight times larger than the exports of Kazakhstan in 2004.

Over the next ten years and beyond, China's overall oil imports as well as the share from the Middle East are expected to increase significantly. During the above period, particularly before 2010, China's best hope to alleviate but not necessarily to reduce its dependence on Middle Eastern oil will be continuous oil imports from faraway places such as West Africa. Russia also has a role to play, although uncertainty over Russia's far east Asian oil pipelines has shadowed that role.

As for Central Asia, the construction of long-distance crude pipelines from Kazakhstan to China's remote Xinjiang will raise Kazakhstan's oil exports to China substantially. Overall, however, the role of Central Asia in China's future oil supply will increase but will remain marginal. For instance, China is expected to have net oil imports of approximately 5.5 million b/d. Even if the Kazakh-China oil pipeline is running at full capacity, the share of Kazakh oil will be around 7 percent of China's overall net oil imports. After all, Central Asia has traditionally been oriented toward the Russian energy market in the north and European markets in the west.[11] Without drastic increase in oil and gas production, and more pipelines, Central Asia's energy exports to China will be constrained in the foreseeable future.

However, over a longer period of time, more Central Asian oil and gas exports to China could become viable beyond the current pipelines being built. For Kazakhstan, if its oil production keeps expanding, more oil could become available for China. Likewise, the chance is likely to be significantly better for China to seriously consider massive natural gas imports from Central Asia—Turkmenistan in particularly—and Russia's western Siberia beyond 2020.

CONCLUSION

China's primary energy consumption is dominated by coal but the importance for natural gas is rising rapidly while the share of oil is steady. China is currently a net energy importer, and its import dependence, represented by rising oil imports, has been growing. From the 1980s to the 1990s and beyond, China has evolved from Asia's largest oil exporter to a large net oil importer and the imports are rising at unprecedented rates.

Over the next ten to fifteen years, China will continue to rely on coal to support its basic energy needs, but coal's share is expected to decline. The rapidly increasing oil and gas demand, coupled with flat domestic oil production growth and limitations on gas production, will lead to rising oil and gas imports and therefore pose serious challenges to China with regard to its energy security. How China will deal with these and other changes will have profound impacts on the overall energy and economic developments in China as well as in Asia.

Central Asia appears to be well positioned to supply oil and gas to China. With the construction of the Kazakh-China oil pipelines underway, Central Asia's oil exports to China will increase drastically during the remainder of the decade, though the starting point is rather low. Compared to the Middle East, the role of Central Asia in China's overall oil and energy supply will still be rather insignificant in the foreseeable future. However, over the longer period of time, the chances of more oil and gas pipeline connections with China are likely to improve significantly. Central Asia will eventually become an important alternative source of oil supply to China in addition to the Middle East, Africa, and Russia.

NOTES

1. Primary commercial energy is defined as including coal, oil, natural gas, hydroelectricity, and nuclear power only. For convenience, I use the term "primary energy" as a short form for "primary commercial energy."

2. Unless otherwise specified, the Chinese data in this paper is from the East-West Center Energy Database as well as the Database of FACTS Inc., a Honolulu-based energy consulting firm. These data draw on various sources of information from China. The primary energy data for other countries here are derived from BP, *BP Statistical Review of World Energy 2005,* www.bp.com/genericsection.do?categoryId=92& contentId=7005893 (June 2005).

3. See C. Yan, ed., *China's Energy Development Report* (Beijing: China Metrology Press, 2001).

4. *BP 2005.*

5. Kang Wu, *Periodic Review of Energy and Economic Developments in China with a Special Emphasis on Oil and Gas* (Washington, D.C.: U.S. Department of Energy, Office of Natural Gas and Oil Import and Export Activities, 2003).

6. Kang Wu, "Oil Demand and Supply Structures and Market Developments in China: Current Situation and Future Prospects," in *Proceedings of the Cross-Straits Energy Forum* (Taipei: Taiwan Research Institute, 2002).

7. Kang Wu, *China's National Energy Policies for Oil and Gas under the Tenth Five-Year Plan* (Washington, D.C.: U.S. Department of Energy, Office of Natural Gas and Oil Import and Export Activities, 2001).

8. International Energy Agency, *World Energy Outlook 2002* (Paris: World Energy Outlook, 2002).

9. Yan, *China's Energy Development Report;* Y. Tang, "China's Economic Situation and Energy Strategy" (paper presented at the China Fuel Oil Conference, Guangdong, October 28–29, 2002).

10. Kang Wu and F. Fesharaki, "Central Asia's Potential as Asia-Pacific Oil Supplier Limited for Years to Come," *Oil and Gas Journal* 100, no. 31 (2002).

11. Kang Wu and S. Han, "Chinese Companies Pursue Overseas Oil and Gas Assets," *Oil and Gas Journal* 103, no. 15 (2005).

10

Central Asia and Asian Pacific Energy Requirements

Robert Smith

This chapter examines Asian Pacific energy requirements and the role Central Asia can play in meeting those requirements in the coming years. It will first examine what types of fuels the Asian Pacific region employs to meet its primary energy requirements. It will then discuss the supply sources for the fuels employed and examine which ones are imported. This will show where there may be room for Central Asian energy supplies and how Central Asia may play a role in contributing to Asian Pacific energy security. Central Asia's energy resources will then be discussed briefly to see what fuels are potentially available to alleviate Asian Pacific energy concerns. Coal resources will not be discussed in Central Asia, as coal reserves are abundant in Asia Pacific; rather, the focus will be on Central Asia's oil and gas resources. The chapter will then examine how Central Asia's energy resources may or may not be used in the Asian Pacific region and briefly explain why.

ASIAN PACIFIC ENERGY REQUIREMENTS: WHAT ARE THEY?

The Asian Pacific region uses fossil fuels (oil, coal, and natural gas) to fuel 90 percent of its primary energy requirements. In 2004, oil and coal each supplied 30 percent or more of the region's energy. Natural gas made up 10 percent, leaving only 8.5 percent for the combined total of hydroelectric power and nuclear energy. Solar, wind, and geothermal energy sources make up less than 1 percent and are not included in the figures below. Renewables, which play a significant fuel role in many countries, are not included because reliable consumption data does not exist. Because renewables are not imported

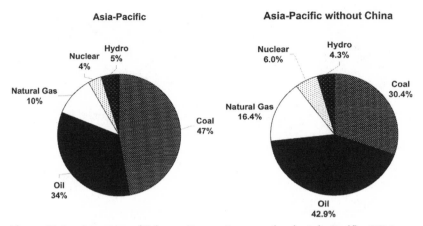

Figure 10.1.   Structure of Primary Energy Consumption in Asia Pacific, 2004

and are unlikely to grow significantly, thus minimizing their relevance to the issue of Asian Pacific energy security, they will not be discussed here. The two pie charts in figure 10.1 show the breakdown of the region's energy sources in 2004, both with and without China.[1] When China is excluded from the picture, coal use drops by nearly 17 percent, indicating just how large a coal user China is and how large China's energy use is relative to the region's. Removing India would lower the coal percentage by another five points. In contrast, the United States relies on coal for less than 25 percent of its primary energy while Europe relies on coal for less than 20 percent.

Another important component of Asia's primary energy mix is oil. With or without China, oil occupies at least 30 percent of the region's primary energy mix. While the high oil percentage is not a problem in itself, it becomes a problem when we look at where Asian Pacific energy supplies originate.

The Asian Pacific region depends heavily on imported energy sources, especially oil. This is one of the primary reasons why energy security is such an important topic in the Asian Pacific region. Table 10.1 shows the region's fossil fuel energy reserves, production, and consumption.[2] Only fossil fuels are shown, because they make up 90 percent of the region's primary energy mix. Note that Asia Pacific has a significant portion of the world's coal reserves. Both its oil and natural gas reserves are too limited to allow the region to survive without imports.

For energy production, the region produces over 50 percent of the world's coal but only 10 percent and 12 percent respectively for oil and natural gas. Coal is the only fossil energy source in Asia Pacific that is evenly matched with its production rates and has ample reserves. The region can consume

Table 10.1.   Asian Pacific Region's Share of Fossil Fuel Energy in the World, 2004

	Reserves		Production		Consumption	
	Amount[1]	Share of World (%)	Amount (mmtoe/y)[2]	Share of World	Amount (mmtoe/y)[2]	Share of World (%)
Oil	4.1	3.5	379.5	9.8%	1,090.5	28.9
Coal	296.9	32.7	1,506.3	55.1%	1,506.6	54.2
Natural gas	501.5	7.9	290.8	12.0%	330.9	13.7
Fossil energy total	—	—	2,176.6	25.6%	2,928.0	32.7

Source: BP Statistical Review of World Energy, 2005
1. Oil: billion barrels; coal: billion tons; and natural gas: trillion cubic feet (tcf)
2. mmtoe/y = million tons of oil equivalent per year

more gas, but much still comes from imports, by pipeline as well as by ship in the form of liquefied natural gas (LNG). Gas demand growth, however, is more difficult than oil growth, as it requires significantly greater capital-intensive investments in infrastructure. For example, kerosene or propane, two oil products that can be used for heating and cooking, can be easily transported in containers. Gas, on the other hand, requires pipelines from either an import terminal or a gas field. The pipelines must be constructed all the way from the source to the burner tip of a stove or furnace. Much of the region's current gas use, especially in developing countries, is confined to areas close to the gas source.

Oil consumption stands at approximately 30 percent of the world total. The Asian Pacific region must import nearly two-thirds of the oil it uses. This translates to more than 15 million barrels per day (mmb/d), or more than all the oil that is produced in North America. This also means that nearly 75 percent of the region's oil supply consists of imports and 22 percent of the region's primary energy consumption consists of oil imports.

HOW ASIAN PACIFIC ENERGY REQUIREMENTS
ARE CURRENTLY MET

Unfortunately for the Asian Pacific region, North America cannot supply its oil import requirements. Occasionally, oil from North America is imported to Asia, as is oil from Europe and South America, but generally large consistent volumes do not flow from these regions to Asia Pacific. Canada and Mexico export oil primarily to the United States. As a result, oil is at the forefront of Asian Pacific energy security discussions.

With oil imports accounting for nearly 25 percent of the Asian Pacific region's primary energy supply, it is important to look at the security of the imported oil's source. In 2004, 12 percent, or 1.9 mmb/d, of the region's oil imports came from within the region. The supplies are primarily from such countries as Australia, Brunei, Malaysia, Indonesia, Thailand, and Vietnam. By 2010, under current economic growth scenarios, however, this number is forecast to decline to 10 percent or 1.8 mmb/d, meaning that the additional imports will have to come from outside of the region.[3] Only 16 percent comes from the combination of Africa, the Americas, and Europe, with the vast majority coming from Africa.[4] Imports from Africa, the Americas, and Europe are expected to remain constant at 15 percent through 2010. Imports from Africa, the Americas, and Europe are often driven more by the price of oil and freight costs than by the actual demand. For instance, when the price of a barrel of oil in Asia becomes higher than the price of a comparable barrel of oil in the Atlantic basin plus the cost of shipping it to Asia, then crude oil traders will ship those barrels to Asia. Over the past decade, such shipments of crude oil to Asia have consistently averaged out to approximately 15 percent of Asia's imports.

The balance of the Asian Pacific region's oil imports comes from the Middle East. The Middle East is defined here as consisting of the countries of Bahrain, Iran, Iraq, Kuwait, Oman, Qatar, Saudi Arabia, the United Arab Emirates, and Yemen. The Asian Pacific region has become the natural market for several reasons. The first is proximity. The distance between the Asian Pacific markets and the Persian (Arab) Gulf is shorter than that to key markets in northern Europe or the United States. The second is the type of crude produced in the Middle East, which is generally higher in sulfur content and lower in higher-end petroleum product yields than many of the Atlantic basin or Central Asian crude oils. Most Asian Pacific oil refineries were designed to use crude oils similar to those exported from the Middle East. This issue, however, is becoming less significant as fuel quality specifications are rising in Asia Pacific and will meet those of North America and Europe in the next decade. In some countries such as Japan, fuel quality specifications already meet Western standards. Figure 10.2 illustrates the source of the region's oil imports from 2000 to 2010.[5]

Figure 10.2 illustrates that oil imports from the Middle East to Asia Pacific are larger than all other oil imports combined; they also exceed Asia Pacific's own oil production. In 2000, Middle Eastern imports represented roughly 70 percent of the region's total oil imports. By 2010, imports will have increased to just over 75 percent of the region's total oil imports or by 4.1 mmb/d, the equivalent of the entire current oil production of Iran. In the context of Asian Pacific primary energy consumption, oil imports from the Middle East account for 18 percent of all the energy consumed in the Asian Pacific primary energy mix.

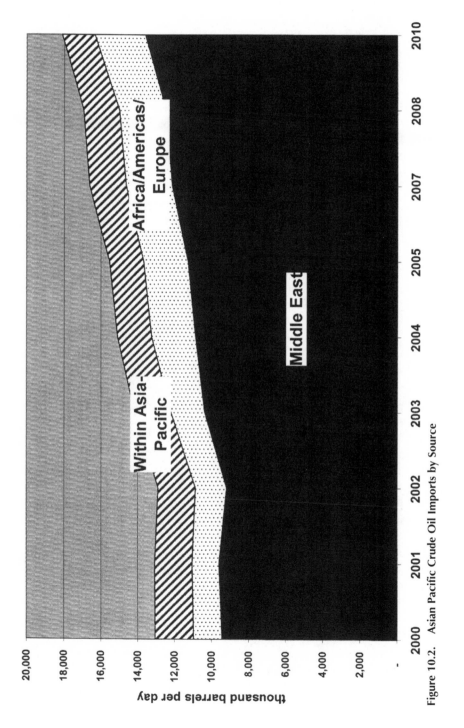

Figure 10.2. Asian Pacific Crude Oil Imports by Source

Aside from oil, other fuels such as coal, nuclear, and hydroelectricity are used, mostly domestically and in proportion to their supply. For instance, both China and India have an abundance of coal, which is relatively inexpensive when compared to alternative fuel sources. As a result, both countries use a large amount of coal for energy. In spite of rising prices, coal is one of the most affordable energy sources; even countries such as Japan and Korea import it.

Natural gas, at least in its piped form, is similar to fuels such as coal, nuclear power, and hydroelectricity in that it is affordable when used near its source. In the Asian Pacific region, however, most of the natural gas is located far from demand centers. To transport the natural gas to demand centers, significant investments are needed, and to date, only countries that have been able to provide a sovereign guarantee have been successful at importing natural gas. Currently more than 90 percent of the region's gas imports are in the form of LNG, which means that the gas is delivered by ship. Right now there are only four places importing LNG in Asia: Japan, India, South Korea, and Taiwan. China will also begin importing LNG by the end of 2006. While the more developed LNG importers can sustain imports at higher gas prices, India's LNG imports were initially delayed over arguments on the price of the gas. India will have difficulties increasing LNG use as lower-priced LNG contracts become harder to negotiate in the face of rising energy prices. Like LNG, long-distance pipelines also require a large long-term investment and are rarely built without extensive involvement on the part of the importing country's government. Even the Japanese government finds piping Siberian gas home too costly versus LNG imports.

The Asian Pacific region first began importing LNG from Alaska to Japan in 1969 with the goal of improving Japan's energy security by reducing the island nation's dependence on imported crude oil. Then Japan began importing LNG from Southeast Asia, the Middle East, and finally Australia. Recently Russia's gas fields in the Sakhalin II project have been committed to Northeast Asian LNG buyers. Of the Asian Pacific region's existing LNG importers, Taiwan imports no LNG from the Middle East, though it has signed a contract with Qatar to begin later in the decade. While Japan imports 23 percent of its LNG from the Middle East, Korea imports 47 percent. India imports 100 percent of its LNG from Qatar in the Middle East and has recently signed another LNG import contract with Iran. In spite of regional LNG use initially being driven by concerns over energy security, the Middle East now supplies gas as well as oil to the region. Korea, for example, has expressed concerns over reducing both its oil and gas (LNG) dependence on the Middle East.

CENTRAL ASIA'S FOSSIL FUEL RESOURCES

As mentioned earlier, the Asian Pacific region depends on fossil fuels for 90 percent of its primary energy consumption. While coal is a significant part of this 90 percent, the Asian Pacific region has little need for coal imports from outside the region. Asian Pacific coal reserves are abundant and, if anything, the region is trying to replace coal with cleaner energy resources. The focus in the future will be on Central Asia's oil and gas resources.

Of the Central Asian nations, only Kazakhstan currently has proven crude oil reserves that are large enough to warrant large-scale exports outside of the region. Current proven reserves stand at 40 billion barrels of oil.[6] The other Central Asian nations each have proven oil reserves of fewer than 1 billion barrels. Uzbekistan, a significant oil producer, presently imports crude oil. The majority of Kazakhstan's crude oil reserves are located in western Kazakhstan, either bordering the Caspian Sea or located offshore in the Caspian Sea. Such locations have shifted much of the export route focus toward the West, rather than toward Asia, for economic reasons. However, with rising oil prices and Chinese oil demand growing at nearly 800,000 barrels per day (800 kb/d) in 2004 and an intended 500 kb/d in 2005, the Chinese government has taken a renewed interest in bringing Central Asian oil east to Xinjiang and onward. This decision is driven more by politics than by economics and will be discussed in more detail below.

Unlike the oil reserves, Central Asian natural gas reserves are located in significant quantities in Kazakhstan, Turkmenistan, and Uzbekistan. The three countries have respective proven gas reserves of 106, 102, and 66 trillion cubic feet, respectively.[7] Turkmenistan and Uzbekistan currently export significant volumes of gas within the Former Soviet Union (FSU) pipeline system. All three would be interested in exporting gas to markets outside of the FSU, as they would have more credible buyers and receive significant export revenues. The difficulty with this, however, is that long-distance export pipelines, like LNG, are capital-intensive and require support from both importing and exporting countries. Such support currently does not exist. Turkey was an ideal choice for exports, but it has since found other gas supplies and currently has a surplus of gas through its various import options.

Kazakhstan, on the other hand, is more interested in monetizing its oil reserves, as the oil will yield revenue more quickly than gas will. Because of this, financial institutions have been more willing to lend money to build an oil export pipeline than a gas pipeline. Oil is more readily transportable and its transportation means are less complex and more affordable than those required for gas. Gas needs an extensive system of pipelines to be delivered to the consumer, whereas oil only needs to be brought to the sea and then a tanker can take it to wherever the market demands. Part of this is due to the relative abundance of oil tankers and the relative scarcity of ships that can carry LNG. There are currently fewer than 200 ships that can transport LNG; a new LNG carrier costs more than the most expensive oil tanker.[8]

HOW CAN CENTRAL ASIA HELP MEET
ASIAN PACIFIC ENERGY REQUIREMENTS?

Central Asia has oil and gas to export, and the most economic direction for it to travel is west, due to the proximity of the markets that can most readily use it. Until recently, none of the export routes seriously looked to supply the Asian Pacific region. This section will examine how and where Central Asia can contribute to meeting Asian Pacific energy requirements, as well as where the current and planned Central Asian export routes intend to export Central Asian oil and gas.

THE POTENTIAL EXPORT ROUTES TO ASIA PACIFIC

While gas markets are becoming more and more global as the LNG trade grows, it will be a long time before they reach the global scale of the oil market. This means that any contribution to oil supplies in one region of the world will ease supply pressure in that region and make other supplies available to be shipped elsewhere. In the case of Central Asia, this may mean that oil being exported west increases supplies to Europe in the Mediterranean region, potentially reducing the need for supplies from elsewhere. The supplies that will most likely be made available as a result, however, are from the Middle East. This is perhaps less than ideal for the Asian Pacific region, as it is already heavily dependent on Middle Eastern oil and gas imports.

If direct export routes are examined, even the closest Asian markets are problematic as potential Central Asian oil and gas export routes. To the north, nothing is viable through Russia as the Russians would like to supply Northeast Asia with both oil and gas from their own fields in the east. The Russians and Chinese have had trouble coming to an agreement on oil and gas contract terms, and nothing is presently happening. China, immediately to the east, may need energy that could come from Central Asia. The Chinese demand centers, however, are located far to the east in large urban areas and near the coast. Xinjiang, the northwestern Chinese province that shares a long border with Central Asia, actually produces its own oil and gas and has a surplus. It is a net exporter to other areas of China for oil and will soon send its natural gas east through the west-east pipeline, a major undertaking by the Chinese government to build a gas pipeline across China from Xinjiang to Shanghai. While the thirty-year reserves needed for the life of the west-east pipeline have yet to be fully proven, any imports from Central Asia that would link up to the pipeline as a supply source would still not be needed until sometime in the next decade. The Chinese have also gotten the Russians to join as shareholders in the west-east pipeline, and this may be indicative of Chinese plans to eventually use some of Russia's Siberian gas to fill the pipeline if and when the gas from Xinjiang's Tarim Basin runs out. Thus the opportunity for Central Asian gas to supply the west-east pipeline may be a long shot. In spite of these concerns, which make oil and gas exports to China unviable, the Chinese are proceeding with what may be the only source of Central Asian energy to be directly exported east.

Another option that would enable Central Asian oil and gas to reach Asia would be to build a pipeline through Iran to the Persian Gulf. Such pipelines, however, are unlikely, due to U.S. sanctions against Iran as well as U.S. influence in Central Asia. Iranian pipelines for either oil or gas would be of little use to lowering the Asian Pacific region's dependence on the Middle East. Central Asian oil would have the added drawback of coming from the Persian Gulf and being vulnerable to Middle Eastern security issues. Thus it would not contribute to improving Asian Pacific energy security. For gas, it is unlikely that Iran would be interested in having a Central Asian gas pipeline pass through its territory. Iran's giant South Pars field, which is shared with Qatar, contains 600–900 trillion cubic feet of proven reserves, depending on whom you ask. Consequently Iran is more interested in monetizing its own gas than in helping Central Asia monetize its gas. While this may eventually mean a gas pipeline to India, it may also mean no exports, depending on how conservative a government Iran has in place. Regardless, as of June 13, 2005, Iran is contracted to export LNG to India toward the end of the decade.

Turkmenistan was formerly at the forefront of Central Asian gas exports to the west. The nation may now be more inclined to export its gas to Asia as it currently has fewer options than it did in the late 1990s. Azerbaijan, which was once thought to have oil waiting to be discovered, turns out to have significant gas reserves in its offshore Caspian Sea areas. Thus the pipelines once planned to go west with Turkmen gas are now being planned to carry Azeri gas, though the Azeris have run into their own problems, too. Turkmenistan was unable to come to any agreement to join the Azeris and had the added legal and environmental difficulties of crossing the Caspian Sea. Meanwhile, the Russians entered the game by building a pipeline under the Black Sea to supply the same market in Turkey. As already mentioned, Turkey has no immediate need for Central Asian gas. With the Russians selling their gas to Turkey, they may then buy Turkmen gas for themselves at a discount through the old Soviet pipeline system in Central Asia.

The problem with sending Central Asian gas directly to Asia, however, is that it is too far from the markets that need it. Excluding Iran, the pipelines that would be necessary to transport the gas would have to pass through many areas that would not enhance Asia's energy security while being quite costly. The main route under consideration was a pipeline that would eventually go to either Pakistan or India. The U.S. company Unocal once sponsored the gas pipeline but has since dropped the idea and no longer has any involvement. Unocal has since been sold also. In the mid-1990s, Pakistan worried it was going to be short of natural gas but has since discovered enough to last through 2010. Beyond 2010, Pakistan will likely try to import gas from Iran via pipeline, as any pipeline supplying gas from Turkmenistan would also have to pass through Afghanistan, adding yet another difficult dimension. LNG is another option, but higher costs and prices will likely rule it out.

Overall, there are few viable options for Central Asian energy resources to help meet Asian Pacific energy requirements. For natural gas, it is difficult to imagine any scenario where a pipeline could be built to supply Asian needs. The distances are currently too long compared with those of the plans to supply Western markets, and they require passing over rugged and often politically unstable terrain. Such factors make the costs associated with potential Asian exports prohibitive.

Oil is just as unlikely to see a pipeline sending Central Asian exports to the Asia Pacific. China may be the only exception, but this does not mean that oil exports elsewhere will not influence Asia Pacific's energy security. There is a fundamental difference between the world's oil and gas markets. Oil exists in a world market and gas exists in regional markets, as noted above. If 2 mmb/d of Kazakh exports enter the world market at any place, they potentially free up another 2 mmb/d from somewhere else. While it is highly unlikely that Kazakh oil that is put in a tanker on the Black Sea or the Mediterranean will ever find its way to Asia, the oil that it displaces may. This means that additional supplies of oil are displaced and hence available for anyone, including the Asian Pacific region. The additional supplies could be from anywhere, although Africa and the Middle East are the likeliest places that would send more oil to Asia Pacific.

THE REALITY OF THE PLANNED EXPORT ROUTES

Currently three routes exist to export Central Asian oil and gas, with a fourth, the Chinese route, under construction. For oil, the main export route is that of the Caspian Pipeline Consortium that exports Kazakh oil from the Tengiz field in western Kazakhstan. Pipeline capacity will increase to 1.34 mmb/d by 2008, and last year it exported 450 kb/d.[9] The pipeline's route travels 980 miles out of Kazakhstan, west through Russia, and terminates on the Black Sea where the oil can be loaded onto ships and taken to Mediterranean markets. Kazakhstan's second existing export option is the Atyrau-Samara pipeline that links up to the Russian system. In 2002, Kazakhstan and Russia signed a fifteen-year contract where 340 kb/d will be exported via the pipeline.[10] The third option is swapping Kazakh crude oil with Iran, where it is refined in Tabriz and Tehran in exchange for Iran crude supplies in the Persian Gulf. Current swap volumes are estimated at 30 kb/d.[11]

The fourth export route will be to China and is intended to be completed by the end of 2005. In March 2003, the Chinese National Petroleum Corporation (CNPC) completed a pipeline from its own fields in Kenkijak, Kazakhstan, flowing west to the Caspian Sea.[12] First, this helps bring China's Kazakh oil production to market in the short term. Second, the pipeline can reverse its flow and export Caspian and Chinese Kazakh crude to China once the Kazakh-China oil pipeline is completed between China and Kenkijak. The section of the pipeline to China will travel east to Dushanzi, a town northwest of Urumqi, Xinjiang, that is expected to run portions of the crude in its refinery. Pipeline capacity will begin at 200 kb/d and is hoped to be increased to 400 kb/d as CNPC looks for more oil supplies in Kazakhstan.[13]

The other Central Asian nations export little compared with Kazakhstan. Turkmenistan does export some cargoes by ship across the Caspian to be loaded into a Russian pipeline to the Black Sea. Other exports are by rail, but rarely are these considered a long-term option.

While there are few options for Central Asian oil exports, there are even fewer for gas exports. Nearly all exports have to go through the FSU gas pipeline system, which means they have to pass through Russia. The Russian pipelines are all managed by Gazprom, which also sells Russian gas. This makes it difficult for large volumes of Central Asian gas to be exported outside of the region. The Russians usually charge prohibitive fees to use their pipeline. The only gas pipeline that exports gas from Central Asia and avoids the Russian system is a small pipeline from Turkmenistan to Kurt Kui, across the border in Iran. The pipeline is designed to supply small volumes of gas across the border to northern Iran.

Future oil pipelines may include a pipeline that would cross the Caspian and connect with the planned oil pipeline from Baku, Azerbaijan, to Ceyhan, Turkey. This option, however, may become unavailable as the Azeris plan to use more of their own crude in it.

Currently no viable gas pipelines are seriously being considered for Central Asian exports. The trans-Caspian gas pipeline was planned to run under the Caspian Sea, land in Azerbaijan, and eventually deliver gas to Turkey. As mentioned above, the Russians have completed the Blue Stream pipeline, which crosses under the Black Sea and supplies Turkey with gas. Turkey is having difficulties absorbing all the Russian gas and will have no need for Turkmen gas anytime soon. Even if there were a market in Turkey for the gas, numerous legal and environmental issues would have to be settled before the portion of the pipeline that passes under the Caspian Sea could be built.

Outside of the interregional gas pipelines in Central Asia, there seems to be little hope for the construction of any others, especially to Asia. Turkmenistan President Saparmurat Niyazov and Afghan President Hamid Karzai have expressed a desire to see a pipeline built from Turkmenistan to Afghanistan and onward to India and Pakistan, but neither has the estimated $2 billion to construct it.[14] It is highly unlikely that any international company capable of building such a pipeline will take an interest in the project, for two reasons. First, they would not want to cross both Afghanistan and Pakistan. Second, there would be no credible buyer for a large volume of gas. Pakistan does not need the gas, and even if it did, it would not need the amount necessary to make the pipeline economically viable. India is the targeted market with the potential to consume a lot of gas. The problem with India, however, is that it may have difficulty paying for the gas and does not view a pipeline through Pakistan as contributing to its energy security. India is not in a position to commit to a multibillion-dollar gas import project that would pass through Pakistan.

Overall, the reasons that Central Asian oil and gas are not likely to be exported to Asia Pacific come down to their distance from demand centers and politics. For oil specifically, the pipelines emanating from Central Asia all head west, which is the shortest distance to a market, and hence the least costly. For gas, nothing is happening to export Central Asia's gas outside the region. There currently is no market close enough to justify the costs involved in building a long-distance export pipeline to supply either India or Turkey, which have neither the requisite demand nor the ability to pay for it.

CONCLUSION

With the exception of China, it is not likely that any of Central Asia's energy resources will be used to meet Asian Pacific energy requirements in the near future. This stems from the difficulties that exist in trying to transport Central Asian oil and gas to Asian Pacific markets. This chapter looked at the most viable oil and gas export options and concluded that none of those are to Asia Pacific. It is unlikely that Central Asian gas will have a market anywhere outside of the region in the near future. Central Asian oil does have a market, but the oil market, unlike the gas market, operates on a worldwide basis, and it is unlikely that the oil will come to Asia Pacific. Rather, Central Asian oil exports will take the route that is most economical to deliver it to a viable market. The Black Sea markets are closer than China's Xinjiang, and once in the Black Sea, the oil can go anywhere. Meanwhile, Xinjiang in northwest China is currently an oil exporter. This means that any pipeline sending oil to Xinjiang will have to move the oil farther east to an area that can use it. At the same time, the markets requiring exports via Iran or Pakistan are undesirable for political as well as energy security reasons.

Even though Xinjiang is an oil-exporting region, the Chinese demand for oil has grown at incredible rates, and no forecasts see this declining. Consequently, the Chinese government has embarked on a major plan to increase its refining capacity and secure oil supplies anywhere it can around the world. The Chinese also plan to increase refinery capacity and expand petrochemical output at Dushanzi, the endpoint of the Kazakh pipeline, but this will create a different end product that is still in surplus in Xinjiang. Thus, while Xinjiang is an oil surplus region, plans have been made to remedy this by building both crude and petroleum product pipelines all the way to the western industrial city of Lanzhou. While the imported Kazakh crude may not be currently needed, the Chinese government is taking a more long-term approach in securing supplies that are not necessarily the most economical. The question of Chinese overspending is legitimate in the case of Kazakhstan, but perhaps it needs to be viewed as the price of one option for increasing energy security.

Overall, China's oil demand in 2004 was for 6.1 mmb/d;[15] 200–400 kb/d of crude oil imports from Kazakhstan represents only 3.3 to 6.6 percent of China's 2004 oil demand. Even with smaller growth rates, this percentage will only decrease. The oil pipeline imports are born out of genuine energy security concerns, but their significance should not be overstated as the contribution to China's and Asia Pacific's energy security is minimal. Furthermore, the Chinese will find that the pipeline exposes them to other energy security concerns that they have had minimal experience with in the past. As has been the case in such places as Colombia, or more recently Iraq, sabotaging an oil pipeline is easy. Both the Chinese and Kazakhs may find themselves exposed to a new energy threat stemming from disaffected Uyghurs.[16]

NOTES

1. BP, "BP Statistical Review of World Energy 2005," www.bp.com (June 24, 2005).

2. BP, "Statistical Review of World Energy."

3. Fesharaki and Associates, FACTS Energy Database: Spring 2005 Forecast (Honolulu, Hawaii).

4. Fesharaki et al., FACTS Energy Database.

5. Fesharaki et al., FACTS Energy Database.

6. BP, "Statistical Review of World Energy."

7. BP, "Statistical Review of World Energy."

8. Fesharaki et al., FACTS Energy Database: LNG Data.

9. U.S. Energy Information Administration (EIA), *Kazakhstan Country Analysis Brief,* November 2004, www.eia.doe.gov/emeu/cabs/kazak.html (June 27, 2005).

10. EIA, *Kazakhstan Country Analysis Brief,* 2004.

11. EIA, *Kazakhstan Country Analysis Brief,* 2004.

12. Kang Wu and Shair Ling Han, "China's Overseas Oil and Gas Investment: An Update," *FACTS Energy Insights* no. 46 (Honolulu: FACTS Inc., 2005), 2–3.

13. Kang Wu and Shair Ling Han, "China's Overseas Oil," 2–3.

14. EIA, *Central Asian Region Country Analysis Brief,* May 2002, www.eia.doe .gov/emeu/cabs/centralasia.html (January 17, 2003).

15. Fesharaki et al., FACTS Energy Database: Spring 2005 Forecast.

16. For more complete recent coverage on the subject, see Dru Gladney and Justin Rudelson, "The Role of Xinjiang in China–Central Asia Relations," June 2003, www .csis.org/china/030605.cfm (May 14, 2005).

III

THE GEOPOLITICS OF CENTRAL ASIA

11

Great Power Politics in Central Asia Today: A Chinese Assessment

Shi Yinhong

Central Asia was an enduring arena of competition, confrontation, and indirect conflict among the great powers in the nineteenth and early twentieth centuries, and as such became the pivot linking the western and eastern parts of the modern international system. Both Britain and Russia, the two great flanking powers of the world with their extended intercontinental involvements, regarded the Great Game between them in Central Asia as a major component of their respective imperial strategies. The geographical location of Central Asia was an obvious and unchangeable deciding factor. As a likely annex of British India to its south, a neighboring territory of Persia to its east, and the natural extension to the Russian landmass to its north, Central Asia constituted both a strategic frontier and a buffer zone vital to the security of empires, and the strategic access for invading an opponent's sphere of influence as well as an enticing power vacuum.

International politics has undergone epic changes around the world in general and in Central Asia in particular, while the lessons of history fade. A comparison of the present with the past, however, reveals that some basic political elements remain intact in Central Asia. First, this region is still a strategic geographical pivot or axis. In addition, the great powers still have strong geostrategic concerns, aspirations, and anxieties in the region, leading to mutual precaution and competition. Third, a kind of balance of mutual asymmetrical strategic advantage still exists in Central Asia; one side, like Great Britain in the past, possesses the preponderance of available material resources and the long-distance capability of power projection. The other side, like czarist Russia, enjoys the benefits of geographical and historical adjacency. Fourth, the local authorities or powers in the region are nothing like passive pieces on a chessboard. They participate and influence the regional international game with a logic often not understood or even recognized by the great powers, sometimes playing a crucial role in the game. Finally, Central Asia is both a region consisting of various states and societies with great diversity in terms of nationality, ethnicity, language, cultural and historical tradition, and an area in which the process of building and consolidating state authority is far from mature. Therefore, modern complexities, disorders, and dangers are inevitable, often interweaving two different strands of domestic construction of internal order and great power competition for influence into a complex pattern.

The changes in the international politics of Central Asia, however, are more than its continuities or similarities with the past British-Russian Great Game. The relatively simple pattern of earlier bipolar great power politics has been replaced by a complex polar structure: the United States, Russia, and China have different degrees of confrontation, interests, and notions.[1] Even where their interests and ideas coincide with or parallel each other, there are still operational difficulties involved in concrete policy coordination and cooperation. Moreover, due to the recent implications of the extraction and exportation of Central Asian petroleum for the policies of the United States, Russia, and China, the current international politics of the region have assumed an unprecedented strategic economic importance. Furthermore, the balance of the great powers in Central Asia is quite different from the historic structure of the British-Russian equilibrium in the region. The United States has obtained, or at least is obtaining, a strong preponderance over Russia and China in some critical aspects because of its vast and nearly comprehensive superiority in power resources, especially foreign aid capability. The United States also has the unique status of being a "hyperpower" with a strong drive for security combined with an unusual historical opportunity as the result of the September 11, 2001, terrorist attack.

There are other historical differences. Transnational and subnational factors have resulted in turmoil and are closely related to domestic conditions in Central Asian nations and societies. For instance, Central Asia is one of the main bases for transnational terrorism, which has become a central issue in world politics since September 11. Also, the forces of national separatism and religious extremism in the region, both of which have connections with transnational terrorist organizations, have become a serious concern of China, Russia, and some Central Asian states. They plausibly define national separatism and religious extremism as serious threats to their national integration and the stability of their frontier areas. Therefore, as transnational terrorism has become the common enemy of the great powers since September 11, their traditional competition in Central Asia has been interwoven with a unique collaboration and potential cooperation on counterterrorism. Great power competition has been intermingled with great power cooperation.

Other historic differences also influence the geopolitics in Central Asia. A regional multilateral security regime, the Shanghai Cooperation Organization (SCO), is similarly connected with combating the forces of transnational terrorism, national separatism, and religious extremism. The Shanghai Cooperation Organization, a unique institution in the history of Central Asia, has emerged as a potential contradiction to the military presence and bilateral military arrangements of the great powers. It is possible, however, that the SCO will eventually link up, accommodate, or even partially merge with these great power presences. Last but not least, the era based exclusively on "might makes right" has passed into history. Power relationships between strong and weak states are subjected to the sometimes decisive restraints of international legal and moral norms concerning sovereignty and the equality of states. This means that the positions, attitudes, strategic calculations, and policies of the Central Asian governments influence the behavior of the great powers, the politics among them, and regional situations on a grander scale than any from the Great Game era.

THE IMPACT OF AMERICAN, RUSSIAN, AND CHINESE GEOPOLITICS

The current geopolitical and geostrategic significances of Central Asia must be discussed in relation to the United States, Russia, and China respectively. In this part of the chapter, "geopolitics" and "geostrategy" refer to politics and strategy that rest on fundamental geographical conditions and are relatively enduring. Therefore, because of its dramatic and sudden nature and predictably shorter duration, the issue of the large-scale U.S. antiterrorist campaign will be discussed in a later section, even though it has dramatically increased U.S. presence and concerns in Central Asia, thereby substantially changing the geopolitical and strategic prospect of the region.

American geostrategic objectives or ideals in Central Asia complement the long-term American strategy in the Middle East. Since September 11, the United States has keenly felt its alienation from the governments of some Middle Eastern Islamic countries that it has traditionally relied on. In particular, the United States is thinking in terms of obtaining a forward strategic position to guard against, contain, potentially topple, or subdue Iran. For the United States, Iran represents an anti-American regional semi–great power that may have the intent, capability, and determination to possess weapons of mass destruction (WMD), as well as representing a strong regional destabilizer that might be aggressive and interventionist in spreading Iranian culture and ideology. Moreover, the combination in the Middle East of a vast influence of Islamic fundamentalism, intense popular anti-American sentiment, and autocratic corruption and incompetence of the elites has been fermenting and accumulating immense potential for turbulence and upheaval. In these circumstances, the United States seeks a new geopolitical foothold in neighboring Central Asia, to supplement or possibly replace its potentially unstable base in the Middle East. In other words, the U.S. military and political presence in Central Asia promises at least an ambiguous hope to counterbalance a failing Middle East policy.

For the United States, Central Asia has two other geopolitical objectives, both of which can be categorized as great power geostrategic contention. There is such an overwhelming consensus in China of their existence and importance that they are the only objectives most Chinese observers of Central Asian geopolitics pay attention to. The first U.S. objective is to guard against the expansion of Russian power within the states of the Commonwealth of Independent States (CIS), and to compete with Russia for influence in the former Soviet republics in Central Asia. The second objective is to guard against China, including preemptive and preventive interdiction of Chinese influence in Central Asia, and constructing a Central Asian link in the strategic precautionary perimeter around China—an important component of America's mid- and long-term global geostrategy. A large segment of Chinese officials, professional researchers, and the general public also believe that the United States wants to use Central Asia as a springboard for indirect interference in northwestern China when it is necessary and feasible. To put it briefly, in terms of the great power geostrategic contentions, the United States intends to use Central Asia, first, to manage the failed superpower, Russia, so that it has no hope of staging a comeback and, second, to deal with a possible future superpower, China, by taking precautions against its potential to challenge American preponderance.

The defining Russian geopolitical and strategic objectives in Central Asia have few similarities with those from the former Soviet era as well as some differences with those in the czarist Great Game era. The fundamental determinants of the present Russian posture are the drastic decline of its national strength, the overwhelming precedence of internal economic and social problems, and the vast retrenchment of its external aspirations, together with the end of "the great power mission," the flagging power politics thinking, and the prudent measurements of "objective versus capability" as well as "benefits versus costs" that are so prominent in the statecraft of President Vladimir Putin. The limited definition of national security requirements leads Russia to see, first, that the former Soviet republics serve as a very special buffer zone that can help Russia to interdict and contain the northward drive of the terrorist, separatist, and religious extremist forces. Second, the former Soviet republics in Central Asia serve as an operational ground for Russia to strike against these forces of terrorism, separatism, and extremism either unilaterally or multilaterally when necessary and with the consent of the countries. Third, despite the ethnic and religious demography and Central Asia's role as a major breeding ground of extremists, Central Asia does not take precedence in Putin's strategic priorities. After September 11, Putin took an almost neutral attitude toward the establishment of an American military and political presence in the former Soviet Central Asian republics on Russia's southern border. This lower ranking of Central Asia in Russia's strategic priorities has not resulted in any remarkable opposition from Russian public opinion. Many in China interpret this as Putin's and Russia's leaning toward the United States and the West.

However, Russian aspirations for national prestige and considerations about future strategic prospects require the maintenance of Russia's more or less controlling influence over the southern belt of the Commonwealth of Independent States. This probably has some flavor of expansionism. What is surprising, however, is not that the successor state to expansionist czarist Russia and the Soviet Union would have such an aspiration, but how little Russia has done up to now in this respect.

Many of China's geopolitical and geostrategic interests in Central Asia are similar to Russia's.[2] China wants to prevent the terrorist, separatist, and extremist forces based in Central Asia from endangering the stability and security of China's northwestern frontier area. Since the late 1990s, the separatist and terrorist force of the East Turkestan Islamic Movement (ETIM) has made use of the unavoidable and complicated antagonisms between different nationalities and employed terror as one of the primary means to strive for separation of Xinjiang from China. ETIM has been nourished by an atmosphere of transnational religious extremism and assisted in training, funds, equipment, and spiritual support by al-Qaeda, the chief transnational terrorist organization, and some anti-Chinese forces. In turn, the activities of ETIM aggravate the national friction and antagonism in Xinjiang, seriously threatening the frontier security and integration of China. Because the external bases and channels of support for this movement come mainly from Central Asia, the Chinese geopolitical objective is to limit terrorist, separatist, and religious extremist forces in that region. Its determination to head off extremist forces led China to strive for cooperation with the former Central Asian Soviet republics and Russia through the Shanghai Cooperation Organization. This body is proudly seen in China as a major innovation in the history of China's diplomacy and in the international relations of the Central Asian region.

The SCO is partially a functional international security regime, aimed at dealing with the common threat of the terrorist, separatist, and religious extremist forces faced by the six member states as well as attempting to secure the status quo in their mutual borders and handle potential disputes by peaceful consultation. The short history of this newly established international regime proves that its coherence and policy-coordination capacity are far from sufficiently strong, and the expansion of its present functions needs more time for realization. Moreover, the SCO is still not the only or even primary international instrument chosen by its Central Asian members in preventing and cracking down on transnational terrorism within the region.

Some Chinese expectations before September 11 concerning the SCO have proved too optimistic. However, it has not been regarded as either obsolete or conflicting with the new Central Asian–American connections, although the Central Asian republics introduced the American military presence into their territory and Russian-U.S. cooperation has extensively and dramatically progressed. The two major common interests reflected in the SCO's declared aims are clearly defined, limited, and important to all its member states. Therefore, it still has potential for growth and consolidation.

The maintenance, consolidation, and cultivation of the SCO has become an important geopolitical and strategic Chinese national interest. The SCO will become even more vital to the Chinese national interest if the potential of the organization continues to increase and its channels of mutual consultation become even more useful in preventing an American precautionary strategic buildup against China. As such, the SCO involves a Chinese geostrategic interest in terms of a preemptive interdiction in Central Asia, which will probably become more and more obvious in a mid- and long-term perspective. It is the counterpart of the American preemptive interdiction against influence of China in the region, perhaps similar to the traditional great power competition over a power vacuum. It is an open question when it would result in a balance of mutual asymmetrical strategic advantages, as mentioned in the previous section. Perhaps, as China's economic, financial, and foreign aid strength rapidly increase, together with strengthened geostrategic thinking and sense of diplomatic forward defense, the Chinese-U.S. balance of strength will be gradually transformed.[3]

GREAT POWER GEOECONOMICS IN CENTRAL ASIA

Having explored the geopolitical and geostrategic significance of Central Asia to the United States, Russia, and China, we now need to take into account the remarkable geoeconomic elements of great power politics in the region. The deposit, extraction, and transport of Central Asian energy reserves are the primary economic resources of interest to the great powers. These important geoeconomic characteristics must be considered in an analysis of the international politics of this region.

Among the governments of the United States, Russia, and China, the United States may be the first to perceive the issue of Central Asian petroleum from a strategic angle. On the one hand, the United States starts from the basis that the oil-rich Middle East is politically unstable, and thus it is interested in securing Central Asian energy sources as a potential supplement. In the event of great upheaval or a major war in the Middle East, Central Asian energy reserves might become an alternative source of supply. Additionally, the strategy of preemptive interdiction is as applicable to the issue of energy as it is to the issue of motivation for expanding international political power. That is, to make the potential strategic competitor obtain as little as possible (ideally even deny it) control over production and transport of Central Asian petroleum, because these controls will "naturally" bring to it corresponding political influence and strategic advantage, among other reasons. At the same time, achieving an exclusive and vast energy supply in Central Asia will help reduce dependence on the import of Russian petroleum, thereby decreasing Russian power over the United States or alternately increasing U.S. power over Russia. Until now the government rather than private enterprise has constituted the main American driving force in the search for petroleum rights in Central Asia, perhaps answering questions regarding the strategic nature of the motivation. Due to Russia's rich deposits and gigantic production of petroleum, it does not need a supplementary energy supply, and thus the Russian government's requirement for Central Asian petroleum is mostly political and strategic in nature. Extraction and transport of oil there affect the expansion of Russian political power, regardless of whether this expansion is from the strictly defined Russian security requirements or from a purely expansionist aspiration.

If the U.S. motivation toward Central Asian petroleum is a mix of energy plus strategy and Russia's motivation is wholly strategic, then China's motivation is purely energy oriented. In recent years, one issue has emerged among international specialists and is more and more widely spoken of inside China's informed circles. The supply of domestically produced petroleum is increasingly in short supply as a result of China's rapid national economic growth and corresponding energy demand. Therefore dependence on imported oil has increased so dramatically that it worries many in the strategic studies circle in China. Considering China's vast population, ongoing rapid growth to maintain social stability, and the accelerating change in the energy consumption structure such as the replacement of coal by petroleum, this long-term problem will become more acute. At present, most Chinese petroleum imports come from the unstable Middle East. Consequently, vital national economic security interests will demand that China seek supplementary sources of supply in order to reduce or at least stabilize its dependence on Middle Eastern oil. Moreover, China has a long-standing tradition of refraining from overseas military intervention as well as an inability to protect petroleum facilities abroad and sea lanes for oil transport. The importance of Central Asian petroleum for China rests on these issues.

China's petroleum diplomacy in Central Asia is still in its early stages. To a large degree, China's petroleum diplomacy reflects the main Chinese pattern of behavior in establishing an overseas economic presence along with governmental encouragement of foreign trade and investment by private Chinese enterprises. With the aid of prudent governmental diplomacy, China is using major state enterprises as a leading force to create, consolidate, or develop overseas economic footholds without any direct or indirect coercion and decide whether to establish them and whether to go forward wholly in accordance with the acceptance, encouragement, restriction, or exclusion of the national government. This economic diplomacy conforms to the PRC's fundamental diplomatic tradition, which is helpful in maintaining friendly relations between China and related countries and advantageous in preventing the further spread of the China threat thesis. However, its effectiveness in realizing some of China's vital and legitimate economic requirements is limited. Developing a proper balance between these basic pros and cons in economics and diplomacy may become a controversial question in China's foreign policy making and international relations fields. It also constitutes an important component of an emerging long-term critical debate regarding the type of fundamental international status, roles, and behavior a rising China should have in world politics, especially in its "traditional" area of power politics.

THE U.S. ANTITERRORIST CAMPAIGN

After September 11, 2001, U.S. concerns over Central Asia and its presence in that region increased by leaps and bounds. The Afghanistan war with the expulsion of al-Qaeda and the overthrow of the Taliban regime, together with the overwhelming American preponderance of influence and power in that country, does not need to be discussed here, except that it has allowed the United States to station its troops in the former Central Asian Soviet republics, a development without precedent in history. The United States has established military, political, and financial relations with the Central Asian republics, which are bound to be permanent and profound, seen from today's vantage point.[4] Thus the geopolitical and strategic structure in Central Asia has already changed. Furthermore, the remarkable rise of Central Asia's strategic significance in *The United States National Security Strategy* (September 2002), as well as in other recent American policy-making documents and policy statements, indicate that this structural change is likely to continue to influence the direction of American power penetration and aggrandizement for at least the next few years.

Chinese public and elite opinion indicates concern about this development, although the Chinese government's judgment has been far more sophisticated and sober minded than Chinese public opinion in the aftermath of September 11. In those initial five or six months, there was uncertainty, confusion, and controversy within China around four basic questions regarding how to define the situation of world politics and China's security environment after September 11. First, will U.S. national security priorities be transformed? If yes, will the transformation be transient? Second, will there be a transformation impacting the international distribution of power, especially the balance of strength among the great powers? Third, what is the fundamental intention of the U.S. war on terrorism? What is the relationship between antiterrorist efforts and the drive for American hegemony? Finally, what is the impact on China's geopolitical and security environment in Asia Pacific? These four questions are all closely related to assessments and concerns about the situation in Central Asia.

The mainstream, and most pessimistic, assessment in China regarding the U.S war on terrorism, described here in its original or "unrevised" form, supposes that antiterrorism as the first priority in the U.S. national security strategy and foreign policy will be of short duration and that containing and encircling an emerging China is still the fundamental goal of the U.S. grand strategy. Moreover, the extraordinary American preponderance of power after September 11, resulting from the vast mobilization of its national power and its much greater willingness to assert that power, along with the drastic Russian "tilt to the West," substantially increased the U.S. power potential in containing and encircling China. According to this assessment, the real fundamental intention of the American war against terrorism is to use the opportunities of this war provides for U.S. hegemony or even strive for hegemony under a pretense of antiterrorism, especially in the second phase of the war following victory in Afghanistan. For China, the creation of the American military presence and military cooperation in Central Asia as well as the expansion of American diplomatic, political, and economic influence within the Central Asian republics demonstrates this intention and strategy. From this perspective, the United States is seen as extending its perimeter of containment and encirclement to the Chinese northwest periphery, thus seriously aggravating the dangers in China's geopolitical and security environment.

That this pessimistic assessment constituted the mainstream opinion in the early months after September 11 and still has a major influence is due in large part to the U.S. government's strategic behavior, policy pronouncements, and countless statements from American elites in political, security, and media circles toward China in recent years. Moreover, this assessment does contain accurate elements. For a great part of the general public as well as for many intellectual elite and officials, its relative simplicity and extremeness increases its appeal. In contrast, comprehensive, sophisticated, and balanced points of view are less likely to prevail, unless helped by time and a remarkable improvement in the U.S. government's attitude toward China and U.S.-Chinese relations, as happened in late 2002. The key to understanding the U.S. military presence and expanded influence in Central Asia lies in the relationship between the two major determinants of U.S. behavior: the vital security need of striking against terrorists and the pursuit of long-range geostrategic interests, perhaps more accurately called the pursuit of hegemonic interests. These two determinants are inextricably interwoven in the international arena, in most cases facilitating each other.

In a period when the perception of the danger of a terror attack against the United States, which originated more or less in Central Asia, still seriously exists, one is wrong to assume that the chief U.S. objective is the pursuit of hegemonic interests. Moreover, such a mistake will lead to a grave overestimation of China's security situation, and thereby produce negative effects in China's whole grand strategy.[5] Conversely, one is also wrong to only look at the U.S. security need of striking against terrorist behavior in Central Asia, ignoring or seriously underestimating its geostrategic intentions as well as the automatic impact in terms of power expansion. Such a mistake will result in a lack of appropriate strategic vigilance, together with corresponding planning and other precautionary efforts. The former mistake occurs more readily in China than the latter; hence the greater need to develop a strategy for judging present U.S. intentions in Central Asia.

It is indisputable that the United States has vital and legitimate security needs in Central Asia, which exist outside of the pursuit of geostrategic and geoeconomic interests.[6] This region, especially Afghanistan, was until very recently the largest base of transnational terrorism; the outcome of the antiterrorist war in Afghanistan is by no means perfect in terms of eliminating al-Qaeda, and the antiterrorist tasks left there remain arduous. These two basic facts are vital in determining that the U.S. military presence in Central Asia was and still is needed for the general cause of antiterrorism. Even after the antiterrorist problem in Afghanistan is largely solved, there will still be a need to develop long-term stability in the region. American power there can still play a role for the near future.

Moreover, Russian fissile material could end up in the hands of terrorists if Central Asia is in chaos, which obviously increases U.S. security concerns and strengthens the need for stability in the region. Because of natural ambiguities at the onset of a policy and paradigm shift, a comprehensive, balanced, and open-minded Chinese approach is required concerning a potential U.S. disposition to form strategic precautions against China in Central Asia.[7] In a time when cracking down on terrorism and preventing another surprise attack still constitute the primary American national security objective, there is a vital need to differentiate between a strategic precaution against China as an effect of antiterrorist actions and as a deliberated primary intention. Additionally, some remaining differences that should be taken into account by any sophisticated strategic thinking, regardless of antiterrorism, include the following: the balance of costs restrains the desire for power expansion, the time and concentration needed to plan and formulate a strategy, policy preference differences between the bureaucracy and the policy makers, and the different implications of a large-scale military presence versus a small military presence. Strategic precautionary measures should be distinguished from containment and encirclement, especially in their popular meaning in China. Comprehensive, sophisticated, and proportionate strategic thinking is the sole reasonable approach.

NOTES

1. Shi Yinhong, "A Rising China: Domestic Ambiguities and Controversies" (presentation at the Carnegie Endowment for International Peace, Washington, D.C., February 12, 2002).

2. Zi Zhongyun, "The Clash of Ideas: Ideology and Sino-U.S. Relations," in Suisheng Zhao, ed., *Chinese Foreign Policy: Pragmatism and Strategic Behavior* (Armonk, N.Y.: Sharpe, 2004), 224–42.

3. Suisheng Zhao, "Chinese Nationalism and Its Foreign Policy Ramifications," in Christopher Marsh and June Teufel Dreyer, eds., *U.S.-China Relations in the 21st Century* (Lanham, Md.: Lexington, 2003), 63–84.

4. Elizabeth Van Wie Davis, "New Perceptions of the International System after 9/11," *Political Science and China in Transition,* July 2002.

5. Michael D. Swaine and Ashley J. Tellis, *Interpreting China's Grand Strategy: Past, Present, and Future* (Santa Monica, Calif.: RAND, 2000), 112–40.

6. Michael Pillsbury, *China Debates the Future Security Environment* (Washington, D.C.: National Defense University Press, 2000).

7. Shi Yinhong, "On the Possible Future Orientation of China's Foreign Policy Opinions and the Issue of 'Peace Rising' Doctrine" (presentation to international conference, Madrid, November 25, 2004).

12

Russian-Indian Relations in Central Asia

Sergey Lounev

RUSSIA AND INDIA AS STRATEGIC PARTNERS

India is a natural friend of Russia. There are practically no differences between the two countries on most world problems. The logic of geopolitics dictates the necessity of close relations between them. India can be a reliable partner in the case of a direct threat to Russian security posed by the Muslim world or China. The same can be said about the Russian Federation. If we take the southern boundaries of Russia, India is already playing a positive role by limiting Pakistan's activity in the zone. India and the Russian Federation face similar problems interacting with the Muslim world.

The prospect of a unipolar world disturbs both Moscow and New Delhi. As the developed North further broadens the use of violence, relations between Russia and India will strengthen. Moreover, there are justified concerns that violence will become the instrument of governance over the world system. Russia and India oppose the unipolar position of the North and its present policy. Simultaneously no one wants to challenge the North to an open confrontation. Moreover, the overall strengthening of economic links with the North has become one of the main goals of both India and Russia from the beginning of the 1990s. But the comprehensive cooperation between two countries and collective expression of views may be more persuasive than individual bargaining.

The military cooperation with India is good for Russia. India is one of its most reliable and substantial partners in this sphere. The development of a subsystem of bilateral relations is crucial for India as well. Additionally, the multinational and multiethnic composition of both countries brings them closer. The existence of ethnic and religious separatism prompts Russia and

India to share a similar approach to issues of self-determination, terrorism, and separatism. Finally, the two countries share relative closeness in the sphere of cultural life, too. Spiritualism, an immanent element of their civilizations, is a common ground. It is not a coincidence that more and more Russian political forces have begun to support the comprehensive development of bilateral relations. Only radical democrats oppose it openly.

While the role of India in the world arena has strengthened since the 1990s, it has simultaneously lost its position in the developing South and the former socialist zone, thus leaving New Delhi feeling stronger but isolated. That is why it is so important for India to restore cordiality in its ties with the Russian Federation.

There are good relations between Russians and Indians at the grassroots level. Public opinion surveys in India show that Russia is among the most popular countries. India is the only country of the South with significant levels of sympathy for the Russian Federation, and all sociological surveys in India put it among the five most popular states. Indians have not forgotten the colossal economic aid they received from the USSR in the 1960s and 1980s. It is a good base for Russian rapprochement with India.

Of course, there are some obstacles, particularly in the economic sphere. Both countries have reoriented toward the North. The influential Indian business sector made no secret of its hostile attitude toward socialism. It was the only segment of Indian society that was more or less satisfied with the breakup of the Soviet Union. Today the Indian business sector on the whole is not very interested in rapprochement with Russia. The same can be said of the Russian business sector. In these conditions, only the restoration of some form of intergovernmental economic ties can change the situation. The combination of Russian science and Indian engineering seems promising in this respect.

THE GROWTH OF ISLAMIC EXTREMISM IN CENTRAL ASIA

The end of the twentieth century witnessed the worldwide effect of religious revivalism on internal political processes and on intergovernmental relations. The danger of Islamic radicalism in Central Asia—from Afghanistan and internally—and its spread to Russian territory were considered a great danger for Russia. The search for a common national ideology resulted in the rise of Islam in Central Asia at the beginning of the 1990s. In April 1992, President Islam Karimov of Uzbekistan went on a pilgrimage to Saudi Arabia. Other Central Asian leaders followed him. During the Soviet period, Tajikistan had seventeen registered mosques. Once the restrictions were removed, their number jumped to 2,000. Every village and district in Uzbekistan rushed to open its own mosque. Thirteen hundred mosques were opened in Namangan alone. In three years in Turkmenistan the number of mosques increased ten-fold. The rise in religious self-identification was slower in Kazakhstan and northern Kyrgyzstan.[1] Significantly, members of the younger generation are becoming increasingly involved in the process of Islamization.

This process enhanced the role of social groups critical of the local elite that formed in the Soviet period. The Islamists started vigorous activities in Bukhara, Samarkand, and the Ferghana Valley. In Namangan the local imams formed Islamic militant units. The Adolat Islamic Party, close to the Muslim Brotherhood, emerged in this city. The radical Islamic Revival Party was notably active in Uzbekistan and Tajikistan. Muslim radicals in Kazakhstan tried to provoke public disorder in Almaty.

Realizing the threat to its interests, the ruling elite in Central Asian states began a selective policy of supporting moderate Islamists and containing and even suppressing the extremists. The 1992 constitution of Uzbekistan prohibited organizations calling for religious hostility and creation of political parties on religious principles.

The Islamic Revival Party was banned in Tajikistan and Uzbekistan. The majority of its Tajik supporters fled to Afghanistan. In 1999, the party was again legalized in Tajikistan. The Adolat Islamic Party and the Kokand-based Humanity and Clemency Party were also banned in Uzbekistan. Dozens of missionaries from Saudi Arabia who had brought Wahhabism (the Islamic school of thought that opposes all practices not sanctioned by the Qur'an) to the Ferghana Valley were deported from Uzbekistan. These missionaries moved to the Osh Province of Kyrgyzstan and the Chimkent Province of Kazakhstan from which they are sending money and literature to Uzbekistan.

In 1997, Muslim extremists who had undergone special terrorist training in Pakistan and Afghanistan resumed their activities in the Ferghana Valley. A series of murders of policemen and officials were committed in Namangan. In 1998, many radicals went on trial. The 1998 Law on Freedom of Speech and Religious Organizations came into effect, giving the state authority to limit the spread of radical Islam and take mosques under its full control (the law demanded official registration of mosques, and the number of mosques reduced by more than twofold).

The Uzbek radicals moved to the neighboring provinces of Kyrgyzstan, Tajikistan, and Afghanistan. In February 1999, the extremists carried out a terrorist act in Tashkent that killed sixteen people. The activities of Uzbek Islamists in 1999 and 2000, their direct attacks against Uzbekistan and Kyrgyzstan, led to the deterioration of the situation in the whole region. The Kyrgyz authorities have radically toughened their policy toward Islamic radicals.

Unfortunately, political Islam is present in the southern parts of Kazakhstan and Kyrgyzstan. Islamists share power in Tajikistan and constitute a real force in Uzbekistan. Islamization in Central Asia has an enclave character, which means that Islam plays a lesser role in the region in comparison to regional and clan interests; but the continuation of a protracted economic and social crisis will lead to disappointment in the secular power. The Central Asian states have only begun their journey to democracy, and it will take a long time. If the republics make no progress toward socioeconomic recovery and development, the process of democratization will be extinguished, and radical and extremist Islamists may come to power.

Most Central Asian countries face the phenomenon of Islamic revival in general and the emergence of powerful radical opposition inside their countries in particular. This phenomenon should be regarded in the context of three factors. First, there is the impoverishment of great masses of people, whose values and orientation are determined by an early industrial type of consciousness; hence the appeal of religion is a simple and natural form of social tie. Additionally, there is the subregional elite struggle for natural resources in what had been until recently the common economic space; when the population is multiethnic, religion plays the role of the ideological force that unites its own society, irrespective of the type of economic activity or social or property status. Finally, there are the external influences that come from Afghanistan, Pakistan, Saudi Arabia, and some other Muslim countries supporting Islamic radicals in Central Asia.

The situation is grim but will worsen unless speedy action is taken to remedy it. The deterioration of the situation could bring tragic consequences not only for Central Asia but also for Russia and Eurasia, including India and China.

RUSSIA'S CONCERNS

The Russian Federation is naturally worried about Muslim fundamentalists consolidating in the republics of Central Asia and Azerbaijan and their influence on Russian regions (autonomous units of the North Caucasus and the Volga region). Russia also worries about the possibility of retaliatory measures in Russia and elsewhere as well as the consolidation of existing Christian fundamentalism. Yet another alarming factor is relations between Saudi Arabia and the Russian regions and the active presence of Pakistani and Afghani fundamentalists in Central Asia and the Caucasus. There is no real cooperation in the Russian Federation between the Muslims of the Volga region and the North Caucasus.

The export of the Iranian revolution to Russia or other republics remains highly improbable. The possible Iranian influence, clearly exaggerated by some Western politicians, is quite limited. First, Iranians are racially Indo-Aryans and thus quite different from other ethnicities of the southern region of the former Soviet Union who are Turkic or Caucasian by origin, except Tajiks and some minor groups. Second, Iran belongs to the Shiite denomination of Islam, whereas the majority of the Muslim population of the Commonwealth of Independent States (CIS), except Azerbaijan, belongs to the Sunni majority denomination of Islam. Third, the local elites are not willing to adopt the theocratic form of governance allegedly imposed on society in Iran. Fourth, economically Iran is not in a position to initiate structural modernization in Central Asia and the Caucasus despite having hard currency from petrol dollars. Of course, in the future, Iranian influence has the potential to grow: in Azerbaijan on the basis of religious denominational similarity, in Tajikistan on the ethnic base, and in Armenia due to political factors. Additionally, when the new infrastructure projects are put into operation—railways and subways as well as oil and gas pipelines cutting through the Iranian territory—they may strengthen Iran's influence in the region.

Many Russian experts and politicians find Turkey particularly alarming because of its geographic, cultural, ethnic, and religious proximity to several former Soviet republics as well as its economic potential and Western political backing. Additionally, the Turkish secular model of development could attract the majority of Central Asian regimes that are looking for examples to follow while at the same time remaining concerned about the possibility of Islamic revival in general and the emergence of powerful fundamentalist oppositions inside their countries in particular. Furthermore, Turkish influence in Central Asia and the Caucasus, which started almost as soon as the republics attained their independence, was viewed as a plot to create an artificial *cordon sanitaire* around Russia. Although Turkey hasn't succeeded in its policy of penetration due to reasons such as the incompatibility of economic mechanisms and outside influence, nevertheless it is widely alleged that Turkish influence will remain intact in the future.

There have been dozens of wars between Turkey—the former Ottoman Empire—and Russia, amounting to half of all wars Russia ever had. Influential political factions in the Russian Federation still consider Turkey one of Russia's main rivals in the world, and some political parties even include that assertion in their programs. However, Turkish ideas about Russia as one of the main obstacles to the growth of Turkish influence in the Turkic and Muslim world are well established in Turkey. The growing tension between the Russian Federation and Turkey may lead to a serious conflict, considering Turkey's membership in NATO, Turkey's rivals inside NATO, and the explosive situation connected to Turko-Slavic and Muslim-Orthodox boundaries in Eurasia.

Afghanistan was the major danger for the region and Russia. Afghan influence was destructive in Tajikistan and to a lesser extent in Uzbekistan. The victory of the Taliban in Afghanistan would have led to serious consequences for the Russian Federation, as the whole southern flank of the CIS would have been endangered.

INDIA'S WORRIES

The growth of Islamic fundamentalism in the region has stimulated Russia's rapprochement with not only India but also China. The governments of China and India began to discuss the threat of establishment of Islamic fundamentalist regimes in Central Asia in the 1990s. The Muslim arc stretches from northwestern Africa to southeastern Asia. India (with its 140 million Muslims), Russia, and China (with its Muslim population in the Xinjiang Uyghur Autonomous Region) face similar problems with the rise of Muslim extremism.

India is also on the alert. Taking into consideration fundamental contradictions with neighboring Pakistan and the existence of a huge Muslim minority, the Indian leadership anticipates various future scenarios, including negative ones. In 1999–2001, when the presidents of Uzbekistan and Kyrgyzstan visited India and Indian senior officials visited Central Asia, it was declared that the countries should coordinate efforts to counter the threats emanating from Muslim extremists. Several agreements were signed to face the onslaught of cross-border terrorism from the Pakistan-Afghanistan mujahideen hub. Some limited defense cooperation was also under way. India's main concern was related to Pakistan's policy in the region. New Delhi was sure that Pakistan wanted to increase its political and economic role in Central Asia in order to augment its geostrategic position and promote the process of Islamization.

India had grave apprehensions about Islamabad's attempt to create an anti-Indian bloc of Muslim countries, including the Central Asian states. The Pakistani authorities succeeded in creating a joint terrorist net of Muslim extremists from Afghanistan, Central Asia (mainly from Uzbekistan and Tajikistan), Xinjiang Uyghur Autonomous Region of China, and some Arab countries. The terrorists who had been trained on Pakistani territory participated in militant actions in Chechnya, Central Asia, and Kashmir.

China's perspective on the fight against Islamic terrorists is similar to India's in many regards. Throughout the 1990s, the Uyghur community in Central Asia boosted its activities, and groups calling for the independence of the Xinjiang Uyghur Autonomous Region started emerging. Uyghur separatists were captured and killed in both Kashmir and Chechnya. China had to rush to strengthen its borders and tighten the entry into the autonomous region. On the one hand, the problem of Uyghur separatists is not acute, because there is a predominance of ethnic Han Chinese in the Xinjiang Uyghur Autonomous Region. On the other hand, the autonomous regions are located along the borders of China and constitute more than a half of its territory. The Chinese authorities are worried that disturbances in one autonomous region can spread to the other. Beijing also has reasons to fear growing terrorist problems, even in Tibet, if extremism and terrorism is on the rise in the neighboring countries.

The situation in the triangle formed by China, India, and Russia is paradoxical. The growth of Islamic fundamentalism and the opposition to the unipolar position of the North is pushing rapprochement among these states. But there are great obstacles to their strategic alliance in a form of political-military axis.[2] Moreover, there is no need to create a new military bloc, which would be counterproductive for all countries. Nevertheless, the prospects of a comprehensive cooperation without the military component have improved.

Cooperation among the three countries against terrorism was already developing by the end of the 1990s. Russia and India created the Joint Working Group on Afghanistan and began exchanging information on Muslim terrorist groups. The National Security Council of India and the Security Council of the Russian Federation set up the Group on Terrorism. Russia, China, and the Central Asian republics created the Shanghai Cooperation Organization (SCO) in 1996. One of its primary goals was to accelerate joint activity against Islamic extremists. India was invited to become an observer of the SCO.

OTHER THREATS TO RUSSIAN SECURITY POSED BY CENTRAL ASIA

The unprecedented "sovereignization" of the republics that made up the former Soviet Union has not been supported by appropriate political rules, norms, and mechanisms to ensure civilized cohabitation of the newly independent states. As a result, the dividing line between aspirations of national resurrection and survival and the promotion of aggressive interests at the expense of other ethnic, religious, and cultural groups has dissipated almost entirely. The discrimination against the nonindigenous groups in most southern republics of the CIS (especially at the initial stage), as well as great economic difficulties, gave rise to uncontrolled migration of the Russian-speaking population to Russia. The percentage of Russians living in the states of Central

Asia has dropped radically. Russia, which is not ready to receive millions of immigrants, faces considerable difficulties. The Russian Federation is carrying out various state and international programs aimed at helping the migrants. On the whole, these programs turned out to be ineffective.

Poverty in Russia among these refugees is significant, primarily due to two factors. First, the refugees from hot spots like Tajikistan, Abkhazia, Azerbaijan, and Chechnya have lost not only their property but also their savings. Second, the overwhelming majority of the migrants who live beyond Russia's borders are city dwellers trained in industry, management, education, and health care. Due to the crisis and the suspension of housing construction, they are compelled to settle in rural areas and small towns, where they cannot find work and are automatically deprived of alternative employment. Marginalization of migrants is an acute problem.

There are other problems for migrants as well. Russian migrants experience culture shock in Russia because their previous local cultures made a great impact on their traditions and mentality. The situation with settlers representing other nations and ethnicities is even more difficult, particularly because Russia did not succeed in dampening the common aspiration in the post-Soviet space to create a "national" state and a "national" ideology, which is closer to chauvinism than positive nationalism. In the opinion of many Russians, migrants aggravate the sociopolitical situation. Many migrants believe that the negative manifestations of Russian democracy outweigh its achievements, and many of them adhere to extremely nationalist positions. This is especially dangerous in the frontier areas of Russia, where the percentage of migrants is particularly high. These sentiments may become a catalyst for negative tendencies in the society if democracy cannot meet overly optimistic expectations and subsequently gives rise to mass disappointment in democracy in general—not only in its Russian variant and in market reforms but in reforms generally. There could also be a popular revival of totalitarian ideologies and the spread of ideas such as "order at any cost."

Migration processes also have negative economic, political, and social consequences for the countries that lose migrants to Russia. A number of republics met with considerable difficulties, such as the mounting discontent of small ethnic groups, disruption in the work of industrial enterprises, the shrinking of higher and secondary educational institutions and medical services, and the drain of skilled manpower.

Interethnic relations in the region are aggravated by events in Afghanistan, where the Tajiks and Uzbeks oppose the Pashtuns. In its turn, Pakistan is on the brink of disintegration, and the federal government does not practically control the northern territories inhabited by the Pashtuns. (Pakistan is also a victim of arbitrary borders, which in this case were drawn by the British authorities.) Such conflicts are impacting on the security of Russia and have the potential to sharply increase the already powerful migration flow to Russia.

Other serious threats to Russia include the transit, import, and export of weapons and especially drugs. According to U.N. estimates, two to three hundred tons of pure heroin are transported from the region annually. The U.N. data shows that the production of raw opium poppies and heroin has risen dramatically during the past decade. Only six to seven years ago, Russia was mainly a transit country for the supply of drugs to Europe from the region. Now the Russian Federation is also a major consumer of drugs. The problem of drug addiction is more and more acute for Russia, and the authorities cannot cope with the growing importation of drugs. An effective control over the flow of such goods and their future elimination will be impossible without a consolidation of the regulatory functions of the state.

Russia created some problems for itself. It has no clearly developed policy with respect to the former Soviet republics. There are several Russian foreign policy concepts, complicating Russia's attitude toward the post-Soviet space. Ideologies dominate the elite, while public opinion is contradictory and scantily studied. Russian foreign policy contains all these approaches, which are combined in different ways at each new stage of development. A constant struggle between these ideas and the forces behind them affects the executive power and makes Russian policy very eclectic, with no clear tactical and strategic guiding lines. Ideas and practical steps for their implementation, such as perceiving Central Asian republics as "civilization ballast" or temporarily ignoring them on the assumption that historically these states "are doomed" to a new union with Russia can only result in growing unfriendliness toward the Russian Federation among its neighbors in the South.

This polarization on issues of substance is also reflected in the formulation of Central Asian strategy and in the functioning of foreign policy decision making. The interests of various institutions, political groups, and economic structures contradict each other on issues of Russian-Central Asian relations. There are no effective constitutional, political, or administrative means to negotiate between the differing interests and assist in bringing about a coherent and consistent national policy based on consensus.

The same can be said about the economic subsystem. Relations between Russia and the countries of the CIS in this sphere have tended to deteriorate. There is no economic cooperation between the Russian Federation and India in Central Asia. On the eve of the 1990s, India showed keen interest in developing links with the republics of the region, but India's possibilities turned out to be limited, even in trade. The only valuable goods for India are gas and oil, but the Russian Federation and India treat this problem differently. Political instability in Afghanistan prevents the construction of oil and gas pipelines from

Turkmenistan, Uzbekistan, and Kazakhstan to Pakistan via Afghanistan. The Russian perspective on the possible reduction of Central Asian dependence on the Russian transportation system is a complicated problem that deserves special analysis, but on the whole, the Russian government is not very enthusiastic about the prospect. India, however, is highly interested in energy exports from Central Asia to South Asia.

Nuclear development in South Asia is against the national interests of Russia and the Central Asian states. Both India and Pakistan, which have so far not signed the treaty on the nonproliferation of nuclear weapons, have active nuclear and ballistic missile programs. India's ruling circles invariably connect their ambition for permanent membership on the U.N. Security Council with the possession of nuclear weapons and their delivery systems. This consideration, along with fears of nuclear China and Pakistan's nuclear program, was one of the main factors that resulted in India's nuclear testing in 1998. Now India is ready for almost any concessions on this problem if its nuclear status is officially acknowledged. India's nuclear weapon will not be used against Russia, but India's testing encouraged the ambitions of other threshold states for legal nuclear weapons status. Indeed, Pakistan tested its nuclear devices immediately after India. Pakistan is one of the main state supporters of Islamic terrorists, and Pakistani leaders are constantly repeating the refrain that "the Pakistani nuclear bomb is a Muslim bomb." In December 2002, Vladimir Putin stated Russian fears that Pakistan's nuclear weapons could fall into terrorists' hands. The process of Islamicization that greatly impacted Pakistan's army could mean that Muslim radicals gain access to nuclear weapons in Pakistan. Thus proliferation of nuclear weapons in South Asia is a major challenge to Russia's security.

THE IMPACT OF THE ANTITERRORIST WAR FOR RUSSIA AND INDIA

After September 11, Russia began interacting with the United States on the Afghan problem. The Russian government passed on all information it had on Islamic terrorists and Afghanistan, including the Soviet experience of military operations in the mountainous country. The two countries coordinated all their activities in the Afghan crisis, although due to psychological reasons Russia would not consider taking part in combat operations. New Delhi and Washington also began an immediate exchange of information on Islamic terrorists.[3]

After the terrorist attack on the United States, there were many illusions about possible changes in the position of the West. A considerable part of the

Russian elite was satisfied with the rapprochement between Russia and the United States. Indeed, for the first time since the beginning of World War II, both countries had a joint enemy. Vladimir Putin's U.S. visit accelerated the improvement of bilateral relations. The Russian Federation agreed to the presence of U.S. troops in Uzbekistan and Kyrgyzstan because Washington had failed to create a military infrastructure in Pakistan. Moscow anticipated more than a dozen possible positive results from the American operation in Afghanistan. Unfortunately, not all the forecasts have been realized, but the temporary halt in the spread of Muslim radicalism in the region was one of few constructive outcomes for the Russian Federation.

The drug traffic was not stopped, as there is no effective action against the production of opium poppies and heroin in Afghanistan. The endless stream of hashish, opium, and heroin is still flowing into Russia from Afghanistan via the Central Asian republics. In 2002, the Russian border guards on the Afghan-Tajik border were involved in hundreds of military clashes with armed drug couriers and confiscated three tons of heroin.

On the whole, the position of the Russian-speaking population has even worsened. By the beginning of the new millennium, the republics realized that the Russian Federation guaranteed political stability in the region. The attacks of Islamic fundamentalists against Uzbekistan and Kyrgyzstan in 1999 and 2000 led to the strengthening of military-strategic ties between Russia and these republics. Although Central Asian authorities had to adjust their approach when Vladimir Putin took a firmer stance on discrimination toward the Russian population, stronger links with the United States mean that local elites do not have to be as responsive to Moscow's position.

There has been no significant change in the attitude of the West to the Chechen and Kashmir terrorists. Moscow and Delhi are again being blamed for "the violation of rights of noncombatant citizens." Practically nothing is being done to stop conservative Muslim regimes such as Saudi Arabia and the United Arab Emirates from financing terrorists.

Russia and India have to deal with terrorism without any real external support. As a result, the Russian Federation and India have grown closer. In November 2001, both sides signed the Moscow Declaration on International Terrorism. In 2002, Moscow and Delhi demonstrated a unanimous position on their common neighborhood—Afghanistan, Pakistan, and Central Asia—during the December visit of Vladimir Putin to India. It was decided to expand their close cooperation on Afghanistan. Both sides welcomed the implementation of the Bonn Agreement and declared full support to the Transitional Administration. Russia and India agreed to cooperate closely in the reconstruction efforts in Afghanistan in order to ensure the survival of Afghanistan as a state, free from terrorism, drugs, and external interference.

Both sides stated that they had a vital interest in maintaining security, stability, and a secular order in the Central Asian region. Russia and India proclaimed that the fight against terrorism should not apply double standards and condemned those who supported terrorism and financed, trained, or harbored terrorists. The leaders of the two countries signed an agreement to set up a Russia-India Joint Working Group on Counterterrorism. The significance of this joint cooperation in the fight against terrorism was emphasized by the fact that half of the Delhi Declaration on Further Consolidation of Strategic Partnership between the Russian Federation and the Republic of India was devoted to related problems.

New Delhi was satisfied with Moscow's stance on Pakistan. It had been suspicious of the links between the Russian Federation and Pakistan. For years, the Indian media was full of news about possible Russian weapons supplies to Pakistan. The reaction of India to the establishment of two Russia-Pakistan Joint Working Groups on Terrorism and Stability in August 2002 was rather negative. But in December 2002 the Russian leaders declared openly that Pakistan should dismantle the terrorist infrastructure under its control and reiterated Moscow's support for New Delhi on the issue of cross-border terrorism. They expressed understanding for India's concerns over the infiltration of groups of militants across the Line of Control in Jammu and Kashmir and agreed with the Indian stance that India-Pakistan talks should resume only after the fulfillment of Pakistan's obligations.

American military involvement in the region has produced contradictory reactions in India and Russia. Afghanistan and Pakistan are considered in India to be a part of South Asia, and New Delhi was always against the military involvement of great powers and superpowers in the region. The ruling circles of India regard the task of ensuring their country's security in terms of the entire subcontinent. Therefore it is natural that India strives to keep neighboring countries within India's sphere of influence, consolidate its "commanding positions" in South Asia, and oppose the participation of external forces in the settlement of regional problems. India believes that the attempt to bring controversial issues of bilateral relations to the attention of international forums and the involvement of external forces can only hinder the peaceful settlement of these problems and hurt regional security. India's neighbors, however, do not see any threat to their security from outside the region. Although the different classes of Indian society have a similar view regarding India's role in the region, there are differences over several aspects of regional policy. There are, for example, nuances in the platforms of the Bharatiya Janata Party, the Indian Congress and left-centrist alliances, but they refer not so much to the macro objectives as to the means of their achievement. Moreover, Indian officials are expressing open "disappointment" over the perceived U.S. "approach" of continuing to regard Islamabad as an antiterror ally.

Not all segments of Russian society are happy with the creation of a U.S. military network in Central Asia. For instance, the vast majority of Russian generals consider most of the concessions made by Moscow as traitorous and they oppose the presence of American troops in Central Asia because they predict that soon American bases will be aimed at Russia and Russian interests. Many experts and politicians state that U.S. policy has nothing in common with the fight against terrorism and Washington is simply trying to impose a Pax Americana on the whole world.

CONCLUSION

Russian foreign policy has become more pragmatic and profit oriented. Ensuring normal internal functioning takes precedence over achieving great power status or becoming a member of prestigious international organizations. The return to Asia, especially to such a long-standing and reliable partner as India, should be seen as the main way for solving Russia's external and internal problems. Both India and Russia have common goals in respect to the Islamic world. Both countries want to normalize relations with the region, both oppose the attempts of certain Western forces to impose on the countries the role of a vanguard in the struggle against the Muslim world, and both fight decisively against Islamic extremists. It would be useful to accelerate the activity of the Shanghai Cooperation Organization and admit India as a member. Moscow and New Delhi should not reject Western assistance in the struggle against terrorism, but there are great doubts about the possibility of such a scenario.

Western assistance is vital in another sphere of opposing the growth of Islamic extremism. For more than one century, the indigenous cultural elite who were educated in Russia or brought up in Russian culture was the most implacable opponent of the various versions of Islamic fundamentalism, since this group realized that it would have no place in their own country if government is Islamicized. As Central Asia now has limited cultural links with Russia, it is absolutely necessary for the West to support the expansion of this group that is highly opposed to Islamic radicalism.

NOTES

1. That this region of Kyrgyzstan is less religious is illustrated by the fact that 90 percent of mosque goers in Bishkek are Uzbeks, who make up only 1.5 percent of the population of the Kyrgyz capital.

2. Recently China started gradually leveling relations with India and Pakistan. But India still considers China an ally of Pakistan and a main strategic opponent in Asia from a long-term perspective. Indian military doctrine points to the possibility of waging "one and a half wars" with China and Pakistan. There has been no significant progress in Indo-Chinese negotiations on border problems. India is anxious about the continuation of Chinese-Pakistani military cooperation (especially in the nuclear sphere) and the perfection of nuclear weapons in China. In turn, China reacted negatively when India tested nuclear devices in May 1998. China's identification of India as its strategic opponent, its reluctance to challenge the United States openly, and its refusal to consider India and especially Russia as equal partners makes the establishment of the "strategic political and military partnership" of three giants of Eurasia practically impossible in the foreseeable future.

3. It is alleged that when the U.S. government first approached New Delhi after September 11 the Indian response was, "We have been passing to you all the information on terrorists in Kashmir, Pakistan and Afghanistan during the past fifteen years. We have nothing new to add."

13

Iran, Turkey, and Central Asia: The Islamic Connection

Shireen Hunter

Several important shifts happened simultaneously by early 1990 in Central Asia: the Soviet Union clearly could not survive much longer, cultural and religious Islam was experiencing a revival, and Central Asian countries were undergoing a resurgence of interest in their ethnic and cultural origins. The Islamic revival had a political dimension in the sense that certain groups of Muslim activists wanted to set up Islamic governments possibly modeled after Iran or Pakistan. Others merely wanted to ensure a greater political presence for Islam in the framework of basically secular forms of government. Furthermore, the more ardent Islamists did not rule out violence as a mean of achieving their goals. The moderate majority, however, favored gradual and peaceful change.

The Central Asians' revival of interest in their ethnic, historic, and cultural roots meant a greater interest in neighboring peoples and cultures with ethnic, linguistic, religious, and cultural links to these regions. A similar process was under way in neighboring countries, which after seventy years of nearly complete isolation from their ethnic and cultural kin were suddenly able to communicate with Central Asians freely. Even countries (notably Saudi Arabia, the Gulf states, and Egypt) that were not immediate neighbors of Central Asia and did not have close ethnic and cultural links with the Central Asian peoples beyond the common bond of Islam took a new interest in Central Asia. Nor was the desire to reconnect with ethnic and cultural kin the only motive in prompting these contacts, either on the part of the Central Asians or the neighboring and other Muslim states. Rather, more pragmatic economic and political motives were at least partly behind this newfound interest among the Central Asians and their neighboring kin.

Economically, the Central Asian countries hoped that some of the neighboring states (but even more so the oil-rich Arab states) would become important sources of economic assistance and a potential market. The statement by the president of Kyrgyzstan on the eve of his trip to Saudi Arabia that he "would be happy to make [perform] Hajj for $100 million" illustrates the relative weight of tangible economic factors as opposed to religious bonds.[1]

Countries such as Iran and Turkey were also interested in the economic potential of the region. Furthermore, all of Central Asia's near and distant neighbors were keen to impact the process of their political and cultural evolution and to shape their external behavior, especially the patterns of their international and regional alliances, in ways that would be congenial to their interests.

In some respects, especially as far as the Islamic dimension is concerned, Pakistan and a number of Arab countries exerted great influence in Central Asia on the eve of the Soviet Union's demise and some time afterward. Nonetheless, most Western analysts saw the competition for the hearts and minds of the Central Asians as being essentially between Turkey and Iran. That Iran and Turkey should be seen as the principal competitors was quite natural. Turkey has ethnic and linguistic ties with the region, and the influence of Iranian civilization—pre- and post-Islamic—is deep, even if unacknowledged. In fact, the title of an article by Daniel Pipes, "Turkic Peoples and Persian Cultures," illustrates the ethnic and cultural complexities of Central Asia.[2]

Many analyses of this competition were simplistic and cast in an almost Manichean form: Iran represented the dreaded Islamic model of government with a revolutionary and anti-Western worldview; Turkey, meanwhile, was the model of a progressive, secular, and democratic Muslim country with a pro-Western outlook. The logical conclusion was that the Central Asians should be dissuaded from emulating the Iranian model and that Iran should be prevented from establishing any significant presence in the region. By contrast, the West should promote Turkey as the model to be followed and as the best partner for the Central Asian countries.

In view of the hostile Iranian-Western relations and considering that Turkey was a staunch U.S. ally from a policy perspective, this strategy was natural and understandable. However, the notion that ideological and other competition between Iran and Turkey would determine the internal evolution and external orientation of post-Soviet Muslim republics was simplistic and flawed. The main flaws of this concept were the lack of recognition of Iran and Turkey's financial, economic, and other limitations; the far greater weight and impact of key international actors, most notably the United States but also Russia and Europe, on the processes of change in Central Asia; and the assumption that the Central Asian states would be passive recipients of ideas and models of development rather than active participants in the dynamic and complex process of nation building. Moreover, the pictures of Iran and Turkey represented in this concept did not totally correspond to the realities of the two countries.[3] In particular, Iran in the final decade of the twentieth century was very different from Iran of the 1980s in terms of its domestic challenges and foreign policy practices. To illustrate, by the time of the Soviet Union's collapse, the Islamic factor was a much less important determinant of Iran's foreign policy, although it continued to influence some important aspects of its foreign policy, notably relations with the United States. At the same time, notwithstanding Turkey's secular character, Islam was an important social and political force. Moreover, Turkey was not beyond using Islam to advance its foreign policy objectives, including in Central Asia, whenever it was expedient.

In short, a complex and varied set of domestic, regional, and international factors helped shape the policies of Turkey and Iran toward Central Asia, rather than mere ideological competition between the so-called Turkish and Iranian models of society and government. The same set of factors was also responsible for the successes and failures of Iran and Turkey as they have tried to expand their presence in Central Asia and protect themselves against any potential or actual threats emanating from the region.

IRAN AND TURKEY: DOMESTIC CONTEXT OF POLICY

The domestic contexts in which Iran and Turkey developed their strategy toward Central Asia were completely different, although there were some similarities between the two countries in terms of the identity-related challenges they faced.

Immediately before and after the Soviet Union's demise, the Iranian scene was dominated by the political, constitutional, and philosophical problems of transition to the post-Khomeini era as well as the urgency of postwar reconstruction and economic revitalization.[4] The Islamic regime faced its most serious challenge since its establishment in 1979. Losing its war with Iraq had seriously undermined the people's faith in the soundness and efficiency of a religiously based government. The war, but more importantly the international isolation that Iran faced despite having been the victim of Iraqi aggression, had seriously discredited the ideology of the regime and the foreign policy derived from it. Doubts about the soundness of Iranian foreign policy had even reached the country's key leadership. Furthermore, after eight years of hardship and sacrifice the Iranian people were demanding improved living conditions and were not interested in attaining influence abroad. The gradual but steady erosion of popular faith in the ideology of the regime with its excessive emphasis on Islam also helped loosen their religious values, a process that would accelerate in the next decade. The erosion of popular faith in Islamist ideology led to a revival of Iranian nationalism, which had remained strong despite the efforts of the Islamic regime to eliminate it, especially during the early years of the revolution.

The changes occurring in the Soviet Union, coupled with factors already noted, generated a debate in Turkey about the country's national identity and its Kemalist ideology, especially as it applied to foreign policy. Turkey's application in 1987 to full membership in the European Community (now the European Union) and its subsequent rejection intensified this debate, since many Turks interpreted rejection as the denial of their Europeanness, thus leading to a debate about Turkey's identity and the framework of its foreign policy. During this time, two ideas gained special currency in the basic strategy of Turkish foreign policy: forging a close strategic alliance with the United States and adopting an eastern orientation. Later geographic, economic, and other realities would force Turkey to adopt a combination of these strategies, with the European focus becoming dominant by the mid-1990s.[5] It also led to the emergence of three alternative conceptual frameworks for the future conduct of Turkish foreign policy. The first of these concepts was neo-Ottomanism, which emerged when Turkey's Ottoman past was reassessed and efforts were made to apply some of its features to the new conditions. The second concept was a new version of pan-Turkism. The third idea was an alternative vision of Eurasia with Turkey as the economic and political hub and the geographic linchpin between Europe and Asia.

IRAN, TURKEY, AND CENTRAL ASIA: ASSETS AND LIABILITIES

In their efforts to expand ties with Central Asia, Iran and Turkey each benefited from certain assets and suffered from certain liabilities. In Turkey's case, undue emphasis has been put on its ethnic and linguistic ties with the Central Asian countries, while the lack of such ties was considered a serious handicap in Iran's case. In reality, however, these factors in themselves were neither great help nor serious hindrance.

In Turkey's case certain common Turkic roots and similarities between Turkish and various Turkic languages have been an asset. However, their impact has been less significant than is generally assumed. Turkic languages, even in Central Asia, are not mutually understandable; they are certainly not the same as modern post-Ottoman Turkish. The fact that modern Turkish is written in a Latin alphabet makes it difficult to learn for those who are acquainted with Arabic script or old Turkish. Central Asian countries still use the Cyrillic alphabet, which makes learning modern Turkish difficult. Individual ethnic identities of Central Asian countries are also quite pronounced and cannot be easily submerged within common Turkic roots. Rather, Turkey's other advantages have played more important roles. A major Turkish asset has been its vibrant private sector as well as its nongovernmental organizations, including Islamic organizations. These industrial concerns and NGOs have expanded Turkey's presence, while contributing to the physical and intellectual development of Central Asia.

In Iran's case the lack of common ethnic roots (with the exception of the Tajiks) and linguistic ties is compensated by the following factors. First, the Persian language was the literary language of the region, and every educated person in Central Asia was acquainted with Persian language and literature until the Bolshevik Revolution. Second, the high culture of Central Asia was immensely influenced by the Iranian civilization. Daniel Pipes's characterization of Central Asia as "Turkic peoples, Persian cultures" is correct, although increasingly the Iranian heritage has been denied, destroyed, or given a Turkic veneer. The following comment by Kyrgyzstan's former president Askar Akayev illustrates that had it not been for other systemic factors, Iran's lack of common ethnic and linguistic roots would not have been an insurmountable barrier in establishing ties with Central Asia. President Akayev told the visiting Iranian foreign minister that he was proud to have been brought up in a household that owned such works of Persian literature as *Shahnameh* of Firdowsi and *Gulistan* of Saadi.[6] Iran's principal asset, but one that has remained undeveloped, is its geographic location and its ability to offer economical access to the outside world to the landlocked Central Asian countries by rail, road, and sea. By contrast, physical remoteness of Turkey has limited its value in this respect, despite the establishment of considerable air links between Turkey and the region.

Iran's most serious liability in terms of relations with Central Asia has been the strong U.S. opposition to its presence and Russian ambivalence toward more extensive Iranian-Central Asian ties. Until 1994 Russia, too, was against significant Iranian presence in the region. And even after improvement in Russian-Iranian relations, Russia has not encouraged more extensive ties between Iran and Central Asia. Meanwhile, Turkey's position in Central Asia, including places such as Tajikistan and Afghanistan with which it has neither ethnic nor linguistic affinity, has benefited from Western support. For example, with Western approval Turkey has acted as liaison between NATO and Central Asian countries. Turkey was also made to implement various projects funded by international organizations and the U.S. Aid Agency (USAID). Meanwhile

U.S. sanctions discouraged foreign investment, contributed to Iran's economic difficulties, and handicapped it as an economic partner.

DETERMINANTS AND INSTRUMENTS OF POLICY: IRAN

Iran's policy toward Central Asia and the Caucasus has been security driven. Thus Iran's highest priority has been to safeguard its security and above all its territorial integrity. This security-driven policy, coupled with the de-ideologization of Iran's overall foreign policy and the growing importance of national interest, has emphasized state-to-state relations rather than close ties with the region's Islamist movements.

A good example of this aspect of Iran's policy is its approach to events in Tajikistan between 1992 and 1997. Iran did not provide military assistance to the Tajik Islamic forces in their confrontation with the Rahman Nabiev and Imomali Rakhmanov governments and even failed to give them any ideological support. On the contrary, Iran refrained from identifying the conflict in Tajikistan as an ideological battle between those wanting to establish a new system of government based on Islam and the Soviet-era leadership. Rather, it attributed it to Tajikistan's regional differences and clan rivalries. Iran even played host to Tajikistan's president Rahman Nabiev in June 1992 at a crucial moment in the emerging Tajik civil war. The Iranian government's attitude caused tension in its relations with the Islamic opposition in Tajikistan, especially the faction led by Shaikh Abdullah Nouri, who was close to Pakistan. Nevertheless, Iran retained contacts with the leaders of Tajikistan's Islamic and secular oppositions. Qadi Akhbar Turajanzadeh and Yusuf Shadman lived in Iran for a number of years. These contacts later enabled Iran to play a crucial, albeit largely unrecognized, role in bringing the Tajik civil war to an end.

Indeed, trying to help mediate regional conflicts has been an important feature of the Iranian policy toward Central Asia and the Caucasus. During the early part of 1992 Iran tried to mediate between Azerbaijan and Armenia. However, because of Azerbaijan's domestic power struggles and the opposition of key international and regional actors, including Turkey, Iran's efforts did not succeed. The Turkish prime minister, Suleiman Demirel, expressed Turkey's attitude when he said that the failure of Iranian mediation showed that Azerbaijan should not run to Iran to solve its problems.[7]

Iran's security-driven policy has also led it to emphasize the sanctity and inviolability of existing borders. For example, Iran and Turkmenistan have agreed to their current borders. Even in regard to countries such as Uzbekistan that have not been friendly toward it, Iran has refrained from supporting the Islamic opposition, although the Iranian media, including its official news agency IRNA, has occasionally criticized the mistreatment of Muslim activists and observant Muslims by the Uzbek authorities.[8]

Iran's policy toward Central Asia and the Caucasus has been heavily influenced by its desire to remain on good terms with Russia, even when the latter has been less than enthusiastic for close ties with Iran. In fact, Russian-Iranian relations have been heavily one-sided. Iran's Moscow-centered policy has been largely a function of its troubled relations with the United States and its desperate search for a counterweight to U.S. power and sources of military and industrial supplies. The desire to remain on good terms with Russia is another reason why the Islamic factor has not played a major role in Iran's policy toward Central Asia. Any Iranian manipulation of Islamic forces in the region would have seriously undermined its ties to Moscow.

Iran has tried to establish an economic and political presence in Central Asia against all odds. The main instrument of Iran's policy in advancing its goals has been its geopolitical location. For example, in order to make itself more attractive as an outlet to the outside world despite its financial problems, in the 1990s Iran invested heavily in expanding its rail network and extending it to the borders of Central Asia. A major step in this direction was the inauguration on March 17, 1995, of the 703-kilometer railroad connecting Bafg in southern Iran with the port city of Bandar Abbas in the Persian Gulf. The presidents of Turkmenistan, Kyrgyzstan, Armenia, and Afghanistan and senior representatives of neighboring countries attended the opening ceremony.[9] In 2005, the railroad was extended from Bafg to Mashhad. During the opening ceremonies President Mohammad Khatami and representatives of Central Asian countries were present. With this extension, Central Asia came closer to the Persian Gulf by 800 kilometers.[10] In May 1996, Iran's President Akbar Hashemi Rafsanjani inaugurated the Mashhad-Sarakhs-Tedzhen railroad in the presence of eleven heads of state, including Turkish president Suleiman Demirel.[11] Considering the fact that Iran is connected by rail to Azerbaijan and under the right circumstances— availability of financing and absence of political obstruction—can expand its rail links with Turkey, Afghanistan, and Pakistan, it can greatly contribute to the expansion of Central Asia's and Eurasia's transportation network. The beginning of a weekly train service from Almaty in Kazakhstan to Tehran, the Iranian capital, in March 2002 as part of an agreement to revive the Silk Road in the framework of the Economic Cooperation Organization was another important step in this direction. Iran is also a key link in the establishment of a north-south transport corridor linking India to Russia via Iranian ports and territory.[12] Iran has also tried to emphasize its advantages as an energy export route.

Central Asian energy producers and oil industry experts agree that from an economic and a geographical perspective Iran is the most logical export route for a considerable portion of Central Asian energy. Even without building a long pipeline to the Persian Gulf, in view of the patterns of Iran's energy consumption and production, it can use swap arrangements to serve as an outlet for Central Asian and Azerbaijani energy. Already a limited amount of Kazakh oil is exported through swap arrangements with Iran. And there is a pipeline carrying Turkmen gas to northern Iran. However, pipelines and alternative transportation networks have political dimensions, and hence, decisions regarding them are taken in light of political and strategic considerations. Indeed, from a geopolitical perspective an argument can be made in favor of an export pipeline that does not end in the Persian Gulf, since already a significant portion of oil consumed globally passes through the Persian Gulf. What is less understandable is the opposition to even partial passage of a pipeline through Iranian territory. Be that as it may, because of U.S. opposition despite all its geopolitical advantages, Iran has failed to convince the Central Asian countries and the oil companies that it is a viable export outlet. However, if some reports are to be believed, the governments of Kazakhstan, Turkmenistan, and Iran have been discussing the possibility of an oil pipeline. The main investor would be the French oil concern TotalFinaElf.[13]

Iran's ability to expand economic and trade relations with the Central Asian countries has also been undermined by political factors, notably U.S. opposition and various economic sanctions imposed on Iran and on potential investors in Iran (Iran-Libya Sanctions Act of 1996) that targeted Iran's energy sector. These sanctions have prevented the revitalization of the Iranian economy and hence its attraction as an economic partner.

Iran has managed to establish some economic and trade relations with Central Asian countries nevertheless. According to recent reports, the volume of trade between Iran and Turkmenistan reached $430 million in 2000, from $72 million in 1994, and the level of Iran-Kazakh trade in 2000 was $220 million.[14] According to Kazakhstani sources, in 2002 it reached $500 million.[15] By the first half of 2004 the volume of trade between the two countries had reached $370 million.[16] According to IRNA, the volume of trade between Iran and Uzbekistan for the first ten months of 2002 was $150 million, as compared to $100 million in 2001. In 2005 the volume of trade between Iran and Kyrgyzstan stood at $200 million. The lowest volume of trade has been with Tajikistan. In 2005 the volume of trade between the two countries reached $37 million.[17] In 2001 the total volume of trade was $30 million and in 2002 was reduced to $29.3 million.[18] However, according to some reports, the volume of trade during the first quarter of 2005 reached $75 million.[19] This situation shows that in Iran's case, economic factors rather than bonds of linguistic, ethnic, and cultural kinship have determined the extent of economic and financial relations. In addition to trade, a number of Iranian private companies are involved in joint projects in Central

Asia. Moreover, Iran has been involved in planning and implementing several joint projects with a number of Central Asian countries. Among these are the construction of the Dousti (Friendship) dam along Harir Rud between Iran and Turkmenistan, which was inaugurated in April 2005.[20] In December 2003, Iran agreed to fund the Sangtoodeh hydroplant in Tajikistan at a cost of $360 million.[21]

DETERMINANTS AND INSTRUMENTS OF POLICY: TURKEY

In contrast to Iran, Turkey has assigned security concerns a less important role in its approach toward Central Asia. This is natural because Turkey does not have common borders with Central Asia and does not face the same kind of challenges. The situation has been different in the Caucasus, where Turkey's proximity has made it more vulnerable to regional conflicts. But even in the Caucasus Turkey's vulnerability has been lower than Iran's. Turkey's principal security concern has been that none of its rivals, especially Russia, be allowed to dominate the region and thus prevent Turkey from expanding its own cultural and economic influence. In the Caucasus, Turkey's main focus has been Azerbaijan, largely because of its energy resources. Another reason has been Azerbaijan's proximity to Iran and the existence of extensive historic, religious, and cultural links between the two. Iran could be a significant rival to Turkey under different circumstances notwithstanding the currently tense Iranian-Azerbaijani relations.

A principal purpose of Turkey's foreign policy toward Central Asia and the Caucasus, as well as some other parts of the post-Soviet space, has been to make Turkey the new hub and center of a new version of Eurasianism. Turkey's NATO membership means that its version of Eurasia is Western oriented. Duygu Bazoglu Sezer juxtaposes the Russian and Turkish versions of Eurasia and explains how these diverging views create tension in Russian-Turkish relations. Writing in the pre–September 11 period, Sezer comments, "Russia, still the pre-eminent power in Eurasia, strongly resists a greater regional role for external actors. . . . Trans-Atlantic powers are especially not welcome. . . . Russia entertains a Russia-centered vision of Eurasia. . . . This Russian vision, this impulse introduces an element of systemic tensions into Turkish-Russian relations. . . . *In the case of Turkey it is the country's continuing membership of the Trans-Atlantic system at the southwestern doorsteps of Eurasia, coupled with its aspiration to connect it with an open system, which exerts similar tensions in bilateral relations*" (emphasis added).[22] The best example of this Turkish drive is its effort to become a significant export route for Central Asian energy to the European markets.

Eurasia interpreted in a broad geographic, economic, and cultural sense, rather than an ideological sense as understood by certain schools of political thought in Russia, can accommodate both Russian and Turkish aspirations. In fact, in the post–September 11 international context characterized by better Russian-U.S. relations (notwithstanding tension in 2004–2005 over the U.S. perception of Russia's backsliding on its democratization process and the introduction of trans-Atlantic forces in traditional Eurasia), Turkey and Russia have emerged as complementary centers of an extended definition of Eurasia. In fact, Turks and Russians have lately been referring to each other as two great Eurasian powers. In achieving its goal as the hub (or at least one of the hubs) of a vast Eurasian landmass and as the bridge between it and the rest of the world, Turkey suffers from geopolitical handicaps, notably the lack of common borders with the Central Asian states.

In addition to Eurasianism, Turkey's policy toward Central Asia has been influenced by a mild and mostly cultural form of pan-Turkism. In fact, this ideology is the cultural and to some degree political arm of Turkey's version of Eurasianism. This Turkish policy is also linked with the evolving politics of identity in Turkey and competing influences of westernization and different varieties of Turkism, including one that has a heavy dose of Islam. Hakan Yazuz argues that Turkey's foreign policy is closely linked with its identity politics. This has especially been true in Central Asia and the Balkans. He also maintains that often there is a disconnect between official and popular definitions of Turkish identity.[23]

Turkey's Kemalist ideology was increasingly questioned and Turkism and Islam acquired greater currency following changes in the Soviet Union. However, the identity-related aspect of Turkish policy toward Central Asia should not be exaggerated, especially if Turkism is interpreted as a repudiation of westernization. A more correct interpretation of Turkish identity is its multidimensionality, although the importance of various dimensions may differ in the case of different segments of the population and according to different circumstances. In terms of its relation to foreign policy, identity can acquire a utilitarian and instrumental aspect. In Turkey's case, this has been true of both Islam and Turkism. Turkey has used both its Turkic and Islamic credentials to advance its goals in Central Asia and other Muslim parts of the post-Soviet space.

A principal goal of Turkish diplomacy in Central Asia and the Caucasus has been to shape the characteristics and inclinations of the new generation of Central Asian elites. Another long-term Turkish ambition has been to make the Turkish language the principal instrument of at least intraelite communication in Central Asia and the Caucasus. To achieve this goal, Turkey has pursued an active policy of establishing Turkish schools in Central Asia, the Caucasus, and even parts of the Russian Federation, notably the north Caucasus, and offering scholarships to Central Asian students. In the early 1990s Turkey offered 10,000 scholarships to Central Asian students. By 2001, 70,000 students were studying in Turkey.[24]

Certain Turkish official religious institutions have also tried to export a "soft and nationalized Turkish Islam" to Central Asia. The main institution carrying this task has been the Foundation of Turkish Religious Affairs, known as Turk Diyanet Vakfi (TDV).[25] Two reasons explain this aspect of Turkey's approach toward Central Asia: pragmatic and ideological. From a pragmatic perspective Turkey realized that the growing interest in Islam in Central Asia and the Caucasus meant that if Turkey did not spread its version of Islam, the Saudi, Iranian, and Pakistani varieties would fill the vacuum, thus potentially undermining Turkey's position. Ideologically, some in Turkey, including TDV head Mehmet N. Yilmaz, believed in the Islamic basis of Turkish national identity. Hence, by spreading Islam, Turkey was also spreading the spirit of Turkishness to Central Asia.[26] The TDV has built mosques, renovated holy shrines, and organized congresses. The TDV held the first Eurasian Islamic Congress on October 23–25, 1995. In addition to Central Asian and Caucasian countries, representatives of other countries and autonomous regions were invited. The second congress took place in 1996 and established a permanent secretariat in Ankara. In short, according to one scholar in Central Asia, "the Republic of Turkey has managed to become the main center of Islamic activism and a source of support for Turkish and Muslim communities."[27] All these are ultimately aimed to transform the Central Asian Turkic states into mirror images of Turkey. This goal is reflected in the use of the world "Turkish" rather than "Turkic" when referring to the community of Turkic states.[28]

The growing relationship between the Turkish military establishment and the military establishments of the Central Asian and Caucasian states (including training these countries' military personnel) is another way Turkey has been trying to shape the new generation of Central Asian elite.[29] Turkey's membership in NATO has given it certain advantages in this regard, especially after NATO's Partnership for Peace (PFP) program was set up.

The political dimension of the ideological factors underpinning Turkey's approach toward Central Asia has been the creation of a Turkic (Turkish) bloc. The main instrument for this has been regular Turkic summits. While important as a framework for Turkey's political relations with the Central Asian countries, these summits have not yet been transformed into a structured organization such as the League of Arab States, which some Turkish observers and analysts had hoped for. A principal impediment to building such a bloc has been the region's continuing links to Russia and membership in the

Commonwealth of the Independent States, even if the CIS has not so far been a successful instrument of either economic integration or collective security.

Turkey's economic relations with the Central Asian countries have expanded significantly through the efforts by the government and the Turkish private sector. The main governmental agency active in this field is the Turkish International Cooperation Agency (TICA) established in 1992, which provides project assistance in a variety of areas from agriculture to tourism and insurance. The Turkish Exembank has also granted credits to these countries, amounting to around $797 million in 2001.[30] But the main impetus behind Turkey's presence has been its private sector. According to official Turkish sources, by 2001 approximately 900 Turkish companies were active in Central Asia. The total amount of private investment had reached $3.5 billion. Turkish construction companies had also completed work valued at $7–8 billion.[31] However, the volume of trade between Turkey and Central Asia has remained quite low and amounted to $600 million in 2001.[32] There was no significant increase in the volume of trade during the intervening years.

ASSESSMENT OF TURKISH AND IRANIAN PERFORMANCE AND FUTURE OUTLOOK

Considering the systemic barriers and other limitations Iran has faced, its diplomacy has performed better than expected. Perhaps Iran's greatest accomplishment has been to prevent its demonization in the eyes of the Central Asians. Indeed, by the mid-1990s, Afghanistan and Pakistan and not Iran were viewed as the main sources of Muslim extremist threat to Central Asia. Iran has also established a foothold in Central Asia despite tremendous odds. President Muhammad Khatami's successful visit to Central Asia in April 2002 was evidence of this. He received a good reception, even in Uzbekistan. President Karimov praised Khatami for his initiative on the dialogue of civilizations and called Iran a reliable trade partner and talked about building a road from Termez to Iran through Afghanistan.[33] Khatami also got a reasonable reception in Kazakhstan. Considering the fact that, according to some sources, American officials had "advised the Kazakhstani government to decline Khatami's offer to visit," even paying this state visit was an accomplishment.[34]

Turkey has made great strides in efforts to establish itself as a main force in Central Asia in absolute terms. However, given all of Turkey's advantages, its success has not been as great as could have been expected. Even at the political level, Turkey's relations with Central Asian countries have not been free of tension. In 2000, relations with Uzbekistan suffered seriously because of the activities of the Uzbek nationalist leader Muhamed Salih, who was allegedly involved in an assassination attempt against President Karimov. Recently, Turkish nationals were accused of involvement in a plot to assassinate Turkmenistan's president Niyazov.[35] When the leader of Turkey's ruling party, Recep Tayyip Erdogan, set off for a tour of Central Asia in January 2003, some commentators said that his purpose was to "revive flagging ties" with these states.[36]

In the future, with the growing involvement of Central Asian countries in the world community, the pattern of their relations is likely to become even more complex. Therefore, while Turkey will continue to remain an important partner and a significant cultural presence in the region, its more ambitious expectations are unlikely to be realized. In Iran's case, much would depend on its internal development and the state of its relations with the United States. If they improve, Iran will become a more important player in the region. Otherwise Iran likely will remain on the margins, unless other key players such as Russia, China, and Europe reevaluate their policies toward the region and Iran's potential role in it. As of this writing, however, controversy over Iran's nuclear ambitions cloud the future of its relations with the United States and Europe, thus making any immediate improvement in its prospects in Central Asia unlikely.

NOTES

1. Quoted in Eugene Husky, "Kyrgyzstan Leaves the Ruble Zone," *Radio Free Europe/Radio Liberty (RFE/RL) Research Report* 2, no. 35 (1993): 21.

2. Daniel Pipes, "Turkic Peoples and Persian Cultures," *Middle East Insight* 10, no. 1 (1994): 34–35.

3. Some analysts at the time pointed out these flaws. Shireen T. Hunter, "The Muslim Republics of the Former Soviet Union: Policy Challenges for the United States," *Washington Quarterly,* Summer 1992.

4. On Iran's domestic challenges, see Shireen T. Hunter, *Iran after Khomeini* (Washington, D.C.: CSIS/Praeger. 1992).

5. For a discussion of these issues, see Shireen T. Hunter, *Turkey at the Crossroads: Islamic Past or European Future,* CEPS Paper no. 3 (Brussels: Centre for European Policy Studies, 1995).

6. Quoted in editor's note, *Central Asia and Caucasian Review,* Summer 1992, 5–6. In Persian. The review is published in Tehran.

7. For details of Turkish and Iranian policies toward Azerbaijan in this period, see Shireen T. Hunter, *The Trans-Caucasus in Transition: Nation-Building and Conflict* (Washington, D.C.: Center for Strategic and International Studies/Westview Press, 1994), 161–76.

8. Uzbek president Islam Karimov was the only head of state who supported U.S. sanctions on Iran in 1995. On a 2002 visit to the United States, Karimov warned the

United States about Iranian meddling in Afghanistan. On Iranian media criticism of Uzbekistan's treatment of Muslims, see "Mashhad Radio: Uzbekistan Persecuting Islamist's Family," *FBIS-SOV-98-301,* October 28, 1998.

9. "Rafsanjani Opens Historic Rail Link," *Middle East Economic Digest,* March 31, 1995, 16–17.

10. "Asia-e-miane shatisaf kilometer beh khalij-e-fars nardikvarshod," BBCPersian.com (May 3, 2005).

11. "Iran-Central Asia Rail Link Opened," *Turkish Daily News.* Reprinted in News Archive, www.msedv.com/rai/archive.html (May 6, 2005).

12. The north-south corridor is to link Mumbai (Bombay) in India with St. Petersburg in Russia—the Indian Ocean with the Baltic Sea. Sudha Ramachandran, "India, Iran, Russia Map Out Trade Route," *Asia Times* online (June 29, 2002).

13. "Technical-Economical Support for Kazakhstan-Turkmenistan-Iran Oil Pipeline Is Examined by the Governments of Three Countries As Well As by the Foreign Oil Companies," *Kazakhstan Today,* http://gazeta.kz/art.asp?ai=24453 (February 6, 2003).

14. Quoted in Charles Recknagel, "Iran: Khatami Tours Central Asia to Press for Iran Energy Routes, Lower US Presence," *RFE/RL Newsline,* April 25, 2002.

15. "Torgovo-promyshlenniy oborot mezhdu kazakhstanom i iranom v 2002 godu sostavil $500 mln" (Trade level between Iran and Kazakhstan reached $500 million in 2002), *Gazeta.KZ* (Kazakhstan Today), February 6, 2002.

16. "Kazakhstan Reiterates Interest in Exporting Oil via Iran," *Interfax-Kazakhstan,* October 5, 2004.

17. "Kazakhstan Reiterates Interest."

18. See "Minister inostrannih del uzbekistana posetit tegeran s vizitom v sleduyuschem mesyatse" (Minister of foreign affairs of Uzbekistan will visit Tehran next month), *Iran.RU,* December 20, 2002, www.iran.ru/rus/news_iran.PhP?act_news_by_id&newws_id=1327; "Obyem tovarooborota mezhdu islamskoi respublikoi iran i tadzhikistanom v etom godu dostig 29.3 millionov dollarov" (Trade between the Islamic Republic of Iran and Tajikistan reached $29.3 million this year), *Iran.RU,* December 18, 2002, www.iran.ru/rus/news_iran.PhP?act_news_by_id&newws_id=1327.

19. "Neshast moshtarak bazarganan irani va Tajik" (The joint session of Iranian and Tajik businessmen), BBCPERSIAN.com, May 25, 2005.

20. "Iranian, Turkmen Leaders Discuss Regional Developments at Dam Inauguration," *IRNA,* April 2005.

21. "Iran, Tajikistan Sign Agreement to Implement Hydroplant Project," *IRNA,* December 2003.

22. Duygu Bazoglu Sezer, "Turkish-Russian Relations a Decade Later: From Adversity to Managed Competition," *Perceptions, Journal of International Affairs,* March-May 2001, www.mfa.gov.tr/grupa/perspet/VI-I/dbseszer.05.html.

23. M. Hakam Yavuz, "Turkish Identity Politics and Central Asia," in Roald Sagdeev and Susan Eisenhower, eds., *Islam and Central Asia: An Enduring Legacy or an Evolving Threat* (Washington, D.C.: Center for Political and Strategic Studies, 2000), 193–212.

24. "Turkey's Relations with Central Asian Republics," Republic of Turkey, Ministry of Foreign Affairs, www.mfa.gov/tr/grupa/al/asian/html (May 2005).

25. Quoted in Yavuz, "Turkish Identity Politics," 208.

26. Yavuz, "Turkish Identity Politics," 208. According to Mehmet Yilmaz, "If we [Turks] take those acquired Islamic characteristics out of Turkish national identity there will be little left behind. Islam molds Turkish national identity: Islam is both reason and guarantor of our [Turks] national existence."

27. Yavuz, "Turkish Identity Politics," 209–10.

28. Shireen T. Hunter, "Turkey's Deficient Foreign Options," *Middle East International,* May 17, 1991.

29. For example, Turkey has been involved in training the Azerbaijani military. Turkey also has military cooperation agreements with most Central Asian countries. See "Turkey Trains, Equips Uzbek Military," *Turkish Daily News,* March 7, 2002; "Turkey, Turkmenistan Sign Military Donation Agreement, Financial Aid Protocol," *FBIS/WEU-2002-0313,* March 12, 2002; "Azerbaijani-Turkish Defense Ministers Discuss Expanding Cooperation," *FBIS/SOV-2002-0508,* May 7, 2002; "Turkey to Give Kyrgyzstan $1 Million to Aid Armed Forces," *FBIS/SOV-2002-0615,* June 15, 2002; "Turkish Armed Forces Donates 2 Trucks of Equipment, Devices to Kazakh Army," *FBIS/SOV-2001-0424,* April 24, 2001. This aid "was delivered to Kazakhstan within the framework of the cooperation agreement between the defense ministers of Turkey and Kazakhstan."

30. "Turkey's Relations with the Central Asian Republics."

31. "Turkey's Relations with the Central Asian Republics."

32. "Turkey's Relations with the Central Asian Republics."

33. "Khatami Says Iran Ready to Help Uzbekistan Develop," *FBIS/NES-2002-0429,* April 29, 2002. Also "Uzbek-Iranian Presidents Discuss Afghanistan," Interfax as reported in Eurasianet.org, April 29, 2002.

34. Ibraghim Alibekov, "Khatami in Kazakhstan Asserts Iran as a Critical Partner for Kazakhstan," *Eurasia Insight,* April 26, 2002.

35. Regarding the names of Turkish citizens involved in the coup attempt, see "Prosecutor General Gives Details of Attempted Coup," www.saeedi.4t.com/custom3 .html (November 26, 2002); and Tariq Saeedi, "Turkmenistan Weathers Three Storms in One Month," *Central Asia Mirror,* January 19, 2003.

36. Antonie Blua, "Turkey: Erdogan Begins Tour of Turkic-speaking Countries of the Former Soviet Union," *RFE/RL,* January 7, 2003, www.rferl.org/nca/features/ 2003/1/07012003162214.asp.

14

Chinese-Russian Strategic Relations:
The Central Asian Angle

Feng Shaolei

Located in the intersection of different cultures and civilizations, Central Asia has a strategic value for powers such as Russia, the United States, China, Turkey, and Iran. The great power competition carried out among these culturally diverse powers exerts a profound influence on regional affairs.[1] Zbigniew Brzezinski was right in describing Central Asia as the Balkan Peninsula of the Eurasian continent.[2] It is important, then, to view Sino-Russian relations within the context of the Central Asian region primarily because changed international relations in Central Asia reflect the track of development of Sino-Russian relations in the decade after the end of the Cold War. Additionally, the September 11 incident brought Central Asia into a new stage of development in terms of Sino-Russian relations—the thesis of this chapter.

POST–COLD WAR CHINESE-RUSSIAN RELATIONS

Russia's Central Asian Policies

The breakup of the Soviet Union not only led to the disappearance of a superpower but also created a geopolitical vacuum in Central Asia. However paradoxical it might seem, from 1989 to 1996, this geopolitical vacuum was acceptable to nearly all the governments with an interest in the region.[3] To some degree, Konstantin Syroezhkin is right in saying that during the first phase of the post–Cold War period (1991–1993), this geopolitical vacuum was due to Russian policies toward the region. While making an immense effort to achieve closer ties with the United States and Western countries, Russia forfeited many opportunities to preserve its influence in Central Asia.

Russia unquestionably had opportunities to preserve its influence in Central Asia.[4] These derived partly from objective conditions such as economic ties, a single cultural and intellectual space, the substantial Russian ethnic diaspora in the region, the continuing positive image of Russia as an economic and political partner, and various political levers of influence. Complementing these objective circumstances were the subjective factors. The fear of destabilization in the event of a sudden Russian withdrawal and the uncertainties about independently resolving inter- and intrastate conflicts made the model of mutual cooperation with Russia attractive. The personal factor was also of substantial significance: most leaders in Central Asia were Boris Yeltsin's former colleagues in the former Central Committee of the Communist Party or had obtained their posts with his support.[5]

Many Central Asian leaders still wished to improve their relationship with Russia in the early 1990s in hopes of counterbalancing the damage caused to the relationship between Central Asian countries and Russia by the rise of nationalism. However, with the tendency toward westernization within the Russian regime, Russia failed to take advantage of these circumstances to achieve integration in economic, political, and military spheres.[6] On the contrary, in the summer of 1993 Moscow created a new currency that essentially excluded Central Asia from the ruble zone, thereby precipitating decisions to introduce national currencies in Central Asia and undercutting Russian influence. In terms of trade, prices, payments, and currency exchange, the Central Asian states were now no different from the "far abroad"—countries outside of the former Soviet Union.[7]

Russia's policies toward Central Asia at the time were also influenced more or less by rising nationalism in Russia, which greatly changed the traditional relationship between Russia and Central Asia. However, in spite of its official policies, Russia retained a large influence. One factor was the weakness of the political elite in Tajikistan; Tajikistan's domestic strife gave Russia no choice but to intercede. Moscow also felt that it had to repulse the external threat from Afghanistan. Indeed, as events later showed, the Afghan threat would prove decisive in relations between Russia and Central Asia.

In a divergence from Konstantin Syroezhkin's opinion, Russia still enjoyed obvious strength in Central Asia. Although the Central Asian states attached importance to the United States, Western Europe, China, Turkey, and Iran, Russia enjoyed the most prestige with Central Asian countries. After a short period of chaos, Russian President Boris Yeltsin publicly announced in early 1993 that the Commonwealth of Independent States (CIS) was the basis of Russia's fundamental interests. He further described Russia's relationship with the former Soviet republics as "special." However, in spite of this rhetoric, this policy approach was not adopted into actual diplomatic practice.[8]

In the next phase, from 1994 to 1996, Russia—mired in domestic political struggles, amid the division of property and formation of new oligarchies and financial-industrial groups—lost control over events in Central Asia. The former Soviet republics of Central Asia evolved from protostates into full-fledged states, with all the attendant attributes. From a Russian perspective, negative tendencies already evident in the earlier phase intensified, including the identification of national interests, the preparation of strategies for economic and political development, and the choice of strategic partners. After Kazakhstan's President Nursultan Nazarbaev's proposal in March 1994 to create a Eurasian union, integration took the form of various alliances. In April 1994, three countries—Kazakhstan, Kyrgyzstan, and Uzbekistan—established the Central Asian Union. In 1996, Azerbaijan, Georgia, and Uzbekistan signed bilateral agreements to create a "Eurasian transportation route." For the same purpose, four countries—Georgia, Ukraine, Azerbaijan, and Moldova—established an association called GUAM (later to include Uzbekistan and now identified as GUUAM). Finally, in March 1996, Russia, Ukraine, Azerbaijan, and Moldova established the Union of Four. Russia held only observer status in these alliances and not even that in GUUAM.[9]

In this period, it is hard to see Russia's role as the "locomotive of integration" among the CIS nations. Obviously this is related to the great influence exerted by the United States and other Western countries on Central Asian states. Complications also arose in the relations between nations to the south and Central Asian countries owing to the increasingly active movements of religious extremists.

A third phase in Russian policies toward Central Asia began in the second half of 1996, when the pro-Western orientation of Foreign Minister Andrei Kozyrev gave way to the Eastern orientation of Foreign Minister Yevgenii Primakov. Russia made titanic efforts to restore its influence and played an important role in influencing the Central Asian energy pipelines. However, it was faced with its own internal and external threats similar to those in Central Asia.

Russia's Central Asian policies did not radically change until 1999 and 2000, when Russia's relationship with the West dropped to its lowest point. This was a culmination of the Kosovo crisis, the extremist attacks in Kyrgyzstan and Uzbekistan, and especially Vladimir Putin's rise to presidential power. Consequently, Russia began to accelerate the formation of a collective security system composed of Russia and other former Soviet republics in Central Asia.

At a meeting of the defense ministers of the Shanghai Cooperation Organization in Astana, Kazakhstan, in March 2000, the delegations from Russia, Kazakhstan, Kyrgyzstan, and Tajikistan announced the creation of the

Antiterrorist Center within the framework of the CIS. In May 2000, Minsk, Belarus, hosted a session of the Collective Security Council, composed of members in the Collective Security Treaty. The session examined and adopted a broad package of important documents and decisions that sought to revitalize the Collective Security Treaty and transform it into an effective instrument for ensuring the security of participating countries. In September, Sergei Ivanov, secretary of the Security Council of the Russian Federation, urged the leaders of the security councils of the member states in the Collective Security Treaty to mount joint resistance to international terrorism. At an October summit in Bishkek, Kyrgyzstan, the countries of Armenia, Belarus, Kazakhstan, Kyrgyzstan, Russia, and Tajikistan signed an agreement on the creation of forces and confirmed a plan to create a regional system of collective security.

Meanwhile, Russia was strengthening its control of the oil pipelines. The Russian government at times had used its control of the pipelines as a lever to control the regional states.[10] In the spring of 2000, Kazakhstan opened a valve to the CPC pipeline to transport oil from Kazakhstan to Novorossiisk, Russia. Western media started to claim that "the attitude of the Central Asian leaders toward stronger ties with Moscow" had become "a tendency."[11]

Russia's Central Asian policies had evolved from those adopted by the former Soviet Union in the period prior to the September 11 incident. Relations changed from being close to being loose, and then back to being close. Of course, the above retrospective only serves as a prelude for the greater changes that took place after the September 11 incident.

China's Central Asian Policies

There were no dramatic changes in China's Central Asian policies compared to Russia's policies at the turn of this century. However, China's policies have their own characteristics. Chinese strategists realize that the strategic importance of the Central Asian states will increase and that the region will have a considerable world influence in the twenty-first century. Economically, Central Asia and its surrounding areas will play an important role in the world's energy supply. Politically, the Central Asian states are increasingly manifesting their own unique style, different from that of Russia or the Ukraine and even more different than that of Eastern and Western Europe. They will not follow the example of Iran, where religion and state form one political structure. Although Central Asian leaders are interested in the political system of Turkey, a secular state where religion and state are separate, they are not likely to introduce the "Turkish model" either.[12] China established diplomatic relationships with Central Asian countries immediately after their independence, showing a respect for their independent and individual choice of development. In addition, it consistently aims to promote and develop its friendship and partnership with Central Asian states.

China also views the Central Asian states in the context of Eurasia. They have a linking role, not only in a geographical sense but also in a political and cultural sense. Central Asia has been called a bridge between East and West. China is closely interested in the stability and prosperity of the region because turbulence around that bridge would affect the future of political and economic cooperation on the whole Eurasian continent. Political and economic stability in the Central Asian states is therefore very important for China. It supports any Central Asian move aimed at safeguarding stability and prosperity and opposes any behavior or trend aimed at undermining that stability and prosperity.

With this as its guideline, China has been actively engaging in multilateral cooperation with Central Asian states, which served as an important start for China to learn to participate in multilateral international cooperation. In April 1996 in Shanghai, the presidents of China, Kazakhstan, Kyrgyzstan, and Tajikistan, as well as the Russian foreign minister, Yevgenii Primakov, signed an agreement on confidence building in military affairs in the border region. In April 1997 in Moscow, China signed the Agreement on Mutual Reduction of Military Forces in the Border Region with the four countries. In July 1998, then Chinese president Jiang Zemin, the presidents of Kazakhstan, Kyrgyzstan, and Tajikistan, and Yevgenii Primakov, representing the Russian president, met in Almaty, Kazakhstan, to discuss the strengthening of regional peace, stability, and economic cooperation. The meeting focused on common efforts to fight separatism, religious fundamentalism, terrorism, illegal arms trafficking, and the illegal drug trade as common threats to the region's stability and security. It also stressed the need for consultation and cooperation among the five countries' ministries for foreign affairs, security, defense, and customs. This series of multilateral diplomatic efforts made good preparation for the formal establishment of the future Shanghai Cooperation Organization (SCO).

The most important characteristic left over from the Soviet period was a continuing Chinese respect, or at least caution, toward Russian preeminence. China's caution is still reflected in its priorities. The first priority is that good neighborly relations with Central Asia are in the interest of peace and stability on its own periphery. A second priority is prevention of Central Asian interference in China's internal affairs, especially with regard to minorities in Xinjiang and Tibet. China has cultivated good relations with these states since their independence in order to gain diplomatic influence generally, and particularly to prevent Uyghur or Kazakh exiles from organizing themselves abroad.

Third, China wants good relations with Russia on international issues, especially with respect to Siberia, the Russian Far East, and trade in military equipment. A fourth priority involves the development of diversified transportation corridors to and from the region to facilitate secure trade on a secure basis, especially in energy and minerals. In 1993, China became a net importer of oil and is becoming increasingly reliant on energy imports, making Central Asian energy especially relevant. In June 1997, the China National Petroleum Corporation (CNPC) won the right to own and operate the Uzen oil field in western Kazakhstan. China also contracted to open up the Zhanazhol, Kenjiyake, and Wujing oil fields in Aktyubinsk. In September 1997, the agreement for its largest potential investment in economic cooperation with Central Asia was signed: China planned to construct a 3000-kilometer oil pipeline from western Kazakhstan to western China. In September 2000, the Chinese discussed a feasibility study for the pipeline, while Kazakhstan is already supplying China with modest amounts of oil by rail. The CNPC also agreed to construct a pipeline from the Uzen region of Kazakhstan to the Turkmenistan border. Fifth and finally, to that end, China promotes the internal stability of Central Asian states, with the assurance that the region is not divided into spheres of influence by the major powers and that major power contention in the region is minimized.[13] While showing respect to the traditional relationship between Russia and the Central Asia states and supporting cooperative relations between Russia and the Central Asian states in various areas, China has been also adhering to the five basic principles of peaceful coexistence as well as these five policy priorities in the region.

COMPARISON OF CHINA AND RUSSIA'S CENTRAL ASIAN POLICIES PRIOR TO SEPTEMBER 11

In the 1990s, after the disintegration of the Soviet Union, China and Russia started to construct relationships with the Central Asian states on the basis of safeguarding the stability of the post–Cold War international community, building a new political and economic international order, and promoting the development of multipolarity. Both China and Russia are acutely aware of the danger to the Central Asian region posed by Islamic fundamentalism, ethnic separatism and extremism, and external hegemonic expansionism. Regional and multilateral security has always been a priority. Both China and Russia use the principles of friendship, equality, mutual trust, and mutual benefit in a sincere effort to build up a constructive regional and multilateral cooperative mechanism. The SCO is the fruit of a joint effort by the two countries. China and Russia seek an all-inclusive cooperative relationship, trying at the same time not to harm their respective relations with the West. A balanced attitude has been adopted in dealing with their mutual relations as well as relations with the West. Finally, both countries take nonalliance as a precondition for the development of their mutual cooperation, to avoid the possible negative effects on the Sino-Russian cooperation. Andrew C. Kuchins commented in his congressional address in 2001, "In the past 4 or 5 years, I have been stressing that we should not over-exaggerate the threat to the United States possibly posed by the mutual interests of China and Russia, and their bilateral relations . . . although in the recent years there have been increasing claims in both China and Russia in opposition to the US hegemony and in favor of multi-polarity, I want to say that the Sino-Russian agreement to be signed this summer (2001) does not mean that the two countries have formed a mutual security guarantee."[14] China and Russia have been sensitive to perceptions of a mutual security guarantee. On the one hand, although Russia's Central Asian policies had been in constant flux, it remained the great power with the most influence on Central Asian affairs prior to the September 11 terrorist attack. On the other hand, China's policies regarding Central Asia involved more of a learning process regarding participation in international multilateral cooperation.

CHINESE-RUSSIAN RELATIONS IN CENTRAL ASIA AFTER SEPTEMBER 11

Chinese-U.S.-Russian Relations after September 11

After the September 11 terrorist attack, Chinese and Russian policies toward Central Asia underwent significant changes with U.S. entry into the region. American forces entered Central Asia following the September 11 incident with some strategic objectives. First, the geographic position of Central Asia is important. It sits right between the European Union, Russia, and China. It is vitally important for the United States to control the "bridge" as an access to the Eurasian interior and maintain an advantageous position. Second, Central Asia is a part of the Muslim world. In order to continue its traditional interest in West Asia and South Asia and to contain "hostile Muslim nations" such as Iran and Iraq, the United States must gain a foothold in Central Asia. Third, since there are special relations between Russia and Central Asian countries, the United States wants to control Central Asia to contain Russia's revival. Fourth, the Central Asian region is full of natural resources, including oil and gas. Central Asia will become a potential world supplier. And finally, Central Asia is vital to the American need to counter terrorism and military action in

Afghanistan. The U.S. military attacks on Afghanistan, in addition to destroying the terrorist network in the region, may also build up pro-American regimes to fill the strategic vacuum in Central Asia and turn the geopolitics in Central Asia to the interests of the United States.

Bilateral relations among China, the United States, and Russia evolved after the September 11 incident with varied rates and directions. The development of U.S.-Russian relations is one area where great progress has been made. President Vladimir Putin made a prompt response to the September 11 incident. Russia not only agreed to allow but even coordinated U.S. military entry into the Central Asian region, which historically ended the situation in which Central Asia was Russia's traditional strategic territory. This measure reflected the readjustment of Russia's foreign policies. In late May 2002, Russia and the United States held a summit meeting in St. Petersburg. At the summit meeting between Russia and NATO, the Treaty between the United States of America and the Russian Federation on Strategic Offensive Reductions and the New Strategic Relationship between the United States of America and the Russian Federation were signed and the Russia-NATO Council was established as a cooperative mechanism among the twenty nations. This is a landmark event in the development of U.S.-Russian relations, which historically symbolizes the official ending of the Cold War within a legal framework since the political turmoil in Eastern Europe in 1989 and the disintegration of the Soviet Union.

Although Sino-U.S. relations have not developed as rapidly as Russian-U.S. relations nor have they been formalized with international treaties, the two visits to China by President George W. Bush after the September 11 incident and former President Jiang Zemin's and President Hu Jintao's visits to the United States are sufficient evidence of the importance attached to the bilateral relations by the leaders of the two nations and their shared wish to build up a "constructive cooperative relationship." Continued U.S. support for China's efforts to join the World Trade Organization (WTO), the restoration of the Chinese-U.S. military exchange and cooperation, and the cooperation between the two nations in antiterrorism (including America's inclusion of the East Turkestan movement on its list of terrorist organizations) indicate that there is still huge potential for the two nations to further their cooperative relations. Although there are still sharp differences between China and the United States on a series of bilateral and multilateral issues, including the Taiwan issue, the Chinese-U.S. relationship has been recognized by both nations as well as in the international community as one of the most important bilateral relationships in the post–Cold War era. Such recognition indicates that there are possibilities for the relationship to further develop. Given the background of drastic improvement in the Russian-U.S. relationship, the Chinese government clearly supports this development.

At a time when the U.S.-Russian relationship achieved significant development, the Chinese-Russian relationship made great strides as well. Immediately after the Russian-U.S. summit, the heads of state of China, Russia, and the four Central Asian republics signed the Charter of the Shanghai Cooperation Organization at the St. Petersburg meeting of the Shanghai Cooperation Organization. The meeting also decided to establish a regional antiterrorist organization and announced that the Shanghai Cooperation Organization was "not a bloc nor a closed alliance." These documents and decisions provided a legal and political basis for cooperation between the Shanghai Cooperation Organization and other international organizations and enabled possible participation by neighboring countries. New vitality was injected into this regional cooperative organization, which withstood the troubles after the September 11 incident. Before the St. Petersburg summit, President Putin spoke on Sino-Russian bilateral relations in an interview with the editor of the *People's Daily.* Putin clearly indicated that Russia "and China have provided the world with a new model of national relationship. It is necessary to integrate conscious non-alliance with coordinated efforts. The model of our relationship specifies equality between our partnership and mutual trust, which is the basis to resolve all problems. Such has been Russia and China's great contribution to the establishment of a new multi-polar international order after the Cold War." President Putin's use of the phrases "conscious nonalliance" and "multi-polar international order" indicates the basis of the bilateral relationship between China and Russia. China and Russia have been furthering their cooperation in trade and commerce, especially in energy resources, and in Putin's words, the military technology cooperation has also been of "high quality." The two countries already have strategic cooperation on a series of global and regional issues. All these indicate that, although there has been a great breakthrough in the Russian-U.S. relations, strategic cooperation between China and Russia has not lost its independent raison d'être. As President Putin said, "The consistent working of the 'dynamo' of Sino-Russian relationship does not depend on exterior factors, because it has its own 'energy.'"[15]

Changes in Central Asia since the Iraq War

Judging by changes in the geopolitical setup reflected in a series of events, including the September 11 incident, the Iraq War, and the color revolutions in CIS states, the United States succeeded in entering Central Asia by seizing on the September 11 incident, divided Europe through NATO's eastward enlargement, and attempted to dominate the Middle East after the Iraq War. This setup has enormously intensified U.S. strategic influence on the Eurasian continent and effectively restricted strategic cooperation on the Eurasian continent, which may not seem to be in America's interests. Various American institutions have played a significant role in the course of the color revolutions in CIS countries and thus directly threatened Russia's influence in this region. Such a geopolitical situation has greatly encouraged the eastward shift of Russia's diplomatic strategic focus.

To put it briefly, Sino-Russian strategic relations have been enhanced. Convincing proof of this is the Sino-Russian military exercise carried out in Chinese territorial waters in August 2005. Economic cooperation between China and Russia has been further expanded and the two countries are strengthening their cooperation and assuming closer positions on a series of important issues like oil pipelines in the Far East of Russia. Last, both China and Russia have taken similar positions on the Iraq War, as well as issues of regional concern, particularly after the color revolutions, when they took similar positions of preserving stability in the Central Asian region and resisting intervention by outside forces.

Despite the crises and tests facing the CIS and changes that may take place in its organization, Russia's influence will still be reflected in bilateral or multilateral forms. The SCO summit held in July 2005 displayed the determination of China and Russia to support stability and development within the Central Asian countries and intensify cooperation to balance outside forces.

Features of Post–September 11 Sino-Russian Relations

China and Russia are both facing a completely new international order. Post–September 11 international relations have contributed toward a hierarchical power structure similar to the Roman Empire. However, such a power structure has not been institutionalized. At present, international relations are in a transitional period and there is still ample room for further shaping and developing.

How should the post–September 11 international community cope with the challenge posed by terrorism? Should it be managed similar to the Roman Empire or with a new and practical multilateral cooperation? There is a significant difference between the two possibilities. The United States possesses a uniquely strong power. But if it wants to use this strength-based attitude to resolve issues and problems unilaterally, it will do so without institutionalized international recognition and confirmation. Economically, the World Trade Organization, the World Bank, and the International Monetary Fund are no longer tools wielded by the United States, as they were immediately after World War II. Politically, the United Nations, the most important international organization, is no longer under the instruction or direction of the United States. Strategically, even organizations like NATO have not given substantial support to the U.S. tendency to act unilaterally. After the September 11 incident, NATO only gave nominal support in line with collective security and did not participate as such in U.S.-led antiterrorist military action. Moreover, when America was about to launch its preemptive military security mechanism, Secretary-General Lord George Robertson announced that NATO was still a defensive alliance. NATO should not waste its energy on something irrelevant. Looking back at the Cold War period, the United States had a set of patterns and systems for its bilateral security strategy as an institutionalized guarantor. This is absent today. It is not that the United States is unwilling to make such an institution, but doing so is now very difficult. In the long term, this new situation heralds a more extensive range of choices for great powers like China and Russia to realize their national interests and begin to build a new world order.

China and Russia have adopted similar attitudes to cope with the challenge of unilateralism. There is a sharp contrast between growing unilateralism and the demand for multilateral cooperation. Countries that would be directly affected by such policies like China and Russia, with bilateral, holistic, and long-term interests, have taken a flexible and calm attitude in dealing with the United States and have shown considerable restraint. This is a phenomenon not seen in recent history.

Apart from these similarities, there are a few noteworthy divergences in the Sino-Russian relationship. One important issue, as defined by some Western scholars, is that the United States and Russia are driven to develop a closer relationship by mutual needs like cooperation in antiterrorism, reduction of strategic weaponry and prevention of proliferation, energy supply and investment, but also jointly addressing the fact that China is reemerging as a major power. Although the model in the post–Cold War international code of behavior is that bilateral cooperation should not take a third party as its target, a concern regarding a third party and attempts to influence a third party is complementary to that code of behavior. On one level, the United States and Russia are deepening their understanding of China's reemergence, which is conducive to the joint coordinated development of China, the United States, and Russia. On another level, there are those who regard China's development as a threat, although it is unclear how the United States and Russia would jointly address a reemerging China. Of course, many Russian and Western academics deny that closer ties between the United States and Russia include plans for dealing with the "China problem."

Universal adoption of the priority of "national interest" in great power diplomacy in recent years is inevitably present in the post–September 11 Chinese-Russian relations. The cooperative relationship developing between China and Russia regarding their economic and strategic interests in Central

Asia had included discussions and negotiations concerning issues such as the energy pipeline, the auction of the Slavneft Petroleum Company, and Russia's bid for accession to the WTO. Regardless of any problems bilateral relations may encounter, the profound external changes and the tremendous mutual benefits to the national interests of both China and Russia ensure continuing cooperation between the two nations in their economic and strategic interests in Central Asia.

The Central Asian policies of the two countries are developing in a manner similar to pre–September 11 policies. China's policies continue to be cautious, low-key, and stable, while Russia's in comparison are more changeable. More than a year after U.S. military forces were stationed in Central Asia, on November 20, 2002, members of the CIS Collective Security Treaty Organization decided to reinforce their military presence in Central Asia. Earlier, at the end of October, Russia's Defense Ministry announced a plan to build an airbase and station aircraft at a military airport near the capital of Kyrgyzstan. Russia will allocate US$50 million to maintain this air base. Although the facilities and condition of this airport are not comparable to the nearby U.S. air base, the fact that Russian and American airbases are within such close proximity to each other is significant. New developments in Russia's Central Asian policies will definitely impact the Chinese-Russian relationship.

PROSPECT FOR THE DEVELOPMENT OF CHINESE-RUSSIAN RELATIONS IN CENTRAL ASIA

The Future Security Pattern in the Central Asia Region

Any judgment of the future development of Chinese-Russian relations in Central Asia depends on predictions for the entire Central Asia region. A likely scenario is based on the triangular relations among China, the United States, and Russia. One possibility is U.S.-Russian cooperation in Central Asia. Another likely possibility is the United States taking the predominant role with or without Europe, Russia collaborating, and China participating. Russia is not likely to reemerge as the leader of the Eurasian continent.[16] The United States, Russia, and China should cooperate or even form an alliance to maintain the security and stability of the Eurasian continent based on two facts: Russia and China have already formed the SCO, which aims at strengthening the stability of the continent, and that after September 11, the United States had already entered Central Asia.[17] Western countries have already been playing an important role in Central Asia, but cooperation between China and Russia, with full participation of the Central Asian countries, will take a key role in the regional affairs.

Chinese-Russian Relations in Future Central Asian Affairs

Clearly the Sino-Russian relationship plays an important role in the future of Central Asian affairs. As the biggest neighboring countries of Central Asia, their historic heritage and potential power exert important, even decisive, influences on this region, especially against the background of close and friendly cooperation between Russia and China.

The biggest contribution to the international community made by cooperation between China and Russia is the Shanghai Cooperation Organization, which provides a framework and mechanism to deal with and solve the complicated issues of the Central Asian region at multilateral meetings in a peaceful manner. The SCO is a new institutional mechanism that transcends culture, ideology, social system, or size of country. It is thus very important in post–September 11 international affairs.

The future Chinese-Russian relationship in Central Asian affairs is likely to contribute a new form of friendly cooperation to the international community. Friendly cooperation between the two countries will not be damaging to their individual national interests. Instead, when the international order is undergoing a dramatic change, it is possible to define national interest in a clear and rational way, which is then conducive to the realization of friendship based on mutual complementation and mutual support. The European Union's successful integration provides a valuable experience. It is not only when the national strengths of two countries are similar that effective cooperation becomes possible; discrepancies in the development of the national power of China and Russia will not be a determining factor in future bilateral relations. The economic, strategic, and political interests of both China and Russia are highly or potentially complementary. China and Russia affirm that both countries prioritize domestic development, which is decisive to the general interest in a peaceful and stable neighboring environment, leading to their policies of diplomacy and strategic security. After the Cold War, especially after the September 11 incident, the international community and the Central Asian region are faced with a long-term task. If China and Russia can form a stable relationship, it will contribute to the entire world community. This is consistent with the strategic objectives of both China and Russia.

NOTES

1. Feng, Shaolei, paper delivered at the Conference on Middle Eastern Studies, 1993, Wuxi, China.

2. Zbigniew Brzezinski, *The Grand Chessboard: American Primacy and Its Geostrategic Imperatives* (New York: Basic, 1998).

3. Konstantin Syroezhkin, "Central Asia between the Gravitational Poles of Russia and China," in Boris Rumer, ed., *Central Asia: A Gathering Storm?* (Armonk, N.Y.: Sharpe, 2002).

4. Feng Shaolei, "Russia and CIS Countries," in *System Change and Foreign Relations after 1992* (Shanghai: Shanghai People's Publishing House, 1997).

5. Syroezhkin, "Central Asia."

6. Much has been published on the differences of opinion regarding Russia's Central Asia policies within the Russian regime in the early 1990s, between various parties, and between politic elites and the general public. However, the political forces led by Gerder Kochiliev took control of policy making in regard to Central Asia.

7. Syroezhkin, "Central Asia."

8. K. Soltsin, "Russia's Geopolitical Policies toward Its Neighboring Nations," *Political Studies*, March 1995. In Russian.

9. Syroezhkin, "Central Asia."

10. Charles Fairbanks and S. Frederick Starr, *Strategic Assessment of Central Eurasia* (Washington, D.C.: Atlantic Council, 2001), 79.

11. Syroezhkin, "Central Asia."

12. Xing Guangcheng, "China and Central Asia," in Roy Allison and Lena Janson, eds., *Central Asia Security: The New International Context* (London: Royal Institute of International Affairs, 2001).

13. Fairbanks and Starr, *Strategic Assessment*.

14. Andrew C. Kuchins, address at Capitol Hill, Washington, D.C., February 2001.

15. Vladimir Putin, interview, *People's Daily,* June 1, 2002, 1.

16. Ian Blamur, "The Future of Eurasia Continent," *National Interest,* December 2002.

17. Angela Shafshauwa Stame, "America, Russia, and the EU: Will a New Alliance Be Formed?" *Survival,* Winter 2002–2003; and Robert Lagvold, "Towards an Alliance between the USA and Russia," *National Interest,* Winter 2002–2003.

15

China and Russia in Central Asia: Interests and Tendencies

Sergei Troush

This chapter will discuss the motivations of Moscow and Beijing in formulating their policies toward the Central Asian region, as well as the perceptions of the Central Asian states on the role of great powers in shaping regional interests. These perceptions are partly reflected through their participation in the Shanghai Cooperation Organization (SCO), which is becoming an active cooperative player on the regional scene. At the same time, the interests of regional actors differ and conflict in many realms. The turbulent events in Kyrgyzstan and Uzbekistan in early 2005 and the serious political instability in other Central Asian states draw additional energy from the Russian and Chinese leadership to keep this geopolitically important zone in coherence with their security interests, to prevent it from plunging into further instability. This chapter argues that Russia, China, and the United States (the third visibly powerful external player in the regional security and economic field) have an obvious common ground for developing multilateral approaches toward protecting the region from violence and turmoil. To do that, all three external actors have to modify their strategies, each one in its own way.

RUSSIA AND CHINA IN CENTRAL ASIA

Until a few years ago Central Asia was of secondary importance to Russian-Chinese bilateral relations. But starting from the events of September 11, the military operation in Afghanistan and the turbulent internal dynamics in Central Asia triggered by these events, the region has drawn greater attention from Beijing and Moscow.

Russia considered this region its strategic backyard but was short of political, economic, and military resources to keep it in order. Instead, Moscow was preoccupied with many challenges inside and outside its core territory, such as economic decline of the first half of the 1990s, conflict in Chechnya, enlargement of NATO, and incessant political crises and frictions, especially during the Boris Yeltsin presidency. All of those distracted Russia from pursuing an active and nuanced strategy within the Commonwealth of Independent States (CIS). Similarly, China was preoccupied with the eastern and southeastern flanks of its foreign policy, its shaky relations with the United States and Taiwan being the main vulnerability. Moscow and Beijing were seeking each other's diplomatic, military, and political support. Consequently they were cautious not to intrude in each other's internal affairs and zones of interest, such as Central Asia and the Russian Far East for Moscow or Taiwan and civil rights issues for China.

In contrast to shrinking Russian capacities, the Chinese presence in the region has been growing economically. Along with China's energy import interests, which became a special factor, China's trade with the Central Asian states was growing steadily. According to official Chinese statistics, in 1992, trade amounted to US$463 million; in 1995, it was US$782 million; in 1997, it was US$872 million. In 2002, China's trade with Kazakhstan alone reached US$3 billion. In the first months of 2004, it grew by 87.7 percent.[1] The rapidly increasing trade resulted from the complementarities of Chinese and Central Asian economies—a booming producer on the one hand and a vast post-Soviet new market with over fifty million consumers on the other hand. The relatively cheap (if low-quality) consumer goods from China were appropriate for the limited purchasing capacity of the Central Asian population. Speaking abstractly, Moscow and Beijing were both present in Central Asia but occupied different levels of the same building. Moscow was at the political and security level and China at the economic level, which allowed a harmonious coexistence between the two. This situation started to change gradually in the second half of the 1990s, with Beijing influencing this evolution more actively than Moscow.

The general dynamism and the steady development of the Chinese economy should be mentioned first in this regard. To complement the boom in China's east and southeast, the "opening" of the western and northwestern parts of the country, including Xinjiang, became one of Beijing's key priorities. Given the growing and alarming disparities between China's east and west in economic, social, demographic, and ecological terms, this priority was understandable. In the 1990s, Xinjiang was defined as the future resource base of China's economy and as such needed an adequate infrastructure. Eventually the need for a stable "external" environment for huge investment and development ventures in this strategic area became paramount, too.

The energy factor deserves specific mention in this regard. Facing the growing need for energy and having set up the goal of diversifying its energy import dependence on the Middle East, Beijing linked itself up with Caspian oil by long-term commitments in Kazakhstan. China's ventures in Kazakhstan's oil fields of Aktobe and Uzen are among the largest of China's overseas oil ventures. In May 2002, the output of Aktobe and Uzen reached 82,000 barrels/day (b/d) and 94,000 b/d respectively, thus constituting the substantial share of the China's oil import.[2]

By initiating and carrying out the Kazakhstan-Xinjiang pipeline project and participating in the Turkmenistan-Iran pipeline, Beijing wants to ensure the implementation of its long-term energy strategy. Using the two pipelines from Kazakhstan as pivotal links from the Middle East to Central Asia and from Central Asia to China, China hopes to position itself within an energy system referred to by energy experts as the "pan-Asian global energy bridge." Such a system could connect Asia's existing and potential energy suppliers (Middle East, Central Asia, and Russia) with the key Asian consumers (China, Japan, and Korea). China could certainly benefit from such a pivotal geostrategic position. Again these multi-billion–dollar projects were impossible without China's greater involvement in the security infrastructure of Central Asia.[3]

Also, the secessionist movement in Xinjiang was prompting China to manage closer contact and gain stronger influence over the Central Asian states. This movement was inspired by these former Soviet states, which, as one region analyst (Martha Olcott) precisely put it, "were catapulted to independence." Given the porous border, the numerous Uyghur communities in these countries and the limited control, real or pretended, of the local governments over the activity of these communities, Beijing's anxiety over the Uyghur presence in Central Asia increased. The Chinese started seeking stronger diplomatic and economic leverage over Kazakhstan, Kyrgyzstan, and Uzbekistan—the key bases of the Uyghurs outside China—to make them less conciliatory to the anti-China Uyghurs.

The interconnectedness of these factors eventually led to the six-member Shanghai Cooperation Organization (SCO) founded in 2001. This structure grew from the five-country (China, Kazakhstan, Kyrgyzstan, Russia, and Tajikistan) confidence-building agreements signed in 1996 and 1997. Uzbekistan joined the SCO as a full member in 2001.

SHANGHAI COOPERATION ORGANIZATION: WHO NEEDS WHAT?

Initiated by China, according to many analysts, the SCO would not have been possible if it was not based on the shared interests of all the members, concerning the security, political, economic, and ethno-political situation in the region. Despite being the most influential external power in its "backyard," Moscow needed to share the burden of countering the Islamist threat to the security of the region and to Russia itself, given its porous 6,800-kilometer border with Kazakhstan and the substantial Muslim population residing in Russia. The threat of Islamic fundamentalism emanating from the south, particularly when the Taliban gained control over most of Afghanistan, made the Tajikistan-Afghanistan border guarded by Russian troops very fragile and impossible to secure completely.

Although the SCO was not originally designed as a military and political entity, the diplomatic term "coordination" of activity, mentioned in its key documents, implied joint effort and sharing of resources (military, financial, intelligence) in order to repel a common threat. The formation of the SCO ran parallel to the formation of its "regional antiterrorist structure." This structure is perceived to be the core working and practical unit of the organization and therefore can be seen as a proof of the SCO countries' concern with security.

The Shanghai Cooperation Organization offered Moscow another institutional mechanism of participation and influence in the region, where its influence was gradually fading. Several regional structures, such as GUUAM (Georgia, Uzbekistan,[4] Ukraine, Azerbaijan, and Moldova) and Central Asian Union (CAU, with Kazakhstan, Kyrgyzstan, Tajikistan, and Uzbekistan as members) excluded Moscow. These organizations, loosely structured and economically oriented, have been trying to secure independent regional interests and minimize the pressure of the former metropolis—Russia. The SCO mechanism could be used by Moscow for day-to-day lobbying, negotiating, and mediating on issues of regional and international importance.

All SCO decisions, according to its charter, are to be made by consensus. The consensus principle has its strengths and weaknesses, but it gives Moscow an opportunity to veto decisions that are not in its interest and could endanger its influence in Central Asia. The SCO also provides Russia with an additional lever over China—an influential member of the international community and a permanent member of the U.N. Security Council—while exploiting Beijing's interest in it as a diplomatic partner on a variety of issues. Among these issues are Russia and China's shared philosophy of a multipolar world; arms control and disarmament; relations with the United States, Taiwan, and Chechnya; role of the United Nations, Korea, and Iraq.

Realistically, the other four members of the SCO—Kazakhstan, Kyrgyzstan, Tajikistan, and Uzbekistan—cannot count on exercising the same influence over China. It is unlikely that Beijing will side with them against Moscow on sensitive matters. However, SCO meets the basic interests of these four Central Asian members, too. Their interests, at the current stage of

SCO development, are also focused on security. Having China and Russia as the "big brothers standing shoulder to shoulder" with them against the Islamic challenge is an obvious diplomatic asset for all four capitals. At the same time, each state, due to its specific circumstances, has its own perception of the Islamic threat and its own strategies for confronting it. Hence they differ in accents and nuances of their objectives in the SCO and their stance vis-à-vis Russia and China.

Tajikistan and Kyrgyzstan, small countries with limited military and economic resources, feel themselves most vulnerable to the Islamist challenges, geographically and ethnically, and view the SCO as the obvious diplomatic opportunity to support themselves in the difficult subregional environment and phase of their historical development. The clashes with Islamist militants in the Batken region of Kyrgyzstan in 1999 and 2000 left Bishkek and Dushanbe (as well as Tashkent) disillusioned with the effectiveness of external support. They were especially dissatisfied with the CIS collective security agreement signed by six CIS member states (Armenia, Belarus, Kazakhstan, Kyrgyzstan, Russia, Tajikistan) and therefore treated the emergence and strengthening of SCO as an encouraging process in that regard.

As a result of a social upheaval in Kyrgyzstan in the spring of 2005, President Askar Akayev was ousted, and a coalition of his political opponents came to power. This coalition is based on the alliance of the clans, domineering in the south of the country (lead by Bakiev) and its north (lead by Kulov). Facing the variety of internal social challenges, with economic shortages and infrastructure bottlenecks being the most pressing, the new government is quite unstable. The clan struggle goes on, fueled by interests in wealth redistribution and anticorruption sentiments. This struggle impacts on the foreign policy sphere too. It has been reported that President Bakiev and his minister of defense disagree on the status of the U.S. bases in Kyrgyzstan.[5] Kazakhstan feels more confident geopolitically and militarily, as it is not situated at the forefront of the anti-Islamist defense. Its strong mineral and energy resource base, together with a relatively developed industrial infrastructure in comparison with other Central Asian states, form the basis for a more active and self-reliant foreign policy. At the same time, the ethnic composition of its population, with Kazakhs and Russians comprising the two largest ethnic groups (53.4 percent and 30 percent respectively), its buffer-state position between Russia and China, and the long and almost equally porous border with each of them, set limits on self-reliance in foreign affairs.[6] Due to a combination of reasons— with Russia's indirect opposition being one of them—Astana has not obtained the long-cherished goal of diversifying its energy export routes.

Given all these factors, Astana's interest in the SCO is understandable. Apart from the key objective of joining the collective security structure against Islamist and radical threats, Kazakhstan had more interest than other member states in an institutional instrument for balancing Chinese and Russian interests in Central Asia. The main internal vulnerabilities and geostrategic priorities of Astana are deeply interlinked with Moscow's and Beijing's attitudes. Therefore, looking from Astana's perspective, having all three of them at the same table to discuss an agenda of shared tasks and priorities could be diplomatically beneficial.

Since Kazakhstan is China's key Central Asian energy supplier and the one especially interested in gaining access to the booming Chinese and East Asian markets of oil and gas, it has favored stability of Xinjiang since it is the area of prospective pipelines. Many observers point out that after the formation of the SCO and the decision to establish an antiterrorist structure in the SCO, the political activity of the Uyghur communities in Kazakhstan was more restricted by the Kazakh government.[7]

Uzbekistan's position in the SCO as well as its general stance toward China and Russia is based on another combination of motives. Tashkent as a foreign policy actor has many assets: a large (in regional terms) territory and homogeneous population, a favorable geostrategic location, a rich resource base, and a relatively developed industry. Having all of that, Tashkent traditionally adheres to a more independent posture within CIS and, with an active president, aspires to play the role of a regional hegemon. To support this role vis-à-vis Moscow, Tashkent pursued until recently an active diplomacy seeking Western support.

On the other hand, the security challenges of Tashkent are no less acute than those of its less ambitious regional neighbors. The militants of the Islamic Movement of Uzbekistan (IMU), supported by the Islamist networks in Afghanistan, Saudi Arabia, and Pakistan, are posing a serious irredentist threat. It is believed that the movement, by setting up the flame of struggle on the Uzbek soil, counted on substantial support among certain sections of impoverished population, mafia and clans that were sidelined by President Karimov from power and wealth. The Batken events of 1999 and 2000 proved the reality and the scale of this threat. Disillusioned by Western support to Tashkent in these crises, Uzbekistan decided to reassess its relationship with Russia in late 1999. The Uzbek government suggested that it might reconsider its withdrawal from the CIS collective security agreement and ratified a treaty on defense cooperation with Russia in February 2000.

In the aftermath of the Kyrgyz events in June 2005, a serious military uprising took place in Uzbek city of Andijan, which was decisively suppressed by the Tashkent military. There were reports of hundreds of casualties; thousands of people fled into neighboring Kyrgyzstan as refugees. Karimov's government qualified the Andijan events as actions of the Islamic opposition, although many observers outside the country doubted that. Tashkent declined international demands for an independent international investigation of the events. Eventually Tashkent's relations with the West deteriorated. After the Uzbek refugees were evacuated from Kyrgyzstan to third countries, Tashkent urged the withdrawal of the U.S. military facility at Karshi-Khanabad, which held about 1,500 U.S. troops.[8]

In the face of existing threats, Uzbekistan is making impressive efforts to rebuild its army. It established a new force structure and new bases in all parts of the country. During the Soviet period, most of the bases in Soviet Central Asia were located along the southern border and near the eastern border with China. This resulted in an unequal distribution of bases inside Uzbekistan, inadequate to its new geostrategic situation. According to its new military plans, Uzbekistan is building new bases in the west, in the Ferghana Valley, and elsewhere to strengthen defense structures against threats that could emerge from any direction.

Military analysts consider Tashkent to be the strongest military force of the Asian former Soviet states with the capability to occupy the Tajik and Kyrgyz sectors of the Ferghana Valley, southern Tajikistan up to its mountains, northern and eastern areas of Turkmenistan, and, with more resistance, southern Kazakhstan. In the future, barring foreign intervention, Uzbekistan could conquer all of Central Asia if it chose to do so.

Uzbekistan is ambivalent toward the SCO as well as Russian and Chinese policies in Central Asia. On the one hand, Tashkent's eventual entry into SCO was an obvious sign of its need to have the support of these two regional giants and effective military help in future, particularly in possible clashes with IMU. Tashkent is pretty confident that Moscow and Beijing would be concerned with the outcome of its fight with Islamic separatists. From Moscow's perspective, if IMU militants came to power in Tashkent, this would seriously invigorate Islamic separatist tendencies, especially in Chechnya and north Caucasus. Moscow would obviously need a heavier military buildup on its long border with Kazakhstan and Georgia. Both of these tasks would be difficult to carry out, given Moscow's stringent military budget. From the Chinese perspective, it is much the same. Tashkent's "falling out" with IMU would mean a greater threat of destabilization in Xinjiang through the thin buffers of Tajikistan and Kyrgyzstan. IMU ties with Chinese Uyghur militants are reported to be strong. Overall, Uzbekistan is viewed by both Moscow and Beijing as an important link in the strategic front against the Islamic challenge, which Uzbek diplomacy uses for its own ends.

Tashkent's other reason for joining the SCO is its desire to avoid being sidelined in the region where it wants to be a leader. Remaining outside the SCO structure would give its regional competitor—Kazakhstan—direct and indirect advantages for prime positions in Central Asia in terms of political and strategic stability, economic and investment environment, and diplomatic outreach. Nevertheless, Tashkent considered it diplomatically wise to sacrifice a certain portion of its evenhandedness and step into the SCO structure. By doing so, Tashkent relied on the consensus principle of this organization and hoped that Russia and China would check each other's domination in SCO. In sum, Tashkent believed it paid a reasonable price for gaining a new instrument of its security policy.

Tashkent's role in the SCO, similar to that in the CIS, stems from its own independent understanding of its national priorities. Starting from the beginning, when it had the status of an independent observer, until now, Tashkent has been trying its best to clarify its special circumstances and special interests to other member states. It is noteworthy how President Karimov put it in his interview during the Beijing summit of 2001, when Tashkent joined the organization. Karimov made it clear that Tashkent would not succumb to instructions from Moscow if it later tried to use SCO as an instrument of its own policy, for example, in organizing a "joint effort" to oppose the expansion of NATO and the planned American National Missile Defense system (NMD). Karimov said, "I signed the document, sharing the ideas of the Declaration of the Shanghai Cooperation Organization. . . . The document refers to cooperation, cooperation and nothing more than cooperation. . . . This grouping should never be transformed into a military-political bloc. It should never be aimed against any other country, should not adhere to questionable motives, and should not organize clandestine activities against third countries."

THE IMPACT OF THE SEPTEMBER 11 EVENTS

What was the impact of the September 11, 2001, events on the evolution of U.S. policies in the region and the response of Russia and China, given their interests in Central Asia?

The Chinese leadership worried about what it saw as Vladimir Putin's pro-American tilt after the September 11 events. The Chinese were puzzled by Moscow's calm reaction to the U.S. decision to withdraw from the ABM treaty, the positive results of the two Russian-American summits after September 11, the signing of the SALT 3 agreement, elevating Russia's status in NATO's decision-making structure, and the bold new economic initiatives, including those in the energy sphere. Using the triangle policy approach, any Russian move toward the United States or vice versa is perceived as detrimental to Chinese interests. Such feelings exist within the Chinese elite. However, Beijing was fully aware that Moscow was pursuing obvious pragmatic goals in its relations with the United States after the events of September 11. China's own reaction to the September 11 events was generally supportive of the United States, but more restrained. China was not fully comfortable with U.S. retaliatory moves after the events.

After the tragic events in the United States, Beijing realized an obvious closeness and even a coincidence of its interests and U.S. interests. The threat of political Islamist extremism is clearly growing and endangering the world with new political and economic cataclysms. Despite serious contradictions with the United States, China would not benefit from such cataclysms, especially during this period of steady economic growth and a constant stream of domestic socioeconomic limitations and difficulties.[9]

China is being challenged by Islamic fundamentalism in Xinjiang, with its eight million Uyghurs and other Muslim inhabitants.

Under these circumstances, Beijing expressed solidarity with the U.S. struggle against international terrorism and a readiness to support it, mainly through intelligence sharing. However, the text of China's official reaction blamed "all forms of terrorism" (a direct hint at the U.S. actions in Iraq during 1998–1999 and in Yugoslavia in 1999) that were criticized by Beijing earlier. As the United States prepared for a military operation in Afghanistan, Beijing stressed the need for clear aims and limits to minimize civilian losses. China also stressed the need for a high-profile role for the United Nations in resolving this crisis.[10]

According to various sources, even this qualified support of the U.S. action was not easy for the Chinese leadership, which faced serious opposition from the conservative part of the Chinese political and military elite. In this context, Beijing held a mixed position toward developments in Central Asia, noting both their positive and negative impact on its interests.

On the positive side, as some influential Chinese sources pointed out, the military defeat of Taliban and bin Laden by the United States led to greater regional security from extremist threats. After Taliban was overthrown, Afghanistan—the pivotal link for trade, communications, and energy supplies—became much safer, and the whole energy security context of Central Asia benefited from that. The U.S.-led military operation seriously weakened the activity of the extremist Islamic Movement of Uzbekistan, which was based in Afghanistan.

However, while the situation in Afghanistan and Central Asia was unfolding, the Chinese side was showing increasing dissatisfaction with the abrupt shift in the military–strategic balance in the region, the growing U.S. presence in Central Asia at the expense of Russia, and the possible deployment of U.S. forces there for an indefinite period. It was perceived as detrimental to China's strategic position since its geopolitical competitor—the United States—intruded into the western proximity of Chinese territory and strengthened its positions there.

The earlier situation in Central Asia, with an unstable Afghanistan and frictions among the Central Asian states, was certainly not ideal to its interests. However, the earlier situation gave China more freedom of action and potentially unlimited access to the oil fields and terminals of Central Asia and the Caspian. Even in an unlikely confrontation with Russia, the latter would hardly be able to endanger the flow of oil and gas to China through all the transportation routes and directions in Central Asia. China definitely feels more comfortable within the "concert" of interests inside Central Asia, with the prevailing role of Russia, a country with decreasing military and economic possibilities there. However, Beijing suspects that the U.S. military will stay there forever, due to the uncertainty in this region and due to its importance as an energy and strategic knot.

The Chinese pointed out the Americans' "pragmatic calculations" and their attempts to use the tragic events in New York and Washington as a pretext to penetrate Central Asia and secure their interests in the region. Just a few weeks after the first personal meeting between George W. Bush and Jiang Zemin in Shanghai in October 2001, the semiofficial Beijing magazine *Shijie zhishi* published a very critical article on that issue. Lie Taxing, an analyst from an influential Beijing think tank, pointed out that "the United States is using the fight against the Taliban as a pretext, in order to station military bases in Pakistan and troops in the Central Asia." He noted that this affected the strategic balance in the Central Asian region. Another analyst was even more straightforward: "Just as Saddam Hussein was used as a pawn, who helped the United States to secure its military presence in the Gulf area, bin Laden is being used as a pawn, helping the United States to secure its role to the north of Pamir mountains."[11]

High-ranking experts and consultants of the state energy companies in China urged a reassessment of the country's energy strategy in view of events in Afghanistan and Central Asia. Vice director of the Peking Institute of Energy Studies, Zhu Xingshan, stated, "The events of the September 11 will have an effect not only on the price of oil in China. China should reassess its strategy of oil supply. It should adhere to the strategy of plural sources of supply to secure itself against political risks."[12]

CONCLUSION

The three most influential external actors on the Central Asia political scene — China, Russia, and the United States — seem to be in the phase of uncertainty or "pause" in their strategies. The key origins of this uncertainty are probably the unclear future situation in Afghanistan, the effectiveness and survivability of Islamic fundamentalist networks in Afghanistan and Central Asia, and the scale of the future presence of the United States in Central Asia. The latter issue was targeted by the SCO summit in July 2005, when the organization urged the United States to set a deadline for withdrawal of its bases in Central Asia.[13]

However, notwithstanding the existing frictions on the Central Asian political and security scene, these external actors and the key operational multilateral institutions they support (NATO and SCO) have reasonable grounds for cooperative, rather than competing, approaches in order to guarantee their interests in the region. Their basic priorities are very close.

First, the three states and two institutions are not interested in drastically changing the regional status quo—the origin, domestic orientation, and system of external relationships of almost all Central Asian regimes.

It doesn't mean that each of them—Russia, China, or the United States—is in complete harmony with its Central Asian partners in diplomatic and security terms. However, revolutionary changes probably would jeopardize the overall social stability and efficiency of state control in those differently authoritarian but strongly secular states. As the result of their failures, the fundamentalist challenges to the region would grow exponentially, and all the capitals—Moscow, Beijing, Washington—would lose. Russia, as a minor evil, will loosen its remaining integrative links with the Central Asian states through the CIS network (even as weak as these links already are); as a major evil, it will face an explosive fundamentalist entity on its south flank. China would suffer from a vacuum of power in the region and the negative "demonstration effect" of Central Asian instability in its Xinjiang region. For the United States, losing stability in Central Asia could keep it from obtaining strategic goals in the Middle East.

Second, the West (mainly U.S. companies) and China—the latter to a lesser degree, but both quite substantially—have invested heavily in Central Asian energy projects, including the capital-intensive long-term projects in Kazakhstan and Azerbaijan: the Baku-Ceyhan and Kazakhstan-Xingjiang pipeline projects. At the same time, there is a growing understanding among the U.S. strategists that energy-thirsty China should not be cut off from Central Asian (or any other) resource bases, because a "wounded" Beijing could grow irrational and dangerous.

Third, Moscow could play a positive role in the tripartite U.S.-Chinese-Russian relations in the Central Asian political space. This would be beneficial from the broad perspective of Russian priorities in foreign policy and domestic development. The overall success of Russian internal reforms depends heavily on Moscow's ability to pursue the nonconfrontational, flexible dualistic strategy toward East and West in political and economic realms. The low level of U.S.-Chinese confrontation would benefit Moscow's priorities in the long term.

The regional involvement of all three foreign powers—Russia, China, and the United States—based on the cooperative rather than competitive strategies obviously benefits all Central Asian states. With such cooperation, these states could play the role of real "actors," rather than of "subjects" of the intra-regional international affairs.

To pursue such a cooperative approach, each foreign power—Russia, China, and the United States—should be ready to sacrifice a portion of their interests for the sake of the Central Asian "concert" of states, rather than a zero-sum game among them.

Russia's "sacrifice" should probably be the greatest of the three. Given its former metropolitan status, it is still suffering from "phantom aches," sensing parts of the empire that are not there anymore. With its military resources seriously undercut, its military presence in the region, with the exception of Tajikistan and recently in Kyrgyzstan, is limited. Even if asked, Russia would not be able to significantly enhance its military presence or, more importantly, the effectiveness of its military forces in the face of the threats facing the Central Asian regimes. The inevitability of sharing the security burden there with the other actors—on the terms of parity—is obvious.

Moscow should gradually shift from the unilateral responsibility approach for Central Asian security to a multilateral approach based on the concert structure involving Russia, United States, and China. This decision—however psychologically tough it is—actually means replacing the security mechanism based on the CIS collective security agreement (with Russia as a core of it) with new security mechanisms jointly supported by multilateral structures like SCO and NATO.

It is obvious, however, that Russia would only agree to retreat in this way if her other geostrategic and geoeconomic interests in the region, those dictated by geographic proximity, historical, civilizational, and economic ties, are "solidly" guaranteed by her new partners. Such interests should include acceptance and nonhostility toward Russia's integrationist effort within CIS, reasonably equal role and responsibilities with Washington and Beijing in the antiterrorist and antifundamentalist struggle in Central Asia, securing Moscow's commercial priorities in transporting energy from Central Asia, guaranteeing the rights and security of the ethnic Russians in Central Asia.

China's sacrifice of interests should probably be the smallest, given its relatively modest (compared to the other two) military and political involvement in the region. Its sacrifice paradoxically should suggest a bigger presence and more responsibility. In the other words, it should gradually sacrifice the proclaimed "noninvolvement" or "evenhandedness" in its foreign policy moves, assume greater responsibility for collective support of the Central Asian states, and be ready to grant military, economic, and financial aid, either through the antiterrorist structure established within the SCO or bilaterally.

Previously China tried to avoid such obligations. However, that stance now seems inadequate to the scale of its domestic and foreign policy interests, as well as its strategic outreach and capabilities. The country that has one of the largest economies in the world, that is the world's seventh largest trading power, cannot leave the future of its transportation, trade, and energy routes from Central Asia, its investment and trade there, the stability of its own potentially promising province of Xinjiang at the mercy of the relatively weak Central Asian armies in their confrontation with Islamist enemies.

Although continuing its global "noninterference" rhetoric, China has already started moving away from it. Its 2001 treaty with Russia and its visibly growing profile in SCO activities (vividly shown by the SCO summit in Astana in July 2005) could be considered a benchmark in this realm.

The "sacrifice" of interests on the U.S. side, for the sake of the multilateral, cooperative approach, seems complicated and thus difficult to make. This sacrifice is perceived as the U.S. ability to check its presence in the region within limits adequate to the real threat, and the ability to withdraw when this threat is either eliminated or low enough that the locals can cope with it. This is a difficult task, given that the perception of this stage and the objective criteria of it differ among the various actors.

To meet this goal, the three powers need to develop and upgrade multilateral structures such as NATO and SCO, preparing them to act as multifunctional, pluralistic, effective, and nonconfrontational structures, with the ability to work out generally acceptable decisions.

NOTES

1. "Kazakh Oil Pipeline: The New Silk Road to China," *AsiaNews.It,* April 27, 2005, www.asianews.it/view_p.php?l=en&art=3158 (June 12, 2005).

2. U.S. DOE Energy Information Administration, Kazakhstan Country Profile, www.eia.doe.gov/emeu/cabs/kazak.html (February 3, 2003).

3. For a detailed analysis of the Chinese motivations in the Kazakhstan pipeline project and the concept of the pan-Asian global energy bridge, see G. Christoffersen, "China's Intentions for Russian and Central Asian Oil and Gas," *National Bureau of Asian Research,* March 1998, 24–28. See also Sergei Troush, "Beijing Oil Diplomacy toward Central Asia and Russia: Basic Motivations and the Impact of the Events of 11 September 2001," SAIS Project on Systemic Change and International Security in Russia and the New States of Eurasia, www.sais-jhu.edu/programs/res/workingpapers .html (June 13, 2004).

4. Uzbekistan discontinued its membership in this regional organization in May 2005.

5. *Vremya novostei* (Moscow), July 27, 2005.

6. Official site of the president of Kazakhstan, www.president.kz/main/mainframe .asp?lng=en.

7. Amnesty International Concerns Regarding Uyghurs in the Xinjiang Uyghur Autonomous Region (XUAR), China, March 2004, Amnesty International Canada, www.amnesty.ca/Refugee/Concerns_Uighur.php (July 18, 2005).

8. *World Today* (Russian Independent TV News), www.ntv.ru/news/index.jsp?nid= 70205 (July 29, 2005).

9. The economic consequences of the September 11 events were heavily stressed by Chinese commentators. See "Zai Meiguo de Kongbu Baozha" (Terrorist Attacks on the USA), *Shijie zhishi* (Beijing) 19 (2001): 8–10.

10. *China Daily* (Beijing), September 14, 2001; September 19, 2001.

11. *Shijie zhishi* (Beijing) 20 (2001): 13–14.

12. *Vremya po* (Astana), October 9, 2001.

13. *Vremya novostei* (Moscow), July 6, 2005.

IV

CENTRAL ASIA AND ASIA PACIFIC

16

Shanghai Cooperation Organization: Challenges, Opportunities, and Prospects

Pan Guang

The creation of the Shanghai Five, which eventually became the Shanghai Cooperation Organization (SCO), made it possible for the first time in history to involve China, Russia, and the Central Asian states in a multilateral mechanism of regional security and economic cooperation. Since 1996, this mechanism has played an important role in confidence building in Central Asia, and it has prevented conflicts like the civil war in Afghanistan from proliferating as conflicts did in the Balkans and the Middle East. In a matter of years China and its SCO partners have resolved border issues left over from the past two centuries that impeded the development of good relationships. The September 11, 2001, terrorist attacks and the ensuing U.S.-led war on terrorism have posed opportunities and challenges to this newly established regional organization. Obviously it needs to formulate and perfect its operational mechanism speedily in order to carry out its mission in antiterrorism and economic cooperation in Central Asia. The SCO summit meeting in St. Petersburg in 2002 was a milestone as leaders of the six member states drew up strategic plans for the new organization's priorities. With major steps now taken to address these priorities, a solid foundation has been laid for SCO to better grasp opportunities and meet challenges on its way to steady development.

SEPTEMBER 11, WAR ON TERRORISM, AND SCO'S RESPONSE

After the terrorist attacks on the United States, the SCO prime ministers attending their meeting in Almaty, Kazakhstan, issued a joint communiqué on

September 14, 2001, denouncing the terrorist attacks while expressing sympathy for the American people and the victims. The joint communiqué declared that the SCO was ready to unite with all countries and international organizations, and that effective measures would be taken to wage an unremitting struggle against all forms of terrorism around the world.[1] Then Chinese Prime Minister Zhu Rongji made two suggestions at the conference: speed up the drafting of the Charter of Shanghai Cooperation Organization and open the proposed SCO antiterrorist center as soon as possible.[2]

The lack of strong unitary action by the SCO has a multifaceted rationale. First, the September 11 attack was directed against the United States, and it is natural that the United States initially played a dominant role in the consequent war on terrorism. It is impossible and unrealistic for the SCO to play any other role than that of a cooperative partner. Second, the SCO is by no means a military alliance that demands unitary actions be taken by its members. Moreover, no SCO member state was then under any direct terrorist attack from Afghanistan that called for joint actions of all the SCO members. Third, the permanent secretariat of the SCO had not come into operation yet. The SCO antiterrorist center was still under preparation. Consequently the SCO lacked the capability to make a quick response or take joint action. Fourth, the SCO countries were also members of other organizations or forums, such as the Commonwealth of Independent States (CIS) and the Dushanbe Group (comprising Russia, India, Iran, Tajikistan, Uzbekistan, and the Northern Alliance of Afghanistan), or even NATO's Partnership for Peace. This means they had an obligation to coordinate their actions with their fellow members in other institutions. Hence there were different degrees of involvement in the unfolding antiterrorist campaigns. Finally, the United States exacted differing requirements from the SCO members. For instance, it demanded military bases and territorial space from Uzbekistan and information sharing and diplomatic coordination from China and Russia. This is the main reason why SCO states have played different roles in the war on terrorism. It would have been illogical and premature for the SCO to take a lead role in the U.S. antiterrorist campaigns, considering the nature and status of the organization as well as the U.S. policy stance at the time.

Before the September 11 attacks, SCO members had taken different positions toward the counterterrorism mission of the organization. Kyrgyzstan was the first country to propose the establishment of an antiterrorist center. Uzbekistan and Tajikistan, threatened by terrorism from Afghanistan, attached similar importance to the counterterrorism agency. But Kazakhstan had always maintained that the SCO should focus more on economic cooperation. Russia was also not very interested in the antiterror mission at the beginning. Leading a counterterrorism mechanism in CIS already, Russia expressed its support only when it realized that China's participation was required. After September 11, some SCO members enhanced their cooperation with the United States, thereby ironically lowering their expectations of the SCO's antiterror mission. Russia played its role via the Dushanbe Group, as all the member states shared support for the Northern Alliance in Afghanistan. Meanwhile, bilateral cooperation on antiterrorism between the United States and the SCO member states got under way, as well as bilateral cooperation between the United States and Russia, and between the United States and China. As a result, a dual development was observed. On the one hand, all SCO members took an active part in the antiterror war in Central Asia, and cooperation from SCO members, particularly Russia, Uzbekistan, Tajikistan, and China, proved critical in ensuring the progress of the U.S.-led war. On the other hand, the SCO itself did not play a unitary role in the war, with each member taking its part mainly through bilateral antiterrorist cooperation with the United States.

This development does not mean that the SCO has no significance in the antiterror war in Central Asia. The Shanghai Five was the first international community to call for cooperation in countering terrorist groups in Central Asia. Since 1996, the Shanghai Five/SCO has mounted high-profile opposition to the "three evil forces" of terrorism, extremism, and separatism in Central Asia. On June 15, 2001, three months before September 11, the six member states of the SCO signed the Shanghai Convention, which foresaw the necessity of antiterror cooperation in Central Asia and laid down a solid legal base for combating terrorism.[3] After September 11, SCO members stepped up their coordination and consultation. The foreign ministers and law enforcement leaders of the SCO states held consultation meetings to discuss the situation in Central Asia following U.S. military operations in Afghanistan, and subsequent measures were taken to accommodate the changes. Besides their face-to-face meetings, then President Jiang Zemin and President Vladimir Putin kept hotline contacts. However, the SCO did not work out an effective, comprehensive, coordinated response strategy, a serious lapse in the wake of the unprecedented terrorist attacks and the consequent war on terrorism.

NEW CHALLENGES FACING SCO

Since the events of September 11, the strategic pattern and balance of power in Central Asia have changed, posing a host of new challenges for the SCO. The SCO's leading role in security and antiterror cooperation in Central Asia has been reduced. Before September 11, the Shanghai Cooperation Organization was the leading vehicle for security cooperation and the counterterrorism campaign in Central Asia. The increased American military presence in Central Asia after September 11 made the United States the major player in the antiterror war in Central Asia. Although the United States assumed a cooperative posture toward the SCO, the growing U.S. presence in the region weakened the SCO's leading role in counterterrorism.

The SCO's cohesion was undermined. As noted above, lacking an effective, fast, and coordinated antiterrorism mechanism, the SCO did not play a unitary role in the war on terrorism, prompting its members to focus on unilateral individual cooperation with the United States and other groups. This aggravated the centrifugal tendency in the organization and weakened its cohesive force.

The sluggish pace of economic cooperation in the SCO became a matter of serious concern, too. Given the rapid growth of American influence in Central Asia, the United States and the West will certainly increase their investment in the region. In contrast, the SCO has made little headway in establishing economic cooperation. If this is not changed, the SCO could have its existence and development undermined.

Central Asia is a rare region where four civilizations—Confucianism, Islam, Slavism, and Hinduism—merge. It is of great importance to strengthen the dialogue of civilizations and cultural cooperation within the framework of the SCO. Secular education administered by the former Soviet Union over more than seventy years has more or less dampened the appeal of Islamic extremism. However, in contrast with the Middle East, Central Asia harbors popular pro-American and pro-West sentiments. Given the increased presence of the United States in the region, the influence of the Western culture is certain to grow. This is likely to exert some impact on the cultural links and cooperation traditionally centered on the Silk Road from China to Russia and Central Asia.

At present, SCO members have a clear understanding of the grave challenges they are facing and are determined to strengthen their cooperation, especially by the establishment of the counterterror institution in Tashkent, so that it will be more capable of dealing with the prevailing complex situation. President Jiang Zemin and President Vladimir Putin, in their first meeting after September 11 in Shanghai on October 20, 2001, confirmed that the SCO should be further strengthened, particularly in carrying out the counterterror mission. They also agreed in explicit terms that Chechen and Eastern Turkestan terrorists should be targeted in the antiterror campaign.[4] China and Russia also agreed to establish a counterterror working group to deal with the threat of terrorism. This working group held its first meeting in Beijing on November 28–29, 2001, to exchange views on international counterterrorism and the situation in Afghanistan and reached a wide-ranging consensus.[5] All

SCO member states took similar steps, both bilateral and multilateral, to deal with the grave challenges brought about by the changed situation and, in so doing, laid a foundation for the final unitary position taken by SCO leaders at the St. Petersburg summit meeting.

OPPORTUNITIES FOR SCO DEVELOPMENT

While the SCO faces new challenges, the changed political, economic, and strategic pattern in Central Asia in the wake of the antiterror war has presented new opportunities for further development. Almost all the Central Asian countries have joined the international coalition against terrorism, which is unprecedented in history. This has created a favorable environment for the SCO to further strengthen its security cooperation and establish a regional counterterror mechanism. SCO members had a different position on the security cooperation and counterterrorism mission before September 11. In the meantime, some states were concerned that strengthened security cooperation and the establishment of an antiterror institution could increase the military elements of the SCO, which could arouse concerns from neighboring countries or even the United States and other Western countries. This is one of the reasons for the lack of progress in establishing the SCO counterterror institution since 1999 when the proposal was first put forward.

The emergence of an international coalition against terrorism after September 11 made all the SCO members appreciate the urgency in upgrading security cooperation and establishing the counterterror institution. With all the doubts and differences cleared up, a consensus was soon reached among all SCO members. In fact, since September 11, more bilateral and multilateral cooperation mechanisms have been initiated and established among SCO members and between members and nonmembers. For example, China has so far established bilateral counterterror mechanisms or dialogues with Russia, America, India, Pakistan, France, Britain, and Germany. In addition to its interest in conducting bilateral antiterror cooperation with SCO members, the United States has also expressed readiness to cooperate with the regional SCO counterterror institution. These developments have created a favorable atmosphere for the SCO to further its security cooperation and carry out its regional antiterror mission.

In addition, the collapse of the Taliban regime and the birth of a new Afghanistan have eliminated a hotbed of turmoil in the heartland of Asia, thus opening an unusual window of opportunity for stability and development in Central Asia, and the SCO member states in particular. Since 1996, the Shanghai Five/SCO has been holding high the banner against terrorism, separatism, and extremism. And it was the Taliban regime that supported these three evil forces after it came to power in 1996. Evidence so far clearly shows that the evil forces, whether in Tajikistan, Uzbekistan, or Russia's Chechnya or China's Xinjiang, or even in Kyrgyzstan and Kazakhstan, were closely linked to the Taliban and al-Qaeda. It was recently discovered that Osama bin Laden once informed leaders of the Eastern Turkestan group that he fully supported a jihad in Xinjiang.[6] Therefore, the collapse of the Taliban regime and establishment of the new Afghan government can promote regional stability and development. Since September 11, Afghanistan's neighboring countries, including SCO member states, have stepped up their efforts to crack down on the three evil forces and have made headway in their struggle against terrorism at home. Today, some of the most affected areas adjacent to Afghanistan have showed a tendency toward stability and improvement in economic growth and standard of living. These favorable changes have brightened the region's prospects, making it more attractive to foreign investments. So the process of peace and reconstruction in Afghanistan is a positive contribution to the stability and development of its neighboring countries.

The antiterror war has also helped target such criminal activities as drug trafficking, weapons smuggling, and illegal immigration, which have long found a safe haven in Afghanistan. This is an auspicious development for the Central Asian countries, particularly SCO members, now jointly combating various cross-border crimes and tackling other unconventional security problems. Unfortunately, these cross-border crimes have not disappeared with the rout of the Taliban regime. Crimes like drug trafficking remain a serious issue. It is reported that the Afghan government has cleared up only 15 percent of the drug-planting areas.[7] Drugs continue to be smuggled out of Afghanistan. In 2003, over 30 percent of the heroin around the world and 95 percent of the heroin in Europe came from Afghanistan, and globally ten million people consumed drugs from Afghanistan.[8] However, the cross-border criminal groups have lost state backing, thus putting SCO members in a better position to tackle those regional security and economic issues by means of bilateral and multilateral cooperation.

Finally, geopolitical changes in Central Asia will facilitate economic cooperation in this region and throughout Asia, notably energy cooperation in the Caspian basin. For example, nobody involved in discussions about the alignment of gas and oil pipelines in the past years realistically expected that a pipeline could go from Central Asia to the Arabian Sea by extending through Afghanistan and Pakistan. Yet such a line has now become possible, and even India may benefit from it. This new development will help diversify the outlet of energy development in Central Asia and break the deadlock in the Caspian Sea region caused by the "rivalry of pipelines." In the meantime, the birth of a new Afghanistan and Iran's improving relations with Europe and Japan are also promoting more investments and technology inflow from the West to Central Asia, thereby further pushing forward energy development in Central Asia. All these developments are creating a favorable environment for the SCO to foster economic cooperation and energy cooperation in particular.

AFTER ST. PETERSBURG: SCO'S STEADY PROGRESS

The strategic importance of the Agreement on Antiterrorism Agency in the Region created at the SCO meeting in St. Petersburg in 2002 lies in the fact that it has provided an effective legal basis for initiating substantial cooperation in the security field. Based on the agreement, the official launch of the Executive Committee of the SCO Regional Antiterrorism Structure (RATS) in Tashkent was the most remarkable event at the June 17, 2004, summit, representing a major step in facilitating security and antiterror cooperation within the SCO framework. This summit meeting took two important steps on security and antiterror cooperation. First, the SCO-Afghanistan antiterror partnership was formed when Afghanistan's President Karzai attended the summit by invitation and, second, the strategic initiative of the six SCO leaders signing the Cooperation Agreement among SCO Members on Fighting against Narcotics, Mental Drugs, and Their Precursors, and the inclusion of antidrug campaigns into the SCO antiterror cooperation framework.[9] With these developments, the overall coordination and rapid response capability of the SCO against terrorism and cross-border crimes would be enhanced.

In October 2002, China and Kyrgyzstan successfully conducted joint military counterterror maneuvers in their border area following the SCO antiterrorism guidelines. It was the first bilateral joint military operation within the SCO framework, signifying the formal startup of the SCO antiterror mission. In August 2003, five SCO members took part in the multilateral antiterror military exercise known as United 2003, which reinforced their quick-response capabilities against terrorists. Against the background of the security situation in the region, SCO and its mechanism for combating terrorism will play an increasingly active role in the future.

This mechanism does not exclude or reject any states or groups. It is meant to become an important terror-combating force in cooperation with the CIS counterterror centers in Minsk and Erevan and in cooperation with the United States, Japan, Europe, India, Pakistan, Iran, and other countries. The Interim Scheme of Relations between the Shanghai Cooperation Organization and other International Organizations and States, signed at the meeting of the

Foreign Ministers Council of the SCO on November 23, 2002, in Moscow,[10] and the Regulations for SCO Observers signed at the SCO summit meeting on June 17, 2004, in Tashkent promoted this kind of cooperation.[11]

Counterterror cooperation between the SCO and the United States is ongoing. All SCO members have established bilateral ties of counterterror cooperation with America, and these existing ties have laid down a solid base for an evolving SCO-U.S. counterterror regime. One example is the Sino-U.S. antiterror cooperation. Right after September 11, the main focus was on sharing intelligence and uprooting the financial sources of the terrorist groups. It also became important to maintain political and economic stability in Pakistan, support Pakistan's actions against terrorism, and prevent escalation of the India-Pakistan conflict. In the long term, this cooperation requires much to undertake. Through summit meetings between President Jiang Zemin and President Bush, and summit meetings between President Hu Jintao and President Bush, China and the United States outlined the long-term strategy for Sino-U.S. antiterror cooperation, and bilateral cooperation has made in-depth progress in this direction. The Sino-U.S. bilateral antiterror working groups, including the financial antiterror working group, were established and experts from the two countries consult regularly. In August 2002, the United States officially added the East Turkestan (ET) Islamic Movement to its list of terrorist organizations. Two weeks later, the U.N. Security Council also added the organization to its list of internationally recognized terrorist organizations, and all U.N. members are now obliged to freeze the overseas assets of the group. The opening of an FBI office in Beijing in November 2002 is another positive measure to further Sino-U.S. cooperation in combating terrorism and various cross-border crimes. China and the United States have also reached an agreement regarding the security of containers. In the meantime, other SCO members are carrying out similar cooperative efforts with the United States and fruitful achievements are also being made. All this, while serving the objectives of SCO's counterterror mission, also benefits the U.S. global struggle against terrorism.

To conclude, the Shanghai Five/SCO process has integrated this Sino-Russian-Central Asian group into a stabilizing multilateral institution that will help promote regional stability and cooperation. The U.S. military entry into Central Asia for the first time, the possible expansion of the U.S. war on terrorism, the postwar development in Afghanistan, the internal situation in Pakistan, and the relations between the two nuclear powers on the subcontinent will greatly influence the future development of the SCO. The Shanghai Cooperation Organization, with its dedication to counterterrorism and economic cooperation, will prove to be an increasingly important and effective institution of action, regionally and globally as well.

NOTES

1. "SCO Joint Communiqué," *Kazakhstan News Bulletin,* September 14, 2001.

2. "Prime Minister Makes Two Suggestions at SCO Conference," *Xinhua News Agency,* September 14, 2001.

3. Shanghai Convention, June 15, 2001.

4. *Jiefang Daily* (Shanghai), October 20, 2001.

5. *People's Daily* (Beijing), November 30, 2002.

6. State Council Information Office of PRC, "East Turkestan Terrorist Forces Cannot Get Away with Impunity," January 21, 2002.

7. *Report by U.N. Office for Drug Control and Crime Prevention,* 2002.

8. *Independent,* April 28, 2004.

9. Cooperation Agreement among SCO Members on Fighting against Narcotics, Mental Drugs, and Their Precursors (Tashkent), June 17, 2004.

10. Interim Scheme of Relations between the Shanghai Cooperation Organization and other International Organizations and States (Moscow), November 23, 2002.

11. Regulations for SCO Observers (Tashkent), June 17, 2004.

17

Kazakhstan and Confidence-Building Measures in Asia

Murat Laumulin

The Republic of Kazakhstan, the ninth largest territory in the world, is located near the center of the Eurasian continent and neighbors on Russia, China, Iran, and Afghanistan. Central Asia was on the periphery of international processes and global interests during the first ten years of its independence until the events of September 11, 2001, radically altered the situation. The Central Asian states actively participated in the operation in Afghanistan; Uzbekistan and Kyrgyzstan hosted U.S. military bases, while Kazakhstan allowed use of its air corridors.[1] Kazakhstan, as well as other Central Asian states, is interested in increased security cooperation with other countries. It is timely and desirable to institutionalize cooperation and create new forms of multilateral interaction.

One form of such institutionalization might be the Conference on Interaction and Confidence Building Measures in Asia (CICA), which was an international security initiative by Kazakhstan. Kazakhstan originally convened the Conference on Interaction and Confidence Building Measures in Asia in 1992. After ten years, the first CICA summit was held in Almaty in June 2002, resulting in two documents: the Almaty Act and the CICA Declaration on Terrorism Elimination and Promotion of Dialogue between Civilizations. This meeting marked the initiation of an important institutionalization process that has great potential.

The idea of CICA convening was supported by sixteen key Asian nations. The geographical area of CICA membership is wide. The total area of its members' territories is 38.8 million square kilometers, which is 89 percent of the Asian region and 72 percent of Eurasia. The population of its member states is 45 percent of the world's population.[2] The current members of the

CICA are Azerbaijan, China, Egypt, India, Iran, Israel, Kazakhstan, Kyrgyzstan, Pakistan, Palestine, Russia, Tajikistan, Turkey, and Uzbekistan. Observer status is held by Australia, Indonesia, Japan, Korea, Mongolia, Ukraine, the United States, Lebanon, Vietnam, Thailand, and Malaysia. Considerable progress has been achieved in the CICA on coordinating positions and building mechanisms for cooperation and security on the continent in a relatively short period. The main objective of the CICA is to strengthen confidence between states, conduct open policy, promote interstate security cooperation, ease tension in disputed border areas, support disarmament, and create an effective security system on the Asian continent.

The CICA will be one of the effective mechanisms to promote an atmosphere of confidence in the region as well as an important factor in establishing a security system in Asia. However, the process of CICA development will take a long time and require joint efforts by all the member states. Thus it is important to provide an interaction mechanism between Asian Pacific and Central Asian states within the framework of CICA. More active involvement of Asian Pacific region states into the CICA process would provide a new impetus to their security cooperation, something Kazakhstan strongly supports.

THE DEVELOPMENT OF THE IDEA OF THE CICA

One modern paradox is the opposing assessments concerning the level of security in the world. Some analysts and politicians assess the world as more secure, while others believe that the level of security has significantly decreased as a result of recent radical changes. Both assessments are valid. Nuclear confrontation has decreased, thereby strengthening global security from the Western perspective. The citizens of the former Soviet Union, however, see civil wars, ethnic conflicts, refugee flows, and political tensions escalating into military clashes that do not promote a sense of security. Additionally, the outside world may also consider the Central Asian situation as a potential source of instability as regards international security.

Perceiving the world as a potentially less secure environment, Kazakhstan undertook measures to convene the CICA. Kazakhstan sees it as a new system of relationships between states of the region that ensures sovereignty, territorial integrity, and security as well as cooperative economies and democratic institutions, while preserving cultural and national distinctions. However, security and confidence-building measures will remain the cornerstone in these efforts.[3]

The majority of Asian states need an effective system of security. For confirmation of this, we can turn to recent history and the modern development of Asian states. Most Asian countries became sovereign in the twentieth century after colonial and semicolonial dependence and fell under the oppression of various totalitarian, repressive, or military regimes. Asia was the arena of bloody conflicts, civil wars, aggression, nuclear and chemical attacks, and various social experiments. Consequently the creation of an Asian security system is an absolute necessity.

A central concern is that this region has the largest concentration of armaments, including nuclear weapons, after Europe. There are many regional conflicts and sources of tension, an uncontrolled process of militarization (military expenses in some Asian countries are rising three to four times faster than in European countries), and high levels of economic and political instability.

Asian countries play an important role in world policy. Recall India's proposals to create a nonnuclear and violence-free world, China's concept of a new international political order, Mongolia's initiative to establish a nuclear-free zone, Japan's initiative to set up Asian Pacific economic cooperation, and proposals by the ASEAN (Association of Southeast Asian Nations) countries to create similar zones in Southeast Asia.

Finally, although indivisible from a geographical point of view, Asia has never been united in a political or geopolitical sense. In other parts of the world there are forums to discuss essential problems. In Europe, it is the Organization for Security and Cooperation (OSCE) as well as other structures, in America it is the Organization of American States, and in Africa it is the Organization of African Unity. Asian states could also benefit from a system of international relations that allows them to develop their economy and political systems in an atmosphere of confidence and security.

The Organization for Security and Cooperation in Europe has impacted the development of the idea of CICA. The European experience deserves the closest attention, since Kazakhstan, one of the post-Soviet republics, is a member of the OSCE. Asia, however, needs another system that takes into consideration the complicated history of relationships between Asian states. While cultural polarization in Europe receded with the end of the Cold War, in Asia national peculiarities and the growth of traditional contradictions were strengthened. Additionally, terms such as freedom, democracy, and human rights, which are fixed in the OSCE documents, have different connotations and meanings in Asia. Any attempt to spread these concepts by imitating the OSCE system will be taken by many Asian countries as meddling in their internal affairs. This makes any mechanical copying of the European model impossible.[4]

Kazakhstan's CICA proposal, while not duplicating the European model, would create an Asian security system in which a participant's security would be guaranteed and protected by a whole complex of measures, including international law and concrete measures to reduce the level of military preparations in Asia. The creation of such a system requires ongoing negotiations on matters of arms control, disarmament and strengthening confidence, the creation of a conflict-prevention mechanism, risk reduction, and effective peaceful settlement. The practical benefits of such a system of security are obvious. However, the CICA proposal will also cover such spheres of international relations as the economy, ecological security, and humanitarian cooperation.

The early meetings to establish the CICA are a testimony to the idea that the creation of an Asian security system enjoys support by a substantial number of Asian states and has significant potential for realization. The president of Kazakhstan initiated the idea of the CICA at different international meetings during 1992 and 1993, such as the forty-seventh session of the U.N. General Assembly in October of 1992 and the North Atlantic Cooperation Council meeting in February 1993. The implementation of the idea of CICA was continued at meetings for experts of the Ministries of Foreign Affairs of Asian countries held on the Kazakh initiative: the first meeting in April 1993, the second in August-September 1993, the third in October 1994.

Representatives of ten countries and two international organizations participated in the first experts meeting; at the second meeting the number of participants rose to twenty-four representatives (including seven observers) and four international organizations. There were representatives from Azerbaijan, Afghanistan, Vietnam, India, Iran, Israel, China, North Korea, Kyrgyzstan, Mongolia, Palestine, Pakistan, Russia, Syria, Tajikistan, Turkey, and Uzbekistan. There were observers from Australia, Cambodia, Republic of Korea, Indonesia, Thailand, Turkmenistan, and Japan. The international organizations present included UNO, OSCE, the League of Arab States, and the Islamic Conference Organization. At the third meeting in October 1994, Bangladesh, Egypt, Lebanon, and Nepal joined the CICA process.[5]

During this process it became clear that a significant number of Asian states and authoritative international organizations support the creation of an Asian security system. In addition, a decision was made to establish a special working group (SWG) during the meeting of ministers of foreign affairs. Most participants believed that creating an Asian system for security would be difficult because of existing disputes, conflicts, contradictions, and claims between potential participants. Most participants shared the opinion that the first stage of the preparation of the CICA must involve both bilateral and multilateral consultations to figure out the positions of participants and specify the aims of the process. Obviously, not all of Kazakhstan's proposals on the structure, organization, and principles of the CICA were accepted, and some aspects of the documents were criticized. For instance, some debated proposals to support market reforms, a nuclear test ban, and some aspects of human rights.[6] Nonetheless, in spite of existing differences and contradictions among Asian countries, the idea of an Asian security system found support among a significant number of Asian states.

CHANGES IN THE INTERNATIONAL SITUATION AND THE PROCESS OF THE CICA

In a positive move for CICA, some countries shifted their positions and some regional transformations occurred after the CICA meeting of February 1996. Russia and China began to actively support the idea of Asian security, and the United States also changed its position significantly. In the course of bilateral consultations, American diplomats expressed support for strengthening and developing regional organizations as the main basis of an overarching Asian security system like ASEAN. Positive developments in the Middle East and cooling of the Arab-Israeli conflict also had favorable consequences for the CICA. The negative reaction among some Arab states and the Islamic Conference Organization relating to Israel's participation in the CICA process disappeared.

There were also impulses in Central Asia to promote the CICA process. Uzbekistan initiated the creation of the U.N. Regional Center for Preventive Diplomacy in Central Asia that could become part of the CICA process. Kazakhstan, Kyrgyzstan, and Uzbekistan are also creating a regional interaction system along the same principles and spirit of the CICA. Countries outside of Asia have also begun to express interest in the CICA. Egypt expressed its intention to take part in the CICA process, and Australia is becoming more active.

In spite of existing difficulties, there are favorable conditions, from the Kazakh perspective, for further development of the CICA process.[7] Kazakhstan holds the opinion that a reliable system of security in Asia cannot be created unless all nations participating in the CICA observe certain basic principles: guaranteed territorial integrity, respect for the sovereignty of all participating countries, noninterference in internal affairs, and negotiations as a base for solution of conflicts and crisis situations. These principles are recognized by all members of the world community and are the foundation of international law, the basic documents of the United Nations, most regional organizations, and most bilateral and multilateral agreements. The unconditional recognition of these principles by members of the Asian community is fundamental to the CICA.

The complications, however, are numerous. First, the global consensus on these principles as reflected in the documents, principles, and structures of existing international organizations, especially the OSCE, should be the basis of the CICA. However, while one view asserts that Asia will not accept the CICA proceeding along the path of the OSCE, another view is to follow the experience of the OSCE. Second, although Kazakhstan and other countries consider the rejection of spheres of influence to be a basic principle of international law and order and the concept of spheres of influence is denied at the official level, this policy still exists. While spheres of influence may be explained as an objective consequence of frequently incomparable economic, political, and military potential of different countries, Kazakhstan considers rejection of this concept as one of the main principles of the CICA. Third, the problem of security guarantees should be solved during the process of the CICA. There are also two alternative views on the matter: the participating countries provide the security guarantees to each other on the basis of bilateral agreements, or a multilateral treaty might be signed and provide collective security guarantees to every party. Kazakhstan believes that the problem should be solved on the basis of both views, starting from bilateral agreements and resulting in the Pan-Asian Treaty within the framework of the CICA. Fourth, there is the issue of the implementation of the CICA mechanism. Kazakhstan believes that the most reasonable mechanism might be a regime of periodic consultations as a basis of activity and maintenance of the CICA. Finally, there is the nuclear problem. Kazakhstan realizes how delicate the problems of nuclear weapons, nuclear nonproliferation, and nuclear tests are for some countries. Although taking into account the position of such states as China, India, Pakistan, and Israel, Kazakhstan proposes to discuss and ultimately stop nuclear tests in Asia, freeze and reduce nuclear arsenals, and strengthen the regime of nuclear nonproliferation in Asia as an integral element of the Asian security system. In addition to these main obstacles to Asian security, Kazakhstan presumes that the other issues connected with the creation of this security system—for example, problems of conventional arms, economic and ecological aspects of security, humanitarian cooperation, struggle against terrorism and narcotics, emigration and immigration policy, and the refugee problem—might be resolved after the startup of the CICA mechanism.[8]

Kazakhstan regarded the February 1996 meeting of the deputy ministers as an opportunity to adopt the CICA declaration of principles. Unfortunately, not all participants were ready to adopt this declaration, confirming the difficulty of the process of establishing the CICA.[9] Kazakh diplomats continued to push for the adoption of the CICA declaration at the pan-Asian security and confidence summit in November 2001. The events of September 11, 2001, and the resulting antiterrorist operation in Afghanistan, however, delayed the CICA summit until 2002.

The first CICA summit on June 2002 was an important step in Kazakh foreign policy. Sixteen Asian states signed two documents: the Almaty Act and the Declaration on Terrorism Elimination and Promotion of Dialogue between Civilizations.[10] The summit took place in a difficult international and regional situation, which followed both the antiterrorist operation in Afghanistan and an Indo-Pakistani confrontation. Nevertheless, the CICA summit enhanced Kazakhstan's international reputation and reinforced its position in Asian, Eurasian, and global affairs.

SECURITY AND COOPERATION

The main objective of the CICA is to enhance cooperation through elaborating multilateral approaches toward promoting peace, security, and stability in Asia.[11] In order to achieve this objective, the member states will take the necessary steps to develop the CICA as a forum for dialogue, consultations, and adoption of decisions and measures on the basis of consensus on security issues in Asia. The CICA parties encourage all member states that are parties to a dispute to settle it peacefully in conformity with the principles envisaged in the U.N. Charter.

Globalization is *the* modern challenge. While it offers opportunities for growth and development, at present the benefits of globalization are unevenly shared among the nations, and much remains to be done to ensure that its benefits be comprehensively and equitably distributed at the global level. Joint actions and coordinated responses are necessary to deal with challenges and threats that the CICA states and peoples are faced with.

CHALLENGES TO SECURITY IN THE CICA VIEW

CICA member states seek to promote regional and international security and stability, which will also contribute to peaceful settlement of existing crisis situations and emerging disputes.[12] The continuing existence and proliferation of nuclear weapons, as well as chemical and biological weapons, threatens all humanity. The member states pledge to support efforts for the global elimination of all weapons of mass destruction (WMD), and therefore they commit themselves to increased cooperation for the prevention of proliferation of all such weapons, including nuclear weapons, which constitute a particular danger to international peace and security.

The ending of the Cold War created an opportunity for the international community to pursue nuclear disarmament. All nations should keep options open, including the possibility of convening an international conference to identify ways of eliminating nuclear dangers and negotiating a comprehensive and verifiable nuclear weapons convention. The CICA members support the establishment of zones free from nuclear weapons and other WMD in Asia on the basis of arrangements freely arrived at among the states of the region concerned.

The member states believe in ensuring security at the lowest level of armament and military forces. They recognize the necessity to curb excessive and destabilizing accumulation of conventional armaments. They emphasize the importance of international strategic stability to maintaining world peace and security and to the continued progress of arms control and disarmament. They emphasize the importance of multilateral negotiations for the prevention of an arms race in outer space.

The member states condemn terrorism in all its forms and manifestations as well as supporting it and failing to condemn it. The threat posed by terrorism has been growing over the past decade. Terrorism in all its forms is a transnational threat that endangers the lives of individuals and peoples and undermines the territorial integrity, unity, sovereignty, and security of states. The menace of terrorism has been magnified by its close links with drug trafficking, illicit trafficking of small arms and light weapons and their transfer to terrorist groups, racist ideologies, separatism, and all forms of extremism, which obtain financing and supply manpower for terrorist activities. Member states regard as criminal all acts, methods, and practices of terrorism and declare their determination to cooperate on a bilateral as well as multilateral basis to combat terrorism, including its possible sources. In order to eradicate this menace to peace and security, they pledge to unite their efforts not to allow terrorism in any form to be launched or financed from the territory of any state and refuse to provide terrorists with safe haven and protection. The parties support the elaboration of a comprehensive convention on international terrorism.

Separatism is one of the main threats to the security and stability, sovereignty, unity, and territorial integrity of states. Member states will not support establishment on the territory of another member state of any separatist movements or entities, and, if such emerge, will refuse political, economic, or other kinds of relations with them, will not allow the territories and communications of the member states to be used by the movements and entities, and will not render them economic, financial, or other assistance.

CICA participants reject the use of religion as a pretext by terrorists and separatist movements and groups to achieve their objectives. They also reject all forms of extremism and will work to promote tolerance among nations and peoples.

Illegal drug trafficking is a major threat to internal and international stability and security as well as to human welfare. This problem is closely linked with the socioeconomic and political situation in several regions, terrorist activities across the world, and international criminal groups engaged in transnational crime, money laundering, and illicit small arms and light weapons trafficking. Several states in Asia require priority attention and assistance from the international community in order to combat drug trafficking. The CICA countries recognize the need for effective strategies to reduce production, supply, and demand for drugs. They agree to monitor suspicious financial flows, including issues related to incomes and transparency of bank operations in accordance with existing international legal instruments, and identify the sources of production, consumption, and trafficking of drugs.

In order to assist the practical implementation of these tasks, multinational training courses and exercises as well as exchange of information among the competent authorities of the member states will be promoted. The parties call on major consuming countries to play a more active role in providing equipment, training and educational courses, rehabilitation, and technical and financial assistance to Asian drug-producing and transit countries. Crop substitution plans and alternative development strategies in drug-producing regions in Asia should be encouraged to tackle the menace of illicit drugs more effectively.

The CICA nations recognize corruption as a transnational crime that calls for concerted multilateral action. They emphasize the importance of banning the transfer of illicit funds and wealth and the need for enhanced international cooperation in tracing and repatriating such assets.

The CICA states recognize that illicit traffic in small arms and light weapons poses a threat to peace and security and is directly linked with terrorist activity, separatist movements, drug trafficking, and armed conflict. Accordingly, they underline the importance of the firearms protocol reached in the framework of the U.N. Convention against Transnational Organized Crime and the program of action adopted by the U.N. Conference on the Illicit Trade in Small Arms and Light Weapons in All Its Aspects, which was held in New York in July 2001. They are determined to cooperate with each other on bilateral and multilateral bases to prevent such threats to peace and security in Asia.

Confidence-Building Measures

In the context of achieving CICA objectives, the parties will take the necessary steps for the elaboration and implementation of measures aimed at enhancing cooperation and creating an atmosphere of peace, confidence, and friendship. Such measures should be in accordance with the principles of the U.N. Charter, CICA, and international law. In doing so, they will take into account specific features and characteristics in various regions in Asia and proceed on a gradual and voluntary basis.[13]

The CICA members encourage all states in the region having disputes to solve their disputes peacefully through negotiations in accordance with the principles enshrined in the U.N. Charter and international law. They recognize that the resolution of territorial and other disputes and implementation of arms control agreements may, depending on specific situations, facilitate implementation of confidence-building measures; on the other hand, they also recognize that implementation of confidence-building measures may facilitate or create a conducive climate for the resolution of disputes and arms control agreements.

The CICA nations recognize that disarmament and arms control have a significant role in enhancing confidence building among regional states. They affirm that being a state party to internationally negotiated instruments should not be interpreted as affecting the inalienable right of all parties to those treaties to develop research, production, and use of nuclear technology, chemical and biological materials, and equipment for peaceful purposes in accordance with the provisions of these instruments. They reiterate the importance of negative security assurances to the non–nuclear weapon states and express their readiness to consider steps that could take the form of an internationally legally binding instrument.

NEW GEOPOLITICS IN ASIA AND THE CICA

The terrorist acts of September 11 in the United States and the subsequent routing of the Taliban regime in Afghanistan changed the geopolitical situation in the world forever. Central Asia shares these dramatic changes. The roles played by all geopolitical and regional leaders—Russia, the United States, China, the European Union, Iran, Turkey, and the Central Asian countries—were altered. However, the Afghan conflict no longer affects Central Asia; the situation is stabilizing.[14]

The United States strengthened its ties with south Caucasian and Central Asian states, intruding into the sphere of Russia's vital interests. On the whole, the successful anti-Taliban operation allowed the United States to strengthen its domination of the world. In fact, China, the only country able to oppose the United States, seized the moment to move against terrorists at home and enlist the support of its neighbors in squashing separatists in China.

This explains why Beijing offered no comment on the American retribution in Afghanistan.[15]

By the middle of 2002, the U.S. operation in Afghanistan destroyed the tacitly accepted balance of forces in the region among Russia, China, and itself.[16] Today, the Kremlin is less active in Central Asia, while Washington is stepping up its activity. Despite seemingly closer ties between Russia and the West (and the United States in particular), no historic rapprochement has occurred. On December 13, 2001, Washington unilaterally withdrew from the ABM treaty, while NATO continued its eastward enlargement. Russia's position weakened in several respects. First, it is no longer the only dominating military-political force in the region. The U.S. military bases in Uzbekistan and Kyrgyzstan have become the linchpin of the unfolding American military and political presence in Central Asia. Second, the United States is actively claiming the role of regional security guarantor. Third, U.S. efforts to exclude Russia from the system of hydrocarbon transportation are also indicative. Russia's regional sphere of influence is contracting. Moscow has neither the political nor the economic levers to close the region to other centers of power and maintain itself as the dominant force.[17]

The balance of power in the region has been changing rapidly. The United States came as a military factor and made its influence strongly felt across the region. There is a latent yet accelerating process of displacing Russia from its sphere of military-political and economic influence. By their presence in Central Asia, the United States and NATO have created a military threat to China. There is also a need to neutralize the so-called Islamic threat.

In the wake of the events of September 11, geopolitics in Central Asia changed dramatically. On the whole, new geopolitical developments will bring the region into closer contact with the world's economy and geopolitics. The current security situation is far from stable; the old threat has been replaced with new ones born of the geopolitical rivalry in Central Asia. The Great Game has entered another stage but is far from being over.

Kazakhstan tried to enhance stability in the region after the events of September 11 by holding the first summit of the heads of CICA member states on June 4–6, 2002, in Almaty. Although the participants did not reach reconciliation, the CICA served as a good forum for the establishment of more confident relations among the states of Asia. The CICA helped overcome barriers of mistrust and suspicion by means of dialogue. Although the CICA is not yet a real mechanism of regional security maintenance in Asia, it can play a supplementary role in Central Asia. Nevertheless, for Kazakhstan, the realization of a large-scale international forum strengthened the country's position and increased its authority in the international arena, which in turn raises trust in

Kazakhstan not only as a stable state but also as a state open for cooperation and dialogue.

NOTES

1. Murat Laumulin, "Central Asia after 11 September," *Central Asia and the Caucasus* 4 (2002): 29–38; see also B. Rumer, ed., *Central Asia: A Gathering Storm?* (Armonk, N.Y.: Sharpe, 2002).

2. A. Kozhikhov, "CICA: Realities and Perspectives," *Analytic* 3 (2002): 23–24.

3. Murat Laumulin, *The Security, Foreign Policy, and International Relationship of Kazakhstan after Independence: 1991–2001* (Almaty: Kaziis/Friedrich Ebert Stiftung, 2002), 161–64.

4. K. Tokaev, "It Is Impossible to Copy the CSCE Experience in Asia?" *Panorama,* November 1994, 7.

5. Murat Laumulin, "Asian Security and the CICA," *Kazakhstan and the World Community* 1 (1995): 40–48.

6. Proposals of the Islamic Republic of Pakistan concerning the Formation of the Special Working Group (SWG) for Preparation of the Conference on Confidence Building Measures in Asia, August 1994.

7. Memorandum of the Ministry of Foreign Affairs, the Republic of Kazakhstan, September 1994, 3.

8. Foreign Minister Kasymzhomart Tokaev, speech on the third meeting of the CICA in Almaty, October 28, 1994.

9. See *Documents: Suppl. Kazakhstan and the World Community* 1 (1996).

10. See the Almaty Act of the Heads of State or Government of the Member States of the Conference on Interaction and Confidence Building Measures in Asia (CICA), Almaty, June 4, 2002. In the preamble to this document, the parties declared the following basic political principles:

> Having met in Almaty at a time of profound changes which are taking place in Asia and the world to set up our vision of security in Asia and enhance our capabilities for cooperation on issues of common concern for our peoples; Recognizing the close link between peace, security and stability in Asia and in the rest of the world; Committing ourselves to working to ensure peace and security in Asia and making it a region open to dialogue and co-operation; Believing that the CICA process presents new opportunities for co-operation, peace and security in Asia; Declaring our determination to form in Asia a common and indivisible area of security, where all states peacefully co-exist, and their peoples live in conditions of peace, freedom and prosperity, and confident that peace, security and development complement, sustain and reinforce each other; Reaffirming our commitment to the UN Charter, as well as to the Declaration on the Principles Guiding Relations Among CICA Member States, which is an integral part of the Almaty Act, as the basis for our future co-operation; Considering that all aspects of comprehensive security in Asia, including its political and military aspects, confidence-building measures, economic and environmental issues, humanitarian and cultural co-operation, are interdependent and interrelated and should be pursued actively; Confident that full, equal and com-

prehensive implementation and observance of the principles, provisions and commitments enshrined in the Almaty Act will create the conditions for advanced co-operation among the CICA Member States and will guide us towards a better future, which our peoples deserve; Have adopted to cooperate in the security sphere.

11. Almaty Act, pt. I.

12. Almaty Act, pt. II.

13. Almaty Act, pt. III.

14. See *New Challenges and New Geopolitics in Central Asia: After September 11* (Almaty: Kaziss, 2003), 4–8.

15. Xia Liping, "Sino-U.S. Security and Strategic Relations after September 11," *SIIS Journal,* August 2002, 29–37; Xuewu Gu, "China und die USA," *Internationale Politik* 2 (2002): 7–16; and Yang Jiemian, "Sino-US Relations in the New Triangle," *SIIS Journal,* August 2002, 1–10.

16. See E. Rumer, "Flashman's Revenge: Central Asia after September 11," *Strategic Forum,* December 2002, 1–8.

17. *New Challenges*, 89–93.

18

The Legacy of Sovietism in Central Asia and Mongolia

Orhon Myadar

The collapse of the former Soviet Union triggered unprecedented changes that galvanized and refashioned world geopolitics. The countries that evolved from the dissolution of the Soviet Union, as well as countries that had to reform entirely because of their dependence on the former Soviet Union, felt the impact of this event to the greatest degree. The recent waves of popular dissent and civil upheavals that have taken place in the post-Soviet space — Georgia, Ukraine, and Kyrgyzstan — have illuminated the consequences of what Russian president Vladimir Putin recently called "the greatest geopolitical catastrophe of the century." While Putin's lament over the demise of the Soviet Union may not lead to the conclusion that post-Soviet countries are worse off now or that it was a genuine tragedy, the remark illuminates the complexity of the changes that accompanied the fall of the giant multinational state.

The Soviet collapse had a profound effect on the countries that formed the greater socialist orbit in general. Though independent (at least superficially), these countries were deeply impacted by the Soviet Union and were led by communist parties that essentially served as agents of Soviet domination in their respective countries. Furthermore, the countries that gained their independence with the Soviet collapse have faced a challenging venture in crafting their own statehood detached from their former metropolitan center. Following the Soviet disintegration, most of the countries stumbled into economic and political limbo with the abrupt discontinuation of assistance from their former master. The basic formula of the governance of the newly independent states largely replicated the former Soviet system, resulting in a blend of bureaucratic authoritarianism, corruption, and crumpled welfare systems.

Although the list of countries affected by the collapse of the Soviet Union stretches across the former socialist camp and beyond, this chapter primarily focuses on the Central Asian republics and Mongolia. It comparatively analyzes the role that the former Soviet Union played in refashioning the societies of Central Asia and Mongolia. It examines the impact of Soviet policies and the resulting cultural and social effects in the respective societies. Finally, the chapter analyzes post-Soviet conditions and entertains a comparative discussion of recent political situations in these countries.

MONGOLIA'S RELEVANCE TO THE REGION

When Central Asia emerged into world geopolitics following the Soviet collapse, whether to include Mongolia in the region was debated by Mongolian policy makers and scholars. Proponents of Mongolian alignment to the region argued that Mongolia shared a common history and culture with the Central Asian societies. Baabar posited that the new Central Asian zone should include both Mongolia and Turkey, whose influence in the region has been significant and should not be underestimated.[1] Opponents of including Mongolia in the Central Asian zone advocated aligning Mongolia with the northeastern region of Asia instead, as it has been for decades. For example, Olzvoi argued that Mongolian alignment with the Central Asian countries would not help Mongolia, since Central Asia is essentially landlocked and Mongolia needs to try to overcome its own landlocked predicament.[2] Regardless of this debate, Central Asia has become almost universally understood to include the five former Soviet republics exclusively.

Although Mongolia does not "belong" to the Central Asian region, various scholars have noted the importance of Mongolia in the region, particularly its historical significance. According to Martha Olcott, "The imprint the Mongol conquest set on Central Asian society was more powerful than that of the Russians and Soviets."[3] The Mongolian empire played an unequivocally important role in mixing the populations of the region and thus had a lasting impact on the regional societies.[4]

The legacy of Genghis Khan occupies a prominent space in literature recording the historical impact of Mongolia in the region.[5] "All the dynasties following Mongols in Central Asia (Timurids, Uzbeks, and Moghuls) claimed descent from Genghis Khan."[6] In his comprehensive narrative on Genghis Khan's legacy,[7] Chesney notes that "in order to comprehend the ascendancy of legitimate political communities in Central Asia, one must begin with Genghis Khan."[8] He argues that "the career and 'meaning' of Genghis Khan provided a kind of constitutional framework[9] for later generations within which to consider the evolution of the political environment of Central Asia—from his death in 1227 to at least the end of the eighteenth century."[10] Thus, the influence of Genghis Khan and his successor empires on the political culture of Central Asia should not be underestimated.

Mongolia's recent history also provides significant fodder for a comparative analysis. Although Mongolia was outside the Soviet Union, Soviet influence swept through the Mongolian space and Mongolia was by no means free from the Soviet leash. While the Central Asian societies and Mongolia had a different degree of affiliation to and dependence on the former Soviet Union, there are disquieting similarities in terms of the policies that were implemented in the respective countries. For the entire Soviet period, both the Central Asian states (under the framework of the greater Soviet Union) and Mongolia were ruled by a single dominant party and were formed by the policies of their respective party leadership. Both were ruled by a pyramidal governmental structure, with the "supreme party" at its apex. Administrative, cultural, and political structures were engineered through the mill of the Soviet party machinery. Thus the shared history among the societies of Central Asia and Mongolia not only illustrates the scope of the Soviets' reach among their satellites but provides important parallels for those who examine the comparative impact of sovietism inside and outside the formal Soviet demarcation.

While there is a common history among the Soviet-dominated societies, an important distinction between Mongolia and the Central Asian states should not be overlooked. Compared to the newly independent states of Central Asia, Mongolia has enjoyed decades of history as an independent state. Having gained its independence in 1924 and joined the United Nations in 1961, Mongolia has carved for itself the symbolic trappings of an independent state and necessary codes of conventional statehood, including well-defined national borders, a constitution, a flag, an anthem, and diplomatic ties. As the result of the breakup of the former Soviet Union, Mongolia reasserted its de facto independence rather than the de jure independence of Central Asian republics. Therefore, its role as an independent state for several decades could offer lessons to the newly emerging states.

As illustrated in table 18.1, its geopolitical location bestowed on Mongolia the potential to build bridges between the predominantly landlocked Central Asian countries and East Asia. (Although Kazakhstan and Turkmenistan border on the Caspian Sea, it is an inland waterway with limited transportation value.) Mongolia is separated from the region by sixty-seven kilometers east of Kazakhstan, while ethnic Kazakhs comprise the majority of the population in western Mongolia. Mongolia's geopolitical proximity to the northeastern Asian region and its relations with East Asian states—Japan, China, and South Korea—could serve as a passageway by which Central Asian states

Table 18.1. Population and Topography

	Population (Millions) 2000	Surface Area (Thousand sq. km) 1999	Land Boundaries	Coastline
Kazakhstan	15	2,717	Kyrgyzstan, PRC, Russia, Turkmenistan, Uzbekistan	Borders the Caspian Sea
Kyrgyzstan	5	199	PRC, Kazakhstan, Tajikistan, Uzbekistan	Landlocked
Tajikistan	6	143	Afghanistan, Kyrgyzstan, PRC, Uzbekistan	Landlocked
Turkmenistan	5	488	Iran, Afghanistan, Uzbekistan	Landlocked
Uzbekistan	25	447	Afghanistan, Kazakhstan, Kyrgyzstan, Tajikistan, Turkmenistan	Borders the Caspian Sea
Mongolia	2	1,567	Russia, PRC	Landlocked

Sources: For population, see *World Development Report 2002: Building Institutions for Markets* (Washington, D.C.: World Bank, 2002), 232–33; for surface area, see World Bank, *2001 World Development Indicators* (Washington, D.C.: Development Data Center, 2001), 12–14

could broaden their network of relations with East Asia and as a corridor for trade routes for both regions to penetrate these markets.

SOVIETIZATION IN CENTRAL ASIA AND MONGOLIA

Totalitarianism

If totalitarianism aims at and succeeds in organizing the masses and eradicating plurality of men [persons], as Hannah Arendt articulated, what Mongolia and the Central Asian states experienced was a form of totalitarianism, at least to a significant extent.[11] In the discourse of "totalizing" entire peoples, various elements of social, political, and economic cultures of the preceding societies were deeply constrained if not entirely eradicated during the Soviet era and were replaced by new codes and artifacts of the artificial nation.

In the process of the Soviet nation creation project, both Central Asia and Mongolia (to a lesser degree) experienced Soviet totalitarianism, hence sovietism. As Olivier Roy argues, "What was stamped on the [them] was neither communism nor socialism but Sovietism."[12] The Soviet ideology was transformed into a tool to inculcate its ideological implications into all aspects of the lives of various peoples. Soviet propaganda swept through the nation, serving a critical role in creating a national psyche.

Politically, both the Central Asian states and Mongolia were ruled by a single dominant party for the entire period of sovietism. This domination by governing parties was totalitarian, with leaders neither elected by a popular vote nor representative of different voices. The new political elite passed through the mill of the governing apparatus and its official ideology. During the Soviet era, elites in Mongolia and the Soviet republics "followed a fairly uniform professional training (as engineers), they joined the party, they underwent a formal russification, and they accepted (or rather internalized) the rules of the game (respect for an ideological code)."[13]

Given the purpose of creating a thriving socialist world in opposition to the West generally, and the rationalization of the worker in contemporary capitalism specifically, the Soviet command economy served as the blueprint for satellite countries of the socialist orbit with respect to their economic systems. The societies of Central Asia and Mongolia were no exception.

The centralized command economic module was intended to create "a more egalitarian society, to meeting the basic needs of its citizens (especially the working class), and to making the amenities of a modern society available to all."[14] As a first step in the pursuit of this utopian goal, most productive resources were made the property of the government, both in the Soviet Union and Mongolia, facilitating the central administration of production. In earlier decades of socialist leadership, as was the case in the Soviet Union, Mongolian leaders launched an extensive campaign against private ownership. The ruling parties in the respective societies planned, administered, and controlled the production and distribution of goods and services. "The economy itself was conceived as a well-ordered machine, where everyone would simply produce goods of the description and quantity specified by the central state's statistical bureau, as Lenin had foreseen."[15] The daily existence of functional members of the societies revolved around their allotted contributions to this end. Thus the Soviet-modeled command economy served a greater role than merely maximizing productivity as purported by its engineers.

Cultural Revolution: Social (De)Construction

In the process of creating a supernation, Central Asian and Mongolian societies were collectively deconstructed, constructed, and reconstructed during the Soviet era. As a part of this process, the law, courts, and penal codes were transformed. "The legal powers of the Islamic establishment were terminated with the final abolition of the *Shari'ah* courts (Quranic law), and of the *adat* (customary law) in 1927" in Central Asia.[16] In Mongolia, the new constitution initially adopted in 1924 was amended twice during socialism, resulting in a largely imitated version of the Soviet constitution.

Campaigns to promote atheism and suppress religious rituals were pressed in the Islamic societies of Central Asia and predominantly Buddhist Mongolia. "In the first decade of Soviet power polygamy, the wearing of the veil *(purdah)* and the Arabic script in which the Qur'an is written were abolished" in Central Asia.[17] Similarly, starting as early as 1937, the purges began their rampage in Mongolia, suppressing both Buddhism and shamanism for many years to come. During the purges, ritual sites were destroyed and lamas as well as shamans were killed or deported. The full extent of this destruction will probably never be known, however, recent studies have unveiled the unfortunate fate of thousands of Buddhist monks who vanished in the periodic purges from the 1930s through the 1960s.

In the process of molding the peoples into an orderly society, manufacturing a national *habitus,* rapid Russification took place in both Central Asia and Mongolia. Although Mongolia never adopted the Russian language to the same extent that the republics did (Mongolian remained an official language and Russian was confined to elite groups), the change in writing was adopted equally. The traditional Uyghur script was replaced by Cyrillic in Mongolia in 1941. In the case of Central Asia, Roy observes that "the changes went from reformed Arabic alphabet (1923–29) . . . to Latin (1929–40), then to Cyrillic (1940)."[18] This clearly went beyond ideological censorship or perhaps Foucauldian surveillance. Although the majority of the people were declared literate after an extensive public education effort, the old literature (including religious writings) could no longer be read by the new generations. In addition, the transformation of script was a long process. It took years before the majority of the population grasped the new writing and became literate. Mongolian was retained as the official spoken language in Mongolia, but Russian words penetrated into the everyday vocabulary. The gravitational center of the Russification was education, which paved the path of upward social mobility. More and more children were exclusively educated in Russian schools and thus became native Russian speakers, with Mongolian a second language. Moreover, Mongol students increasingly received their higher education in the Soviet Union.

In Central Asia, the degree of russification varied from republic to republic, with the greatest occurring in Kazakhstan, given the higher proportion of Slavic migration. Elites in Central Asia and those "wishing to be promoted to the higher echelons of Soviet institutions were required to be fluent in Russian and, ostensibly at least, demonstrate their Communist credentials."[19]

Ironically, the reverse pattern, in which Russians were molded into local cultures, was virtually nonexistent. The same picture can be observed in all Central Asian countries, which shows that "it was the indigenous people who lived their lives according to a double code under the Soviet control."[20] In Mongolia, elites intermarrying with Russians became trendy. However, time and again, even at the marital level, it was the Mongolians who learned Russian and became russified, even while residing in Mongolia. For instance, former MPRP general secretary Yumjaa Tsedenbal's wife, Tsedenbal-Filatova, who was Russian, persisted in addressing the children of Mongolia in Russian throughout her decades-long reign as the head of the Mongolian Children's Fund.

The elements of educational, juridical, and economic life in the societies of Central Asia and Mongolia were undermined in a few decades under the pressure of wholesale social transformation. Collectivization, purges, and the imposition of an ideological model eradicated traditional customs and cultural societies in Central Asia and Mongolia.

POST-SOVIET TRAUMA: TRANSITIONAL EPOCH

Given the intensity of the Soviet influence on Central Asia and Mongolia, the breakup of the Soviet Union unequivocally marked the modern history of the countries. Whether the republics and Mongolia were ready for such a dramatic change of course, this historic event encapsulated a political impetus for Mongolia to rebuild its nation-state along an unpaved path and for the

Central Asian republics to assert (reassert) their independence and identity.[21] As would be expected in any unprepared civil society, political turmoil was widespread in Central Asia and Mongolia. This political vacuum urged the peoples to revisit the political and economic effects of Marxist praxis and communist psyches in which they had been systematically indoctrinated for decades. It also encouraged them to find a way to carve out their statehood in a better fashion than their exiting societies.

The transition has by no means been a simple task. The dissolution of the former Soviet Union not only marked the collapse of communism but also hallmarked the disintegration of the federation and subsequent independence for the respective states. The newly independent states of Central Asia were by-products of this historic event. There was no single model or process of transition that could be followed and replicated. Furthermore, all Central Asian states, and Mongolia to a somewhat lesser degree, depended heavily on the former Soviet Union and the Council for Mutual Economic Assistance (CMEA). Thus the abolition of the intensive economic and technical assistance of these sources has negatively impacted each country.

The general tendency among the regional states has been "to maintain close alignments with and to continue to depend on the former metropolitan center, now represented by the new Russian state."[22] Russia continues to display an unequivocal influence in the former Soviet space, because of its geographical location, size, economic and military weight and because of its historical legacy. Despite its current relative weakness, Russia remains a dominant power among the former Soviet puppet states (it possesses the largest population, highest GNP, and strongest military, including a nuclear arsenal) and is still capable of spinning the present situation in any direction. Central Asian regional security and stability, therefore, is deeply contingent on the role that Russia plays, given that the countries of the region evolved within and then diverged from the empire. Venturing a path divorced from the past or the present Russia thus has been neither realistic nor desirable.

Action or Reaction?

The recent history of Mongolia offers an interesting divergent path from the regional countries of Central Asia. At the outset of Soviet dissolution in the early 1990s, Mongolian civil society formed different political groupings for the first time in at least seven decades. These groupings included, in various forms, groups, unions, and parties, even those radically opposed to the former party (which would have been unheard of just months earlier). On March 7, 1990, a political group representing the Mongolian Democratic Union began hunger strikes in Sukhbaatar Square outside the Mongolian parliament.

Realizing that potential instability in the country could trigger political chaos or even civil war, the entire Political Bureau and secretariat of the Mongolian People's Revolutionary Party (MPRP) capitulated within days, agreeing to an open national election in June. This event ushered in unprecedented changes in Mongolia. The constitution was consequently amended in May 1992, introducing new electoral laws and legislation for political parties.[23] The reform gave birth to a one-chamber parliamentarian government and elected president.

As for the Central Asian states, McChesney observes that "from a politically quiet and submissive role within the former Soviet Union, [they were], without warning or preparation, forced to assume full responsibility for political organization, economic policies, and the well-being of its citizens."[24] Unlike many other former Soviet republics, none of the regional states experienced any significant independence or pro-democracy movements; therefore, their independence came as a surprise rather than hard-earned sovereignty.

The unexpected arrival of sovereignty for the Central Asian states came with a price tag attached. The sudden withdrawal of Soviet assistance created a huge economic limbo in each regional state. All five Central Asian states were underdeveloped and depended on central government assistance to a greater extent than the other Soviet republics did. Tajikistan, for instance, relied on the central government for 80 percent of its fuel and 75 percent of its foodstuffs, while Uzbekistan received 6.4 billion rubles from Moscow in 1990, 43 percent of its total expenditures that year.[25] Furthermore, all Central Asian states suffered from handicapped industrialization. In the decades prior to the collapse of the Soviet Union, the region counted for the lowest level of per capita industrial output of the Soviet republics. By the Mikhail Gorbachev period, the per capita industrial output of the region was less than half that in Russia proper.[26] In addition, in all Central Asian states a large proportion of the population remained in agricultural ventures, with extremely low rates of urbanization compared to other titular nationalities.[27]

Other factors accounted for further shocks in the Central Asian states in the post-Soviet period. The almost complete withdrawal of financial and technical assistance from the former Soviet Union and the abolition of CMEA plunged the countries into a long-lasting recession, leaving the regional countries ranked far behind most of the world economies as illustrated in table 18.2.

The countries thus faced an enormous challenge to establish and develop institutions necessary for transition to a post-Soviet economy. The lack of preparedness among the political leaders and economic agents of the regional countries has made this transition a great challenge for all the regional states.

Table 18.2.   Rankings of Economies Based on Gross Nationsl Income (GNI) Per Capita

GNI Per Capita 2000 World Bank Atlas Method	Global Rankings	Regional Rankings	GNI Per Capita 2000
Kazakhstan	125	1	1,260
Kyrgyzstan	184	5	270
Tajikistan	197	6	180
Turkmenistan	143	2	750
Uzbekistan	171	4	360
Mongolia	164	3	390

Source: *2002 World Bank Atlas* (Washington, D.C., 2002), 19.

Governance: Rules of the Game

In the initial years after the dissolution of the former Soviet Union, a significant number of the political, economic, and military leaders elites in Central Asian republics and Mongolia were the ex-communists. Political parties in Central Asia evolved into a professional class of politicians or an entrenched elite oligarchy, resulting in an authoritarian type of governance. This was the case in all Central Asian republics including Kyrgyzstan, where "the gradual monopolization of political and economic power within the hands of (former) President Askar Akaev and his closed circle of allies, and on the other, the expanding corruption within the ruling elite, the government, and the civil service."[28] This growing authoritarianism in Kyrgyzstan, which was once the most democratic Central Asian country, paved the way for increasing public dissatisfaction and resulted in the recent rapid opposition takeover of the Kyrgyz government.

As illustrated in figure 18.1, the region on the whole demonstrates a highly authoritarian type of governance with each state consistently below zero on the scale of 0 to 10 (the vertical axis registers democracy scales with 10 representing the highest democracy score).[29]

Consistently, authoritarian leadership among the regional countries poses the question of whether it was inevitable that the post-Soviet republics would embrace some sort of controlled rule in the chaotic aftermath of the Soviet disintegration. Jean-Jacques Rousseau contends in his *Social Contract or Principles of Political Rights* that "in rare cases, public safety is provided through a special act, which makes the *worthiest* man responsible for it."[30] He argues that dictatorship works "when the state does not yet have sufficiently stable basis to be capable of sustaining itself by the strength of its constitution."[31] In a cauldron of potential turmoil, political instability, and overall social chaos resulting from the destruction of the previously existing political tapestry,

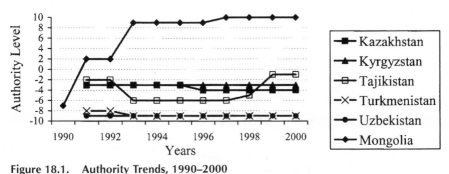

Figure 18.1. Authority Trends, 1990–2000
Source: Monty G. Marshall and Keith Jaggers et al., "Polity IV Project: Political Regime Characteristics and Transitions, 1800–2003," www.cidcm.umd.edu/inscr/polity (April 12, 2005).

Rousseau's hypothesis demonstrates that it may have been "necessary" for some sort of authority to provide safety for the Central Asian peoples. However, Rousseau also notes the importance of the limitations of such power. He warns that the dictatorship must be limited in duration, which has not been the case in the region as the governments have continued to curtail political rights and individual liberties. In terms of the comparative measures of freedom (provided by Freedom House), all regional countries suffer from very low levels of political rights and civil liberties (1 represents most and 7 represents least free, respectively; see table 18.3).

"[The governments of Central Asia] have pursued a policy of zero tolerance toward any type of political activity outside the pro-government one."[32] Thus opposition movements have been contained and have lacked the political unity and cooperation necessary to significantly threaten the authoritarian leadership. Even before the 2005 Kyrgyz color revolution, opposition forces to the Kyrgyz government suffered from internal division.

The countries have also failed to embrace freedom of the press and information, reduce inequality of resources, increase the accountability of nonelected

Table 18.3. Comparative Measures of Freedom

	Political Rights	*Civil Liberties*	*Freedom Rating*
Kazakhstan	6	5	Not Free
Kyrgyzstan	6	5	Not Free
Tajikistan	6	5	Not Free
Turkmenistan	7	7	Not Free
Uzbekistan	7	6	Not Free
Mongolia	2	2	Free

Source: Freedom House, *Freedom in the World 2005, Table of Independent Countries*, Comparative measures of freedom, www.freedomhouse.org/research/freeworld/2005/table2005.pdf (April 5, 2005).
Note: The ratings in the table reflect events from December 1, 2003, through November 30, 2004.

individuals and organizations, decentralize decision making, or, most importantly, better educate all citizens (bearing in mind that the perceived incompetence of the masses could be the result of lack of opportunity for responsible involvement rather than a justification for permanent denial of such opportunity).[33]

This leaves the question why Mongolia took such a divergent path from the Central Asian republics. Both figure 18.1 and table 18.2 show that Mongolia, on the other hand, enjoys a relatively high freedom rating with a high level of political rights and civil liberties. Mongolia had a decades-long history of independent statehood (even if constrained by the Soviet Union), which has played an important role in determining the country's emergence from post-Soviet shock. Unlike the former Soviet republics of Central Asia, Mongolia had strong ties with international bodies, with a seat in the United Nations and diplomatic relations with many countries prior to the Soviet Union's dissolution. While the Mongolian central government was largely dependent on the former Soviet Union, Mongolia's identity as an independent country was strongly felt by both civil society and the leaders. Therefore, autonomous self-determination and self-governance detached from the former Soviet Union came naturally compared to the Central Asian societies.

Another possible explanation is that Mongolian opposition to the major power unified at the outset of the post-Soviet transition. While multiparties and various interested groups were formed at the beginning of the 1990s, they joined forces against the MPRP. In addition to the effective unified opposition force, MPRP made a historically crucial decision at the right time. The resignation of the entire cabinet not only deescalated the ongoing political unrest but also prevented the eruption of a civil division.

Whether overly romanticized or not, Mongolia achieved a relative degree of democratic governance, at least measured against Western norms. While struggling economic conditions, a widening gap between rich and poor, and a crumbling social welfare system may undermine such achievement, Mongolia appears to be a step ahead of the Central Asian states.

CONCLUSION

This chapter provided a discursive analysis of the role the former Soviet Union played in reshaping the societies of the Central Asian states and Mongolia.

The chapter further analyzed the situation in which Central Asian states and Mongolia found themselves in the aftermath of Soviet dissolution. Mongolia's ability to emerge from the shadow of authoritarianism to construct a new democratic society and the failure of the Central Asian states to make a similar transition suggest that Mongolia was less dependent on the former Soviet Union and hence embraced its post-Soviet status quo more readily. Also, Mongolia managed the transition from centralized rule and command economy more capably.

While Soviet totalitarianism has made a lasting, deep impact on post-Soviet space, these lingering effects should not prevent the societies from venturing down a new path that is autonomous and attuned to the best interests of their citizens. The 2005 Kyrgyz color revolution may serve as an exemplar of the citizenry taking charge in refashioning society and modifying the political discourse of which they are an integral and defining part.

NOTES

1. B. Baabar, "The Central Asian Security Zone," *Mongolian Journal of International Affairs* 2 (1995): 18–32.

2. Kh. Olzvoi, "A Mongol's View of Economic Development and Cooperation in Northeast Asia," *Mongolian Journal of International Affairs* 3 (1996): 65–66.

3. Martha B. Olcott, "Central Asia: Common Legacies and Conflicts," in *Central Asian Security: The New International Context*, ed. Roy Alison and Lena R. Jonson (Washington, D.C.: Brookings Institution Press; London: Royal Institute of International Affairs, 2001), 28.

4. For admixtures of "races," especially intermarriage with Mongols, see Dilip Hiro, *Between Marx and Muhammad* (New York: HarperCollins, 1995), 2.

5. "Genghis" is the most common Western spelling. It is believed to be a variation of the spelling "Jenghiz," which is the transliteration of the Chinese Cheng-ji-si (Ch becomes J in certain older European transliterations). So therefore the beginning sound of Genghis should be a Ch, not the English G. "Chinggis" is commonly used among Mongolians and generally agreed to be the most probable in accuracy to the original. Other variations of Genghis: Cheng-ji-si (Chinese pin yin), Jenghis, Jenghiz, Chingis, Cingis, Chinggis, Chinggiz, Tenggiz.

6. Olivier Roy, *The New Central Asia: The Creation of Nations* (New York: New York University Press, 2000), 6.

7. For more detailed accounts on Chinggis Khan and his empire, see R. D. McChesney, *The History and the Life of Chinggis Khan,* trans. Urgunge Onon (Leiden: E. J. Brill, 1990).

8. R. D. McChesney, *Central Asia: Foundations of Change* (Princeton, N.J.: Darwin, 1996), 121–22.

9. The Great Yasa of Chinggis Khan is a key historical source that informs discussion on any kind of constitutional framework of the Mongolian empire. This comprehensive legal code represented the norms of relations between citizen and society, man and nature.

10. McChesney, *Central Asia,* 6.

11. Hannah Arendt, "The Origins of Totalitarianism," in *Princeton Readings in Political Thought: Essential Texts since Plato*, ed. Mitchell Cohen and Nicole Fermon (Princeton: Princeton University Press, 1996), 575.

12. Roy, *New Central Asia*, xii.

13. Roy, *New Central Asia*, xii.

14. James C. Scott, *Seeing Like a State: How Certain Schemes to Improve the Human Condition Have Failed* (New Haven: Yale University Press, 1998), 345

15. Scott, *Seeing Like a State*, 195.

16. John Glenn, *The Soviet Legacy in Central Asia* (London: Macmillan, 1999), 89.

17. Glenn, *Soviet Legacy,* 88.

18. Roy, *New Central Asia*, 76.

19. Glenn, *Soviet Legacy*, 98.

20. Roy, *New Central Asia,* 82.

21. Tsarist Russia began its dominance of these republics back in the 1850s, and the domination continued for seventy years under the Soviet system.

22. Roy Alison and Lena Jonson, eds*., Central Asian Security: The New International Context* (London: Royal Institute of International Affairs, 2001), 1.

23. Frederick Nixon and Bernard Walters, "The Transition to a Market Economy: Mongolia 1990–1998," *International Journal of Economic Development* 1 (2000): 35–66.

24. McChesney, *Central Asia*, 3.

25. Hoomon Peimani, *Failed Transition, Bleak Future: War and Instability in Central Asia and the Caucasus* (Westport, Conn.: Praeger, 2002), 14.

26. Glenn, *Soviet Legacy*, 95.

27. Glenn, *Soviet Legacy*, 95.

28. Peimani, *Failed Transition*, 49.

29. For the construction of the index, refer to Monty G. Marshall and Keith Jaggers et al. at www.cidcm.umd.edu/inscr/polity/index.htm#data.

30. Jean-Jacques Rousseau, "1762 Social Contract," in *Rousseau's Political Writings: Discourse on Inequality, Discourse on Political Economy and on Social Contract*, ed. Alan Ritter and Julia Conaway Bondanella, Norton critical ed. (New York: Norton, 1988), 160.

31. Rousseau, "Social Contract," 164.

32. Marshall and Jaggers, "Polity IV Project."

33. James L. Hyland, *Democratic Theory: The Philosophical Foundations* (Manchester: Manchester University Press, 1995), 256–57.

19

The United States, Asian Security, and Central Asia before and after September 11

Thomas W. Simons Jr.

Asia is a region of extraordinary diversity in its societies, economies, politics, and range of security interests. Bringing it under a single rubric therefore is extremely difficult. Being centered on the Chinese landmass does not make it one region; having the United States present everywhere does not make America the common denominator, either. Moreover, U.S. policy is almost always defined in global terms and is based on values rather than geostrategic considerations. According to the definition in the National Security Strategy issued by President George W. Bush in September 2002, the key U.S. strategic goals are political and economic freedom, peaceful relations with other states, and respect for human dignity. In his second inaugural address in January 2005, President Bush resoundingly confirmed his determination to support freedom worldwide. Operationally, the main task is to defeat global terrorism; the most striking innovation is a new stress on preemptive action, unilateral if necessary. The relations the United States pursues in various geographic regions are functions of these larger global purposes. As a result, concrete U.S. regional policies tend to emerge at the intersection of global goals and specific developments and events.

It has not been particularly difficult for the United States to make good Asian policy with such an approach. It provides for great flexibility, and over the years the United States has been rather successful in defending and promoting its interests in the region in ways that are advantageous to its local partners, too, despite communist rule in China and the setback in Vietnam. But such an approach encounters difficulties when it tries to make coherent policy for the whole Asian region. As a result, the United States tends to have policies for Asia's multiple subregions, including Central Asia with its southern hinge, Afghanistan. This chapter will look briefly at how U.S. policies have moved in recent years and will investigate whether any changes since September 11, 2001, have been fundamental.

THE DECADE OF THE 1990S

In the 1990s, Central Asia was in some sense paradigmatic. Of course the first post-Soviet decade witnessed enormous change there, but it was also a decade of drift and gridlock in the area's international situation. After some initial confusion, the Central Asians learned that Russia could not be replaced by the United States or China or any combination, and they settled into a delicate balancing game among them.

The U.S. approach was active but basically modest. The United States provided about $1 billion in humanitarian and technical assistance, an amount comparable to other countries and institutions. Some military ties developed; after NATO's Partnership for Peace program was formalized in 1995, all area countries except war-torn Tajikistan joined. In 1994, Kyrgyzstan, Kazakhstan, and Uzbekistan came together in their own organization, and by September 2001 they were providing troops to the Central Asian Peacekeeping Battalion that exercised with the U.S. 82nd Airborne Division. But since 1992, most Central Asian states were also parties to the Collective Security Treaty (CST) of the Commonwealth of Independent States along with Russia. While Uzbekistan withdrew (along with Georgia and Azerbaijan) in 1999, the CST also conducted exercises focused on terrorism in 2000 and 2001.

Central Asian governments joined almost every international organization they could in these years. Very soon, however, it became apparent that to prevent their standard of living from bottoming out, Central Asians were going to have to rely on their energy resources, not on memberships in international organizations. Their cotton was a glut on the market, and their minerals would take years to commercialize. Energy could be developed more quickly if a way could be found to get it to world markets from this landlocked region. This was the origin of the Caspian basin pipeline diplomacy that dominated the area's international relations and was a large part of the U.S. agenda for most of the decade. It was driven by three features: Russia had the existing pipelines; new pipelines require considerable new private investment; and investment adequate to build the most efficient new routes, south through Iran or through Afghanistan and Pakistan, was hostage to politics. Investors were awaiting developments in U.S.-Iranian relations or stabilization in Afghanistan; meanwhile Russia was able to delay non-Russian routes like the one ending on the Mediterranean in Turkey long enough to modernize its own routes as temporary outlets. Routes from the Caspian basin to the Pacific through or around China were barely in the talking stage.

Economic and social conditions deteriorated steadily, and beginning in 1993, one Central Asian government after another moved to neutralize its parliament and extend its presidency. In searching for new national identities, all five countries focused on self-generated, pragmatic definitions above ethnicity or religion. In practical terms, this was a formula for orientation toward Russia. By the end of the decade, the upshot was an interlocking series of stalemates in politics as well as economic and international ties. Authoritarian personalism was the norm, economic reform lagged, and corruption flourished. Yet there was still room for independent political activity, the economies made room for the market, and neither politics nor economics was completely criminalized. Russia had consolidated its role in the area, but this fell far short of reabsorption. Just as there was no external ascendancy, there was also no dynamism. Every country faced the danger of subsiding into bipolar political confrontation between a fearful post-Soviet dictatorship and a radical Islamism that was becoming the only possible ideology of opposition.

The United States sought to base its Asia policy on the triple axes of economic partnership, democratic development, and nuclear nonproliferation; but there was little energy for the task, and consequently there was not much forward movement. The United States sought its partners in the evolving community of market democracies, linking economic and political development along the way. This caused particular problems with China and Indonesia and also Central Asia, increasingly as the countries turned toward authoritarian personalism, and then with overtly nuclear Pakistan, which in 1999 turned for the third time in its history to military rule.

While the United States did not neglect the military aspects of security, in the 1990s its Asia policy stressed economic instruments. The United States offered carrots in the form of aid and support for trade and investment. It wielded a stick in the form of sanctions it applied against countries as varied as Iran, Myanmar, and Pakistan throughout the decade, against India after its nuclear explosion in 1998, and against Indonesia almost from the outset of its political crisis in mid-decade. In general, the United States sought to expand bilateral relations beyond nuclear nonproliferation, to include new issues like terrorism, drugs, democracy, and human rights. But most of its diplomatic energy still went into large multilateral nonproliferation efforts: indefinite extension of the Nuclear Nonproliferation Treaty (NPT) and then agreement on a Comprehensive Test Ban Treaty (CTBT). As a result, nuclear nonproliferation remained the political centerpiece of U.S.-Asia policy. A further result was a kind of American version of Asia's own Brownian movement: plenty of activity but little direction.

As a final result, thinkers about U.S.-Asia policy tended to focus a bit fearfully on Asia's economic boom and incipient military modernization as potential threats to U.S. interests. Paul Bracken's book brooded about a coming paradigm shift for U.S. power and engagement in Asia.[1] Writing the same year, the venerable Robert Scalapino was more moderate and less alarmist but still saw danger in a yoking of rising nationalism and rising military strength, in China as elsewhere in Asia. "Yet in the long run," Scalapino concluded, "the fundamental issue may be that of American commitment."[2]

Before September 11, the George W. Bush administration did little to change this picture. Although it advertised more interest in Asia and the military dimensions of security than its predecessor, its initial policy shifts amounted to little more than a new stress on bolstering U.S. alliances in the region that could hedge against emerging Chinese power in the twenty-first century. But that stress reflected an impulse rather than a policy. To make it a policy would have required a degree of engagement and a range of resources that were just not there. By September 11, therefore, Scalapino's question about American commitment in Asia was still the right one to ask.

ASIA AND U.S. POLICIES SINCE SEPTEMBER 11

The Overall Approach

The initial U.S. response to the September 11 attacks was characteristic: at the high end, a declaration of war on global terrorism, paired with an overwhelming immediate focus on Afghanistan. As usual, this made it hard to come up with an articulated, comprehensive strategic vision. But it left the United States plenty of flexibility to deal with the whole range of issues between globally defined issues and the war it was fighting in Afghanistan.

Still, that flexibility was not total. Both the very general and the very particular in U.S. policy involved specific choices that then pushed the policy process along like sheepdogs. For instance, the option of attacking Iraq as well as Afghanistan surfaced immediately, but before two weeks were out was set aside for the time being because it would make the kind of coalition needed to prosecute an Afghanistan war impossible. But this was only one instance of the general rule that the United States makes policy through an iteration of specific decisions.

Afghanistan

It was clear from the outset that humanitarian and financial aid had to be major components of the Afghanistan campaign. Air power alone could not defeat the Taliban, and the United States wanted and needed to minimize the American ground contribution. For that it needed to build enough support among Afghans so that Northern Alliance troops could carry most of the ground war, supplemented by small U.S. special-purpose forces: Special Operations units, the 10th Mountain Division (at the outset), and Marines from offshore. Humanitarian airdrops and covert funding of opposition forces therefore began almost immediately. So did high-level policy statements that the United States would not abandon Afghanistan again, that reconstruction was integral to the policy, that we were in for the long haul this time. In other words, Afghanistan was a military-political-economic operation for the United States from the outset.

It has remained one ever since, and policy has continued to bump forward through decisions that address specific problems as they arise and then commit the U.S. government. At the decisive political meeting outside Bonn in December 2001, the United States was obliged against its initial inclination to accept international peacekeepers in Kabul (though not outside, at least initially), because that was the price Afghans demanded for a political deal. At the aid donors' meeting in Tokyo in January 2002, despite its distaste for nation building, the United States emerged as the largest single first-year contributor, with a pledge of $296.75 million to a multilateral package worth $4.5 billion over five years.

At the Virginia Military Institute in April 2002, President Bush pledged to stay the course in Afghanistan, though without specifying resources. During the summer, tension built between Afghans and allies over how to provide the security needed to get assistance through. By July, defense secretary Donald Rumsfeld and regional commander General Tommy Franks were acknowledging that U.S. troops would stay for years to keep Afghanistan from reverting to a terrorist haven. By August, in a "midcourse correction," the United States was willing to back deployment of peacekeepers outside Kabul, so long as others did it.

Despite a successful Loya Jirga that established an interim government under President Hamid Karzai in July 2002, the issue of how to tame the warlords to stabilize the government and get aid through continued to bubble along as a political issue. In September, Special Forces accompanied Afghans on a raid against renegade police, and Afghan troops sent a southeastern warlord packing into the hills. In October Douglas Feith, undersecretary of defense, revealed in Kabul that the United States would soon emphasize "stability" rather than military operations, and special envoy Zalmay Khalilzad mediated a dispute between two major warlords in the north. In December 2002, coalition forces (not peacekeepers) joined government troops threatening warlords in the dangerous southeast, and donors pledged $1.2 billion in fresh aid at Oslo. In January 2003, finally, the United States unveiled its new strategy of sending small joint regional teams (JRT) of seventy soldiers, civil affairs officers, engineers, medics, and diplomats to seven or eight locations around the country by the summer, with more to come thereafter. As he ratcheted up the pressure on Iraq, President Bush called President Karzai on January 28, 2003, before his State of the Union speech, to assure him once more that the United States remained committed to a "prosperous, democratic, and stable Afghanistan."

Step by practical step, the United States had undertaken a political, economic, and military commitment in Afghanistan that could scarcely have been imagined on the morrow of the September 11 attacks. Faced with stubborn resistance from neo-Taliban forces and debilitating tensions among ethnic groups in Karzai's government, in mid-2003, the United States announced a new program of "accelerating success" for Afghanistan and then rolled it out piecemeal over many months. By October it had committed $2.4 billion for the next year alone. That winter Ambassador Khalilzad went to work on improving ethnic balance in the government and military. Serious training of Afghan troops and police began, and a new Loya Jirga set the framework for national elections in 2004. By the spring of 2004, the JRTs had morphed into provincial reconstruction teams (PRTs) and were in place throughout the country; they included some run by the British and Germans, but most were staffed by Americans. A new pledging conference in Berlin produced promises of another $4.5 billion for the following year. By the time successful elections took place in October, U.S. troop levels had risen from 12,000 to 17,000 despite the difficulties in nearby Iraq. By 2005 the resistance was losing traction, and Khalilzad could be transferred to Iraq. After all, it was a country where many of the lessons learned in Afghanistan—the sequence of assembly, interim government, constitution and elections, the need for adequate forces and resources, the importance of ethnic balance—had already been applied for more than a year.

Central Asia

The same incremental process was at work when it came to building the coalition that would be required to win the war in Afghanistan. As strong as the United States was militarily, additional forces and assured access arrangements would still be needed. Immediately after September 11, the whole world was with the United States in principle. Not only did NATO invoke Article 5, its collective self-defense clause, for the first time in history, but even Russia and China joined the cascade of immediate offers of support. But everyone wanted concrete U.S. recognition of what that support meant, quids for all those quos. Mustering the quids faced the United States with immediate policy challenges that went far beyond the military.

It already had a substantial military presence on the southern side of the nutcracker it now wished to build around the terrorist heartland: bases in Saudi Arabia and on Diego Garcia in the Indian Ocean, assets in Kuwait and Bahrain. It quickly proceeded to negotiate for new ones in Oman and Qatar in the Gulf area and to expand its naval presence in the Arabian Sea. Building out is easier, even politically, than building from scratch. To the north and east, Pakistan and Central Asia were the key staging grounds for military action in Afghanistan, and a radically new presence was needed there; new prices would have to be paid.

In Central Asia, neutral Turkmenistan limited its contribution to use of its airspace and territory for transit of humanitarian supplies, so the United States was later free to criticize the savage political crackdown, which began there as 2002 drew to a close. Elsewhere the Western and especially U.S. buildup was startling. Within a year the United States and other coalition members were using large bases at Khanabad in Uzbekistan and Manas in Kyrgyzstan, the French were using Kulyab in Tajikistan, and the United States and Kazakhstan had agreed the United States could use Kazakh airfields for emergency landings.

Military-to-military relations that the United States had nurtured in Central Asia since 1992 proved precious assets when the time for expansion came, but more would be needed. Part of it would be material, and that meant more than outlays for new infrastructure. Direct U.S. assistance outlays to the area more than doubled the first year; by 2005 nonmilitary aid to the five countries had swollen to $2.67 billion, and the United States also supported vastly expanded inputs from international financial institutions. Part of the price, however, would be political.

The problem for the United States was how to reconcile political support for the increasingly authoritarian, personalist area regimes, on the one hand, and its principled support for democratic and market development and respect for human rights, on the other. To its credit, the administration was aware of the tension from the outset. It also faced a drumbeat of reminders from Congress and the media that in Muslim Central Asia, political repression creates Islamist radicals and terrorists, so that acquiescing in repression is not sound policy. As it proceeded to build its presence and its relations in the area, therefore, the United States kept up steady and public pressure on the regimes concerning human rights, democratic development, and market-oriented economic reform. Commitments on these issues were formalized in the treaties signed with Kyrgyzstan in February 2002 and with Uzbekistan in March, but they have been consistent features of the U.S. agenda in public and private.

The regimes chafed under the pressure, and the results were mixed. Administration statements like the congressional testimony of assistant secretary of state Lorne Craner in July or the State Department fact sheet on U.S. "successes" in Central Asia issued in November 2002 freely characterize Central Asian performance on these issues as "poor" or "extremely poor." But among the mixed results, some are positive. Contrary to expectations, outside Turkmenistan there have been no mass arrests in the area until political turbulence hit Uzbekistan in 2005. Coalition government continued to hold in Tajikistan, and in Kyrgyzstan and Kazakhstan, political oppositions not only exist but have grown since September 11; part of the growth has to do with U.S. pressure.

Here, too, by 2005, tension among U.S. objectives that surfaced with September 11 had become a pattern. In Central Asia, authoritarian and personalist regimes remain in place with U.S. support, but the United States continues to press them toward more representative governance and market-oriented economic management (with international financial institution support)—but they continue to chafe. The tension is reinforced by developments elsewhere in the post-Soviet space: the Rose Revolution in Georgia at the end of 2003 and the Orange Revolution in Ukraine at the end of 2004. They were worrisome to post-Soviet authoritarians in their own right, but since the United States supported both, they also put a large question mark over U.S. support for the Central Asian status quo. In 2005 the "pattern" appeared to spread to Kyrgyzstan and to threaten Uzbekistan in May. Central Asian leaders increasingly found the United States hard to predict; so did their large neighbor to the north. Whether that created the makings of a new "holy alliance" of conservative regimes remained to be seen.

Russia

Given the weight of history and the strong continuing Russian presence in Central Asia, Russia has been the second necessary element in the support structure for the war on terrorism the United States has been trying to put together in Central Asia. For both Russia and the United States, the issues extend far beyond Central Asia. President Vladimir Putin used September 11 to seal political ratification of a strategic choice for Russia he had almost certainly made earlier: rather than resist the United States at a moment of national weakness, Russia would rebuild in order to reemerge later as a great power, and part of rebuilding meant joining forces with the United States against terrorism and thereby gaining the means to shape the international system in which they both operate.

With regard to duration, the position on Afghanistan (developed through the summer of 2002 and announced by Secretary Rumsfeld and General

Franks in August and by local commander Lieutenant General Dan McNeill in September) is that coalition forces will stay until the Afghan army and government can provide security and prevent the resurgence of "terrorist organizations." The U.S.-Russian debate on the duration of the U.S. military presence in Central Asia has been carried on via Uzbekistan and Kyrgyzstan, where U.S. forces operated beginning in December 2001 under a renewable one-year status of forces agreement. In principle, Kyrgyz officials have affirmed it would be extended for as long as the war on terrorism required. But Russia evidently needed something, too, and after months of pounding, in June 2002, Kyrgyz National Security Council secretary Misir Ashyrkulov told his Russian counterpart, Vladimir Rushailo, that international forces would leave Kyrgyzstan within six months of their agreed mandate. Then Rushailo announced that the two countries would consult if the terms changed. But that construct merely provided the platform for continuation of the competition at another level.

Admittedly, that level took a while to reach. Clearly Russia has required a substantial payoff for its new approach, but the shape of that payoff has changed over time. Again, Central Asia is only one element. It has been outshone in the policy firmament by the Treaty of Moscow committing both sides to substantial reductions in nuclear weapons even as the United States scrapped the ABM (Anti–Ballistic Missile) Treaty of 1972, or by the Prague summit in November 2002, which agreed to include formerly Soviet republics in a further expansion of NATO. The main payoff was to be an expanding, comprehensive strategic relationship, in which the United States systematically recognizes Russia's status and consults with it on all-important questions. But Central Asia was to be an integral part of this new relationship. At the Moscow summit in May 2002, the joint statement "reaffirmed" the two countries' "shared interest in promoting stability and in upholding the sovereignty and territorial integrity of all the states of the south Caucasus and Central Asia," and they undertook to support economic and political development and respect for human rights there. These commitments constitute a platform that can scarcely be improved. Once again, however, the proof of the pudding has been—and will continue to be—in the eating.

Like the Central Asians, Russia requested compensation for joining the U.S.-led war on terror in the form of U.S. acquiescence in repression of whatever opposition can be labeled "terrorist," and most particularly of Chechen armed resistance. As a political issue, Chechnya is more than a decade old and remains the most neuralgic in Russian politics; to some extent the price has been paid. The United States has never stopped harassing Russia about Chechnya and about the need for a political solution, but starting September 11 it lowered the decibels. The Moscow theater crisis later in the fall heightened world sympathy for Russia's Chechen dilemma, and further outrages have kept it up. But on the first anniversary of September 11, Russia was unable to parlay this sympathy into a new right to intervene militarily in Georgia.

With parameters reestablished, brisk movement within them has been the rule. The new Russian air base in Kyrgyzstan was opened in 2003, and 2004 was a year of great activity. In midyear the United States initiated public discussion of plans to withdraw 60,000–70,000 troops from Europe and Asia, with the implication that some could be moved nearer to the sources of the new threats, in Eastern Europe or even, perhaps, Azerbaijan. Russian defense minister Sergei Ivanov snorted that Russia was aware of U.S. plans, and they were of no concern. In July, nevertheless, when the NATO meeting at Istanbul announced a new "special focus" on Central Asia and the Caucasus, Russia announced a new base of its own in Tajikistan, which Putin then opened in October. In between, Russia and its Central Asian neighbors conducted a surge of "successful" military exercises, some under CST auspices, some bilateral, and Russia secured permanent legal existence for its bases, something the United States has never enjoyed.

By early 2005, the tugging and hauling appeared to have brought matters full circle: with Afghanistan stabilizing, Central Asian leaders returned to the issue of how long the U.S. military would remain in their countries. For Uzbekistan's Karimov, it was till U.S. troops left Afghanistan; for Kyrgyzstan's Akayev (not long before his ouster), it was until stability in Afghanistan "is achieved." But then defense secretary Rumsfeld's underpublicized visit to Baku in April rekindled speculation about a new U.S. base or facility in Azerbaijan. Nothing was clear. Although Secretary Rice assured President Putin that the United States was no threat to Russia's interests in the post-Soviet space; in real terms there was no end in sight.[3] In July, the Shanghai Cooperation Organization "suggested" that the United States give a timetable for withdrawal from Khanabad; Uzbekistan followed with a bilateral ultimatum; and the United States was gone by November. Simultaneously, Kyrgyzstan reaffirmed its willingness to see the United States use Manas until Afghanistan was stable (although at a higher price). The balancing continued.

FRAYING AT THE FRINGES

While the United States focused on winning in Afghanistan and securing its northern rim, the southern rim of the terrorist heartland was not neglected. Already in October 2001, the United States was using Pakistani bases in Sindh and Balochistan and beginning to provide President Pervez Musharraf the political and economic support he needed to sustain reengagement with the

United States politically. The same month, the Philippines requested U.S. military assistance in fighting its Muslim rebels in the south, and in January 2002 the two countries set up a joint command to combat terrorism, with 600 U.S. troops landed. In March 2002 the United States announced it was sending 100 troops to Yemen to train Yemenis in counterterrorism; the number later rose, and the navy was helping patrol Yemeni coastlines. By September there were 800 U.S. troops in Djibouti preparing for action targeted at the terrorist-infested Yemeni-Saudi border across the Red Sea. In both the Philippines and Yemen, most trainers left after their work was done, but some stayed, and campaigns continued. In November, a suspected al-Qaeda leader was taken out in Yemen by a U.S. missile fired from a Predator drone (with Yemeni intelligence help). In June of that year, the White House announced its intention to resume direct military training aid for Indonesia, which it did in August; with ups and downs, the U.S.-Indonesian military relationship has grown apace, with some rough edges smoothed by U.S. help in the tsunami crisis of 2004.

Meanwhile, however, new tensions were appearing at the extremities of the Asian region. As the war in Afghanistan shifted toward chasing al-Qaeda remnants and nation building, U.S. policy attention turned increasingly toward Iraq, so that Arab support came at a higher and higher price, including U.S. reengagement in the deteriorating Israeli-Palestinian situation. Tension rose in both South and Northeast Asia, and in both areas it raised the specter of nuclear war, which many in the 1990s had hopefully consigned to the dustbin of history.

After September 11, there was massive U.S. reengagement in the subcontinent, and it took new forms. To be sure, it meant reengagement with an old partner, Pakistan, which almost immediately turned against the Taliban regime it had supported and offered use of its airspace, some bases, and intelligence. The trouble was that elements of Pakistan's government were involved with Islamist extremists. They had protected and supported not only the Taliban but also insurgents crossing the Line of Control into Indian-held Kashmir. Even without September 11, India's size and dynamism would probably have made it an attractive new Asian partner for the United States. Now the two countries could tell each other they were facing the same threat.

To be a good U.S. ally, Pakistan had to extricate itself from the Islamist swamp it had waded into in the 1980s, and that was hard. It substantially reversed course in Afghanistan and was making progress against radicals at home, but support for the Kashmir insurgency had always been consensus politics in Pakistan, and Pakistanis hoped to continue it. So the attack on the Indian parliament in New Delhi on December 13, 2001, should have been a watershed. India responded with a full mobilization, demanded total elimination of Pakistani support for insurgents, and was supported by the United

States. With a million men facing each other on a hair trigger, India welcomed U.S. engagement for the first time in its history. It found strategic partnership with the superpower attractive for the long term, and valued U.S. pressure on Pakistan as well.

Yet there were limits to the pressure the United States could exert on Pakistan, and such pressure could produce unintended consequences. In terms of Kashmir, Musharraf renounced support for terror in principle and ramped it down in practice but did not end it. He remained an indispensable U.S. ally in Afghanistan, and a large U.S. aid effort was rolling out to help him stay that way. The middle course for the United States was therefore to join what civil society Pakistan had in calling for a return to democracy on the deadline set by Pakistan's Supreme Court for three years after Musharraf's takeover, in October 2002. Musharraf accepted, but he then made serious political mistakes that alienated Pakistan's main parties and thereby provided an electoral opening for religious parties and put them in control of two frontier provinces and made them the swing factor in the national parliament. It would take years before they discredited themselves and returned to their normal place on the margins of national politics.

India meanwhile found a better way off the hook of confrontation in Kashmir: it held state elections in its part of Kashmir that were free enough to produce a credible result, at about the same time Musharraf was botching his return to democracy. Deescalation followed immediately, but resumption of Indo-Pakistani dialogue—now the main U.S. policy objective—took another year (and two assassination attempts on Musharraf). Underway since 2004, dialogue has reduced tension but produced only limited concrete results. Both sides value their U.S. relationship, however, to the point where Pakistan sat still as India and the United States lunged toward a new nuclear cooperation relationship in July 2005 and March 2006 summits. If triangular diplomacy has brought new strategic stability to the subcontinent, it is still tentative.

China

If China is not fully the sun around which other Asian subregions turn, it is more than the hole in the Asian security doughnut: it is the necessary ingredient to all Asian security solutions. But China is also the most opaque of Asian subregions. It is still ruled by a dictatorship that controls information and plays its policy cards very close to the vest. Most aspects of Chinese policy are related in some way to its proclaimed national strategic priority— economic development. But, like the U.S. pursuit of "freedom" or "human dignity," it does not tell observers much about the specifics of Chinese policy. It leaves China lots of flexibility, and in fact Chinese policy, like U.S. policy, has been decisively shaped by events.

In April 2002 in Tehran, Jiang Zemin chastised "strategies of force" and the U.S. military presence in Central Asia. The Bush-Putin summit in May was thus a setback to Chinese hopes of keeping Russia in any "antihegemony" front. Putin made the situation perfectly clear in his subsequent interview for *People's Daily* on June 5. Russia had "special interests" in Central Asia, he said, if only because 20 million Russians lived there, but he was "not concerned" at the stationing of U.S. troops in the area. Each country has the right to choose its partners in the fight against international terrorism, he went on, although those choices should not inflame local or interstate frictions or have a destabilizing effect. Still, the occasion for the interview was the SCO Asian security summit Putin hosted in St. Petersburg, and it helped calm the waters. A Chinese spokesman "took note" of U.S. statements that it had no interest in extending its military presence in Central Asia. Putin assured the Chinese that they were still Russia's main strategic partner, and the Six signed a twenty-six-point charter and began discussion of a secretariat and an antiterrorism center in Kyrgyzstan's capital at Bishkek (but was eventually established at Tashkent).

A Kyrgyzstan Paradigm?

As the story continued to play out, it evolved in interesting directions. As in the past, the lines of the future began to cross in vulnerable little Kyrgyzstan. Much of the tussle has been over the new U.S. military presence there, but Russia also had significant military facilities in this small country, and in June 2002, the Kyrgyz government extended permission for these installations by "seven to fifteen" years. Now, however, China and Kyrgyzstan signed a border delimitation agreement that proved politically controversial in Kyrgyzstan. However, in October they went on to announce that they were holding joint maneuvers (preparing forces to combat terrorism) on both sides of their common border. It was the first time in living memory that Chinese troops had participated in maneuvers outside Chinese territory.

Matters came to a head in December. The bubbling political opposition in Kyrgyzstan was driven less by the border agreement with China than by declining living standards and mounting disgust with elite corruption. On December 2, the media suddenly announced a new Russian deployment to Kant air base not far from Bishkek. It was small in size, so that as a pendant to the U.S. presence it was mainly symbolic. But it was accompanied by hefty new Russian economic inputs—rollover of Kyrgyz debt and big new trade deals. Its legal status was more secure than that of its larger U.S. counterpart at Manas, and two years later it was joined by a new Russian base in neighboring Tajikistan. That, too, was mainly symbolic (the Russian 20lst Motorized Rifle Division had been the mainstay of Tajikistan's external security since 1991), but the symbolism meant Russia was in Central Asia to stay, to support regime stability.

All three countries then moved to reassure China. Putin took off on an extensive Asian tour in which he replaced previously tepid Russian participation in China's favorite multilateral vehicle, the SCO, with vigorous support. On December 12, Kyrgyzstan and China signed a bilateral agreement to combat terrorism, separatism, and extremism, especially from Uyghurs, after discussions "within the SCO." And the United States put the Eastern Turkestan Independence Movement (ETIM), a Uyghur outfit fighting to free Chinese Xinjiang, on its official list of terrorist organizations. By the end of the month, China was holding joint maneuvers with Kazakhstan; by late 2003, the SCO countries held counterterrorism exercises. There were rumors that China, too, wanted to station forces in Kyrgyzstan. What was true was that in 2002, the United States, China, and Russia all introduced military forces into this small country on the roof of the world. Even if those forces did not stay, they foreshadowed a new U.S.-Russian-Chinese trilateralism emerging from the welter of bilateral and multilateral activity that Central Asia had witnessed up to that point. It had not been intended or planned and was not formalized, but it was nevertheless real.

However, if a new Kyrgyzstan paradigm was in fact established in 2002, subsequent events have shown that its effects were more complex than simple defense of the domestic status quo. For under Kyrgyzstan's new tripartite proto-umbrella, President Askar Akayev permitted a degree of political activity and political opposition unique in Central Asia, and in March 2005, that opposition coalesced following tainted parliamentary elections to bring him down and send him into exile. The new authorities have reassured Russia and the United States about their bases, and the latter have been correct and tentative in their approaches, similar to China but in contrast to their conduct vis-à-vis Georgia and Ukraine earlier. But if the proto-condominium in Kyrgyzstan has dampened the competition, it has left larger strategic questions open. For Akayev, his country's new multilayered security may have permitted some liberalism, but his neighbors may conclude that liberalism leads to the door and then tries to nail it shut forever.

FUNDAMENTAL CHANGE?

In his State of the Union address on January 28, 2003, President Bush gave new vigor to the case for preemption and unilateral action against freedom's enemies that his administration had been steadily bulking up since it came to office. But as the Iraq crisis has drawn on, that vigor has waxed and waned in policy statements, thus it remains worthwhile to keep one's eye on the intersection between lofty principle and vulgar circumstance, just as it did before and after September 11. It may well be asked whether anything fundamental has changed in U.S. policy concerning Asian security.

Speaking at an Asian security conference in New Delhi just before Bush's 2003 address, U.S. Ambassador Robert Blackwill expressed a firm conviction that Asia's century is now under way. But he drew a sharp contrast between Europe—where the next decade promises unparalleled peace and prosperity—and an Asia where U.S. power and influence face major challenges if a "durable and robust political framework" is to be maintained in which the United States, its allies, and its friends "can prosper in freedom." As Asia prospers, Blackwill argued, it becomes susceptible to acute instability. It contains the most threatening sources of global terrorism, the most severe international territorial disputes and "nondemocratic rivalries over the right to rule," large militaries, and the potential to "develop, acquire, use or export WMD."

Blackwill returned to Washington to work on Middle East strategy and Iraq and then retired. But despite all the changes since September 11 described in this chapter, the Asia he sketched out in January 2003 is still very much the Asia of the 1990s, before September 11, and it remains accurate today. Asia is mainly dangerous in the same ways and mainly hopeful in the same ways. Which adjective will apply in the years ahead depends very much on the depth and durability of U.S. engagement in the region. U.S. engagement is no panacea, as we have seen in Pakistan and Kyrgyzstan. But in today's Asia much depends on it: it permits experimentation and movement in new directions that are impossible without it. To recall what Robert Scalapino wrote at the end of the past decade, "In the long term, the fundamental issue may be that of American commitment."[4] September 11 and its aftermath may have strengthened the experiential and political bases for sustained U.S. engagement in Asia to the point where that commitment is assured. But that is still uncertain. The fundamental question remains the question Scalapino posed.

NOTES

1. Paul Bracken, *Fire in the East: The Rise of Asian Military Power and the Second Nuclear Age* (New York: HarperCollins, 1999).

2. Robert A. Scalapino, "The American Response to a Changing Asia," www.ndu.edu/inss/symposia/pacific99/SCALAPINO.html (February 2, 2002).

3. Steven R. Weisman, "Rice Tells Putin United States Is NO Threat in Region," *New York Times,* April 12, 2005.

4. Scalapino, "American Response to a Changing Asia."

Selected Bibliography

Abdullaev, Kamoludin, and Catherine Barnes, eds. *Politics of Compromise: The Tajikistan Peace Process*. London: Conciliation Recourses, 2001.

Allison, Roy, and Lena Jonson, eds. *Central Asian Security: The New International Context*. London: Royal Institute for International Affairs, 2001.

Azizian, Rouben, and Yongjin Zhang. *Ethnic Challenges beyond Borders: Chinese and Russian Perspectives of the Central Asian Conundrum*. New York: Palgrave Macmillan, 1998.

Davis, Elizabeth Van Wie, ed. *Chinese Perspectives on Sino-American Relations*. Lewiston, N.Y.: Edwin Mellen, 2000.

Ebel, Robert, and Rajan Menon. *Energy and Conflict in Central Asia and Caucasus*. Lanham, Md.: Rowman & Littlefield, 2000.

Fairbanks, Charles, and S. Frederick Starr. *Strategic Assessment of Central Eurasia*. Washington, D.C.: Atlantic Council/Central Asia–Caucaus Institute, 2001.

Fayzieva, Dilorom. *Environmental Health in Central Asia: The Present and Future*. Billerica, Mass.: Computational Mechanics, 2003.

Gleason, Gregory. *The Central Asian States: Discovering Independence*. Boulder: Perseus, 1997.

Hunter, Shireen T. *Islam in Russia: The Politics of Identity and Security*. Armonk, N.Y.: Sharpe, 2004.

Hunter, Shireen T., and Huma Malik, eds. *Modernization, Democracy, and Islam*. New York: Praeger, 2005.

Kalyuzhnova, Yelena, and Dov Lynch. *Euro-Asian World: A Period of Transition*. New York: St. Martin's, 2000.

Kaplonski, C. Truth. *History and Politics in Mongolia*. New York: Routledge, 2004.

Kleveman, Lutz. *New Great Game: Blood and Oil in Central Asia*. New York: Atlantic Monthly Press, 2003.

Laumulin, Murat. *The Security, Foreign Policy, and International Relationship of Kazakhstan after Independence: 1991–2001*. Almaty: Kaziis/Friedrich Ebert Stiftung, 2002.

Lubin, Nancy, and Barnett R. Rubin. *Calming the Ferghana Valley: Development and Dialogue in the Heart of Central Asia.* New York: Century Foundation Press, 2000.

Luong, Pauline Jones. *The Transformation of Central Asia: States and Societies from Soviet Rule to Independence.* Ithaca, N.Y.: Cornell University Press, 2003.

Manz, Beatrice. *Central Asia in Historical Perspective.* Boulder: Westview, 1994.

McCauley, Martin. *Afghanistan and Central Asia.* White Plains, N.Y.: Longman, 2002.

McNeal, Dewardric L. *China's Relations with Central Asian States and Problems with Terrorism.* Washington, D.C.: CRS Report for Congress, December 17, 2001.

Mehendale, Sanjyot, and Touraj Atabaki. *Central Asia and the Caucasus.* New York: Routledge, 2005.

Menon, Rajan. *Russia, the Caucasus, and Central Asia.* Armonk, N.Y.: Sharpe, 1999.

Naumkin, Vitaly V. *Radical Islam in Central Asia: Between Pen and Rifle.* Lanham, Md.: Rowman & Littlefield, 2005.

Olcott, Martha Brill. *Kazakhstan: Unfulfilled Promise.* Washington, D.C.: Carnegie Endowment for International Peace, 2002.

Oliker, Olga. *Faultlines of Conflict in Central Asia and the South Caucasus.* Santa Monica, Calif.: Rand Corporation, 2003.

Rashid, Ahmed. *Jihad: The Rise of Militant Islam in Central Asia.* New Haven: Yale University Press, 2002.

———. *Taliban: Militant Islam, Oil, and Fundamentalism in Central Asia.* New Haven: Yale University Press, 2001.

Rossabi, Morris. *Modern Mongolia: From Khans to Commissars to Capitalists.* Los Angeles: University of California Press, 2005.

Roy, Olivier. *Globalized Islam.* New York: Columbia University Press, 2005.

———. *The New Central Asia: The Creation of Nations.* New York: New York University Press, 2000.

Rudelson, Justin Jon. *Oasis Identities: Uyghur Nationalism along China's Silk Road.* New York: Columbia University Press, 1997.

Rumer, Boris. *Central Asia: A Gathering Storm?* Armonk, N.Y.: Sharpe, 2002.

Sagdeev, Roald, and Susan Eisenhower, eds. *Central Asia: Conflict, Resolution, and Change.* Washington, D.C.: Eisenhower Institute, 1995.

———. *Islam and Central Asia: An Enduring Legacy or an Evolving Threat.* Washington, D.C.: Center for Political and Strategic Studies, 2000.

Schofield, Victoria. *Afghan Frontier: Feuding and Fighting in Central Asia.* London: Tauris, 2003.

Schwartz, Stephen. *The Two Faces of Islam.* New York: Anchor, 2003.

Sievers, Eric W. *The Post-Soviet Decline of Central Asia.* New York: RoutledgeCurzon, 2003.

Simons, Thomas W., Jr. *Islam in a Globalizing World.* Stanford: Stanford University Press, 2003.

Wheatcroft, Geoffrey. *The Dust of Empire.* Boulder: Perseus, 2003.

Zhao, Suisheng, ed. *Chinese Foreign Policy: Pragmatism and Strategic Behavior.* New York: Sharpe, 2004.

Index

About the Contributors

Kamoludin Abdullaev is currently a Visiting Fellow at Ohio State University with over twenty-five years of experience in the study and teaching of the Modern History of Central Asia. Since 1992, he has been a policy analyst and independent consultant in international nongovernmental research organizations involved in education and conflict resolution in Central Asia and an active participant in the U.S.-sponsored research exchange programs in the field of history and conflict resolution. Dr. Abdullaev did his post graduate work at the Academy of Sciences of the USSR, Institute of the History of the USSR, where he received both his masters and doctorate degrees. He has authored and edited three books in English and three in Russian as well as over forty articles in English, Russian, Tajik, French, and Japanese.

Rouben Azizian came to the Asia-Pacific Center for Security Studies in January 2002 from the Department of Political Studies of the University of Auckland, New Zealand, where he taught from 1994 to 2001 as well as serving as a visiting professor in the Department of Government, Georgetown University in 1997. From 1987, when he acquired his Ph.D. in International Relations from the Diplomatic Academy of the USSR, until 1991 he was a part-time lecturer in the Department of International Relations at the Diplomatic Academy. Dr. Azizian has edited four books and published numerous book chapters, journal articles, and working papers on foreign policy and the security of Russia, Central Asia, South Asia, Northeast Asia, and New Zealand. Prior to becoming a full-time academic, Dr. Azizian had an extensive career in the Soviet and later Russian Foreign Service from 1972 to 1991.

Gaye Christoffersen is associate professor of political science at Soka University of America. She has extensive teaching and research experience in the international relations of Northeast Asia and Southeast Asia and in U.S. relations with both areas, including time spent as a Fulbright Professor in 1992–93 at Far Eastern State University, Vladivostok, and in 1998–2000 at China's Foreign Ministry's Foreign Affairs College. She has written on Asia-Pacific affairs, China's international energy relations, Sino-American relations in East Asia, and Indonesian civil-military relations, and she has published articles in *Asian Survey*, *Pacific Affairs*, *Asian Perspective*, *China Quarterly*, and *Pacific Review*.

Elizabeth Van Wie Davis is a professor at the Asia-Pacific Center for Security Studies. Previously, she was the Fei Yi-Ming Professor of Politics at Johns Hopkins University's SAIS Center in Nanjing, China, also holding appointments at Illinois State University, Mary Baldwin College, and the University of Virginia as well as researching extensively on Asian security and politics in Europe, North America, and Asia. Dr. Davis has two recent book publications and numerous articles that have appeared in journals around the world. She received her Ph.D. in Foreign Affairs from the University of Virginia.

Among his many posts, **Feng Shaolei** is director at the Center for Russian and Asian-European Studies, East China Normal University. Prior to this, he was dean of the College of Humanities at East China Normal University from 1994 to 2001. Professor Feng's specialized areas of research include the history of international relationships after war and foreign policies in China, comparative study on Russian and Chinese reform, and international political economics. He has written many books and articles for major publications.

Shireen Hunter is director of the Center for Muslim-Christian Understanding at Georgetown University. Previously, she was director of the Islam Program at the Center for Strategic and International Studies (CSIS) of Washington, D.C.; an Academic Fellow, Carnegie Corporation; a Visiting Senior Fellow at the Centre for European Policy Studies (CEPS); and a Guest Scholar at the Brookings Institution and Research Fellow at the Harvard University Center for International Affairs. She received her B.A. from Teheran University, her M.S. in International Relations from the London School of Economics, and her Ph.D. in International Relations from the Institut Universitaire de Hautes Etudes Interenationales, Geneva. She has written more than seven books and is the author of numerous book chapters and many articles in leading journals.

Alisher Khamidov, now at Johns Hopkins University SAIS as a Ph.D. candidate, was assistant director of The Center for the Study of Sanctions and Security at Notre Dame University and regional coordinator of the Central Asian Media Support Project in Osh, Kyrgyzstan. He also served as the Volunteer Assistant for Prevention Program, Medicins Sans Frontieres in Osh, Kyrgyzstan. Mr. Khamidov received his B.A. with honors in English and German from Osh State University and his M.A. from the University of Notre Dame. He has published several articles on Central Asia.

Mikhail A. Konarovsky is currently the Russian ambassador to Croatia. He has held various positions in the Foreign Ministry of the Russian Federation and abroad. From February 2002, he was ambassador to Afghanistan. Beginning in May 2001 he was ambassador of the Russian Federation to Sri Lanka and the Maldives. Ambassador Konarovsky was educated at Moscow State University and the Diplomatic Academy by the Ministry of Foreign Affairs. He completed his Ph.D. at the Moscow Institute for Oriental Studies in 1983. He served as a Fellow in the Center for International Affairs at Harvard University in 1991–92. He has authored numerous publications on Russia's policy in Asia as well as on regional security and preventive diplomacy.

Najibullah Lafraie is currently a lecturer at the University of Otago in New Zealand. He is a native of Afghanistan, where he obtained his B.A. in law and political science from Kabul University. Later he received an M.A. and Ph.D. in Political Science from the University of Hawaii. After joining the liberation movement against the Soviet invasion of his home country in 1980s, he was appointed minister of information in the Interim Government of Afghanistan in 1989 and minister of state for foreign affairs in the Islamic State of Afghanistan after the downfall of the communist regime in 1992. He served in that position until the Taliban captured the Kabul City in September 1996. Dr. Lafraie and his family moved to New Zealand in September 2000. He writes on issues relating to Afghanistan.

Murat Laumulin is currently serving as a vice-director at the Kazakhstan Institute for Strategic Studies. His previous positions include first secretary at the Embassy of Kazakhstan to the Federal Republic of Germany in Bonn and Berlin (1998–2002), chief researcher at the Kazakhstan Institute for Strategic Studies (1994–1997), and working in the Ministry of Foreign Affairs, Republic of Kazakhstan (1993–1994). Dr. Laumulin earned his Doctor of History at the Institute of USSR History, Academy of Sciences in Moscow in 1990 for issuing the Western Historiography on Kazakhstan. He is the author of several books and numerous publications on medieval European history, the history of Kazakhstan and Central Asia, foreign investigations in Central Asian history and culture, the development of Central Asian and Oriental studies in Europe, the foreign policy of the Republic of Kazakhstan, nuclear nonproliferation, the U.S.-Kazakh relationship, and Asian security.

Sergey Lounev is currently holding numerous positions, including Leading Research Fellow at the Institute of World Economic and International Relations, Russian Academy of Sciences; Leading Research Fellow, Institute of Oriental Studies of Russian Academy of Sciences; professor of Moscow Academy for Humanitarian and Social Studies; lecturer of program, Stanford University in Moscow; and professor of Moscow State University, Institute of Asian and African Studies. Dr. Lunev received his M.A. from the Institute of Asian and African Studies, Moscow State University; his Ph.D. from the Institute of Oriental Studies, Russian Academy of Science; and a Doctor of Sciences (history) from the Institute of Asian and African Studies, Moscow State University. He has authored/co-authored several books and articles and has organized and/or participated in many conferences, both in Russia and internationally, focusing on the socioeconomic and political development of CIS countries.

Aleksei Malashenko is currently a scholar-in-residence, co-director of the Program of Ethnicity and Nation-building at Carnegie Moscow Center. Additionally, he is a professor at the Institute for Foreign Relations (Foreign Ministry of Russian Federation) and a member of the editorial boards of *Acta Eurasica* (Moscow) and *Centralnaja Asia I Kavkaz* (Stockholm). Since 1990, he has been a visiting professor at Colgate University. He was head of the sector of Islamic studies at the Institute of Oriental Studies, Russian Academy of Sciences. Professor Malashenko has authored or co-authored eleven books.

Orhon Myadar is currently associated with the University of Hawaii at Manoa in political science. She is a native of Mongolia, where she obtained her B.A. from the University of Humanities in Mongolia. Later she received an M.A. from University of Hawaii and is currently finishing her Ph.D. there. She lived first with the Soviet Union's rule under the centrally controlled government in Mongolia, and then more recently as Mongolia has struggled to establish a free market and a democratic-style government. Her research has examined post-Soviet transitional political economy and democratic identity in Central Asia and Northeast Asia.

Pan Guang is director of and professor at Shanghai Center of International Studies and Institute of European & Asian Studies in Shanghai; director of the

Shanghai Cooperation Organization Studies Center in Shanghai; dean of the Center of Jewish Studies Shanghai; and vice chairman of the Chinese Society of Middle East Studies. He is professor of history and political science and Walter and Seena Fair Professor for Jewish and Israeli Studies. He has traveled and lectured widely in North America, East Asia, Russia, Europe, the Middle East, and Australia. He holds a number of prestigious posts in Chinese Institutions on International Studies, Asian Studies, Middle East Studies, and Jewish Studies, and he has published numerous books and articles on a variety of topics.

Shi Yinhong is professor of international relations and director of the Center for American Studies, Renmin University of China in Beijing; former president of the American Historical Research Association of China; a visiting fellow at Harvard-Yenching Institute at Harvard University; a Fulbright research visiting scholar at the University of North Carolina at Chapel Hill;and a visiting professor for postgraduate teaching at the University of Denver. Dr. Shi received a Ph.D. in International History from Nanjing University in 1988. He has published seven books and more than 180 articles.

Manabu Shimizu is currently a professor at Hitotsubashi University, in Tokyo, Japan, specializing in area studies in Central Asia, South Asia, and the Middle East and in development economies. He is a former professor at Utsunomiya University and Sophia University, as well as former director of the Institute of Developing Economies in Tokyo. Professor Shimizu has published two books and numerous book chapters and articles.

After retiring from thirty-five years in the U.S. Foreign Service, his final position as ambassador to Pakistan, **Thomas W. Simons Jr.** is currently director of the Project on Eurasia in Transition at Harvard's Davis Center for Russian and Eurasian Studies. Prior to this, he was a consulting professor at Stanford University. He lived in British India and newly independent Pakistan in a diplomatic family in the 1940s, and he studied Islamic history as a Harvard Ph.D. candidate. Ambassador Simons visited Afghanistan in 1963 and 1998 and Central Asia in 1976 while serving in the embassy in Moscow, and he visited all the Central Asian and Caucasus countries as coordinator of U.S. Assistance to the New Independent States of the Former Soviet Union (1993-1995). He has recently published a book with Stanford University Press.

Robert Smith is presently with Fesharaki and Associates Consulting and Technical Services (FACTS), Inc. at the East-West Center in Honolulu, Hawaii, where he is head of Gas Studies and senior associate conducting independent research on primary energy resources in relation to economic development, market structure, environmental concerns, and fuel competition in the Asia-Pacific and Middle East regions. He is also a China Energy Project member, East-West Center, with his research focus on China's oil and gas industry. In addition, he has conducted several research projects focusing on energy issues in Central Asia and China. He has authored or co-authored several articles in technical journals. Mr. Smith received his B.A. with honors in history/strategic studies from Johns Hopkins University and his M.A. with honors in Asian studies from the University of Hawaii, Manoa.

Sergei Troush is a Visiting Fellow at the Center for Northeast Asian Policy Studies (CNAPS), Foreign Policy Studies. Prior to this he was a Visiting Fellow at the London School of Economics and a Visiting Fellow at Peking University. His area of expertise is in China, Sino-Russian, and Sino-American relations, and in interrelationship of China's domestic and foreign policy. Dr. Troush received his Ph.D. at the Russian Academy of Sciences, Institute of Far East Studies. He has published one book and numerous articles, book chapters, and web publications..

Kang Wu is a Fellow at the East-West Center in charge of research activities, assessing the current situation and future prospects of energy demand and supply in the Asia-Pacific region and their implications for economic development at the Center. Dr. Wu specializes in studies of energy policies, security, demand, supply, trade, and market developments; energy-economic links; oil and gas issues; and the impact of fossil energy and particularly transportation fuel consumption on the environment. Dr. Wu is an energy expert on China; he supervises the China Energy Project at the Center and is also familiar with oil and gas sector issues in other major Asia-Pacific countries and the region as a whole. Dr. Wu is the author and co-author of numerous journal articles, project reports, professional studies, conference papers, books, and other publications.